In memory of
Hans-Judy Jolly-Bunge
whose other-worldly spirit
and this-worldly laughter
laid the foundations
of this book

For Dorota Budzińska
who has restored the memory of
Dąbrowa Białostocka
as a Jewish Space

An Atlas of Jewish Space

Robert Jan van Pelt
Mark Podwal

   PARK BOOKS

On Reading Between the Lines	9
As to Two Jewish Spaces	12
Prologue: On Jewish Habitations	15
An Atlas of Jewish Space	25
Coda—and a New Beginning	295
Bibliography & References	319
Acknowledgments	329
Index	333

A NOTE ON TERMINOLOGY

An Atlas of Jewish Space presents a reading of the history of the ancestors of the Jews that seeks to understand the formation of a number of spatial conceptions that are rooted in the Jewish tradition as responses to particular political and social crises. This is a complex history that also is plagued by overlapping identities. The following explanation of terminology used may help to map this difficult terrain.

Hebrews.
The *Oxford English Dictionary* defines a Hebrew as, "a person belonging to the Semitic tribe or nation descended from Abraham, Isaac, and Jacob; an Israelite, a Jew." It also notes, "historically, the term is usually applied to the early Israelites; in modern use it avoids the religious and other associations often attaching to *Jew*." In this text, the word *Hebrew* will refer to the ethnic group that emerged in Canaan some 3,400 years ago and that Jews recognize as their tribal ancestors.

Canaanites and Jebusites.
The Canaanites were the majority non-Hebrew population of Canaan until the twelfth century BCE. Unlike the Hebrews, a rural and also pastoral people, the Canaanites maintained an urban civilization. One of the Canaanite cities was Jebus (which means "threshing floor"), which was inhabited by a Canaanite people known as the Jebusites. This city was renamed Jerusalem after its conquest by King David.

Israelites and Judahites.
Around 1100 BCE, the Hebrews split in two groups. The larger one, which was a confederation of a number of larger and smaller Hebrew tribes, occupied the highlands of Galilee, Samaria, and the Jordan Valley. This area north of the Canaanite city of Jebus became known as Israel, and hence those belonging to this northern Hebrew group are known as Israelites. The smaller Hebrew group occupied the Judaean hills south of Jebus. They claimed to be descendants of the Hebrew tribe of Judah, and hence are known as Judahites.

In the eleventh century BCE, the Israelites and Judahites were unified in a single state under King Saul, then separated again, later to be reunified by King David in a federated monarchy that included not only Israel and Judah but also the Canaanite city of Jebus, which, renamed as Jerusalem, became David's capital. King Solomon, David's son, changed the federated monarchy into a united monarchy by suppressing Israelite autonomy. After Solomon's death, the Israelites seceded, resulting in two new states: Israel, which occupied more or less the territory of the Israelites before the reign of King Saul, and Judah, which included both the territory inhabited by the Judahites and the originally Canaanite city of Jerusalem.

In the eighth century BCE, Israel is conquered by Assyria and disappears from the map. The Israelites fade as a nation in Assyrian captivity: Israelites who remained in the ancient homeland preserved some but not all original Hebrew traditions, and as they lived in the region of Samaria, they became known as Samaritans. The Judahites held onto an increasingly shaky independence for another 150 years. However, the Babylonian conquest of Judah and the destruction of Jerusalem seemed likely to condemn the Judahites to the same fate as the Israelites.

Jews.
Unlike the Israelites, the Judahites survived as a nation in captivity. But the experience of exile changed their sense of identity. The text now begins to refer to these Judahites-in-exile and Judahites-after-exile as Jews—the English noun *Jew* derives, via the French *Juif*, the Latin *Iudaeus*, and the Greek *Ioudaios*, from the Aramaic *Yehudayi*, which means an inhabitant of Judah.

Judaea.
After a sixty-year period in exile, a minority of Jews returns to the region of origin. The text will refer to this area, before the Babylonian captivity known as Judah, now as Judaea, a Roman name derived from the Greek *Ioudaia*. Judaeans are the inhabitants of Judaea, which included Jews but also Samaritans. Not all Jews lived in Judaea: a vibrant Jewish community remained in Babylon, now Persian-ruled, and another also established itself in Egypt.

Palestine and the State of Israel.
The destruction of the Third Temple in 70 CE and the Bar Kokhba revolt in 132–36 CE lead to a Roman makeover of Judaea that seeks to erase the historical association of the area with the Jews. The area will now be known as Palaestina, a name that is meant as a clear slap in the face of the Jews, as it refers back to the ancient Philistines, who occupied the coast of Canaan 1,400 years earlier and were the antagonists of the Hebrews. The text will use the term *Palestine* when it refers to the ancient homeland of the Jews as it existed under late Roman, Byzantine, Arab, Ottoman, and English rule. Finally, the term *State of Israel* designates the sovereign Jewish state proclaimed in 1948.

Semites, anti-Semitism, antisemitism.
Coined in the late eighteenth century, the term *Semite* referred to the descendants of Noah's son Shem, among whom were the Jews. In the nineteenth century, the adjective *Semitic* was applied to a language family that includes Arabic, Aramaic, and Hebrew, and quickly came to refer to Arabs, Aramaeans, and Hebrews and their descendants, the Jews. In 1879, the term *Antisemitismus* (translated in English as "anti-Semitism") entered the

German language. While it suggested a movement opposed to all Semites, in fact, it focused only on Jews. This lack of precision has given antisemites who preach hatred of Jews an opportunity to plead that they cannot be anti-Semitic because they like Arabs in general and support the Palestinian cause in particular. In order to show that anti-Semitism has nothing to do with an opposition to Semites in general, scholars of anti-Semitism and the Holocaust prefer to use the spelling *antisemitism* instead, as it suppresses the false notion that it opposes some form of *Semitism*. Dropping the hyphen that connects *anti* and *Semitism* establishes that the word is a conventional, unified term for modern Jew hatred that is not connected to, for example, a possible dislike for Arabs.

ON READING BETWEEN THE LINES
Robert Jan van Pelt

An Atlas of Jewish Space explores some aspects of the development of the space of Jews and Jewish space in a dialogue between images and short texts. This project began as a request by my fellow members of the Architectural Advisory Board of the Babyn Yar Holocaust Memorial Center in Kyiv to conduct a seminar on the development of the Jewish understanding of space and place, territory and architecture, synagogue and home, household and family, workdays and holy days, to prepare us for the monumental task of articulating a design approach to the future of the Babyn Yar ravine. Today it is a public park in Kyiv, but in 1941 it was the site of the single largest massacre of Jews during the Holocaust. For various reasons, the Babyn Yar site has not yet been developed as a memorial, and the Babyn Yar Holocaust Memorial Center has assumed responsibility for its future. As a historian who wrote a doctoral dissertation on the Temple of Jerusalem, has spent most of his academic life studying the Holocaust in general and Auschwitz in particular, and has always had a fascination with the peculiar sense of space in the Jewish tradition, I was intrigued by the challenge to put Solomon's Temple, the Altneuschul (Old-New Synagogue) in Prague and its adjacent cemetery, where one of my ancestors is buried in a grave still marked by its original headstone, Auschwitz, and Babyn Yar in a single narrative.

My presentation occurred at the very time that the Babyn Yar Holocaust Memorial Center decided to commission Basel-based architect Manuel Herz to design a synagogue to be constructed close to the ravine. This synagogue is to stand, when not in use, as a closed book at the site, ready to be opened, like the *siddur* (prayer book), when needed to provide space for a service. This architectural project, which is to bring a Jewish liturgical space close to a place of Jewish martyrdom, suggested a more extended meditation on the intersection of how Jews see and interpret the world, how the world—in this case the part of the world that is intensely hostile to Jews and Judaism—saw and persecuted the Jews, and the way that intersection can be understood in spatial if not architectural terms.

In my presentation, I accompanied my argument with images derived from many different sources, but when the chair of the Architectural Advisory Board, Nick Axel, suggested publication of my lecture as a companion piece to Herz's synagogue, I became wary of an approach in which images would simply "illustrate" my written arguments. The essence of Jewish space, and of Jewish thinking, is that it is dialogical, a conversation, and the presentation had been a monologue. I admire the work of New York artist Mark Podwal, with its commitment to Jewish subjects, its imaginative boldness, its sharp wit, and its fearless ability to articulate the complex identity created amid the overlapping iconographies of Jewish aspiration, Jewish persistence, Christian anti-Judaism, modern antisemitism, and Nazi destruction. And so, I sent Mark an email with a simple request: might he be interested in entering in a dialogue with me by choosing from his work images to accompany my argument, to push back at times, to enigmatically smile or even laugh out loud at it, when necessary? Mark immediately agreed, and for a month we dialogued online, with texts traveling from my computer in Toronto to his in New York and scanned images in the opposite direction. Many of the works came from a treasury compiled over forty years; some were drawn especially for this book. At times the match is close, perhaps even too close; at times the friction between art and text is great, perhaps too much so. As in any dialogue, perfect agreement was not the goal. And if the art of reading is indeed located in one's ability to read between the lines—a capacity that is greatest during childhood—then it might be that those very gaps between Mark's art and my words are the doors that allow our book to become your book.

The text stands not only in a dialogue with Mark's art. It also engages the works of authors who have accompanied me on my own journey toward a basic understanding of Jewish space and the spaces of Jews. These include Abraham Joshua Heschel, André Schwarz-Bart, Arthur Koestler, Bella Chagall, Bruno Schulz, David Koker, Ezra the Scribe, Franz Rosenzweig, Hannah Arendt, Heinrich Heine, Israel Zangwill, Leonard Cohen, Lion Feuchtwanger, Peter Weiss, Philo of Alexandria, Sholem Aleichem, Thomas Mann, Vasily Grossman, and others. Their voices were important to me, and I hope that they will also speak to you.

I write these words in the short interval between the last day of Hanukkah of the Hebrew year 5781 and the winter solstice of 2020. The Covid-19 pandemic is at its worst, yet those most at risk are now being vaccinated. It is a time of utter darkness in more ways than one—physically, medically, politically, socially—yet there is a promise of light. The *New York Times* reports that in Utqiagvik, Alaska, the sun has been buried beneath the horizon since November, and the pandemic has arrived there. However, winter darkness was and remains an accepted part of Arctic life, according to Roy Nageak Sr. It is the time when "families would get together and tell these stories of who we are, where we came from."

As Mark and I, blessed to live in warm, well-lit, and well-stocked homes, try to make this record of who we are and where we came from amid the Covid-19 lockdown, we do so in the spirit that, in the end, the "we" in our images and narrative includes not only the Children of Israel and the descendants of "those who," in the words of the Haggadah, "rise against us to destroy us," but all of us who try to figure out who we are, where we came from.

Arbeit Macht Frei (2013)

אמרו
לכו ונכחידם
מגוי

ולא
יזכר
שם ישראל
עוד

AS TO TWO JEWISH SPACES
Mark Podwal

According to the artist Ben Shahn, in his 1956–57 Charles Eliot Norton lecture at Harvard, for an artist, each work is often instilled with doubt. "There are no guideposts, no maps, no geography" to tell the artist that he or she "is on the right path." Nevertheless, I'd like to acknowledge two Jewish spaces that set me on my path: One, Dąbrowa Białostocka, my mother's birthplace, a shtetl in northeastern Poland burned to the ground by the Germans in 1941. The other, a Jewish camp 150 kilometers north of New York City.

In 1929, when my mother, at age eight, immigrated with her family to the United States, her brother David was denied entry based on an erroneous diagnosis of an eye infection and had to remain in Dąbrowa. Letters from eye specialists in Warsaw attesting that David had been misdiagnosed failed to help. Moreover, attempts to arrange a visa for David to immigrate to Latin America were unsuccessful. When the German army reached Dąbrowa in July 1941, in revenge for finding the body of a slain German officer, the command burned down the entire town. Only two small stone houses on the edge of town and a partially destroyed church were left standing. About 300 Jews lived under desperate conditions, finding refuge wherever they could in huts or in storage basements. In November 1942, the Jewish population was forced to run most of the twenty-eight kilometers to Grodno, where they were placed in the Kelbashin camp, previously used for Russian prisoners of war. The Dąbrowa Jews remained there for nearly six weeks before the final trip to the Treblinka extermination camp. My mother's mother, on learning that her son David had perished in Treblinka, became severely depressed and was committed to a psychiatric hospital for the last eighteen years of her life. The closest I ever got to my grandmother was when I helped carry her coffin.

Since early childhood, Dąbrowa Białostocka lived in my imagination. Although for many years I had wanted to visit Dąbrowa, the incentive came when its mayor sent me an invitation to participate in a conference on the history of the town's Jews. Although Dąbrowa was once 75 percent Jewish, no Jews currently live there. My visit on May 24, 2016, resulted in a series of drawings, some of which are published in this volume.

The other Jewish space was Cejwin Camps, where I spent several summers. When at age twelve I first arrived at Cejwin, having grown up in a non-observant home, I was overwhelmed with a Judaism I barely knew anything about—and enthusiastically embraced. More interested in arts and crafts than sports, I spent many afternoons sawing wood to shape into Jewish motifs for the camp's newly constructed synagogue. Little could I envision that five decades later I'd design the textiles for Prague's 700-year-old synagogue, the Altneuschul. Nor conceive that in a forty-year span I would illustrate the works of Nobel Laureate Elie Wiesel or be commissioned by the Metropolitan Museum of Art to create its Passover seder plate.

Preoccupied with Jewish history and fascinated by its traditions, legends, and mysticism, I've tried to imaginatively interpret and faithfully transmit my heritage through pictorial narratives. Much of my art involves inventing visual metaphors adapted from Jewish symbols and iconography. When chronicling an event, although my art at times may include anachronisms, I like to be accurate concerning historical details. Drawing for over forty years for the *New York Times* very much influenced my art. The role of op-ed art is not to "illustrate" but to expand the impact of the word, as opposed to a literal interpretation. Literary critic Harold Bloom said about our book *Fallen Angels*, "Mark Podwal is in every sense an illuminator." The term *illumination* denotes: to reveal information or details; to clarify; to help understand something.

Although museum directors and curators have urged me to broaden my subject matter—to become an artist more universal rather than being limited by Jewish content—my heart is with the Jewish experience. Franz Kafka once described writing as a form of prayer, and that definition has resonated with me. For me, drawing is a form of prayer. To have been asked by Robert Jan van Pelt to collaborate on this volume is a tremendous honor. The artworks chosen for the book represent nearly fifty years of my art on Jewish subjects. Many of the original drawings, paintings, and prints are in the collections of institutions such as the Metropolitan Museum of Art, the Victoria and Albert Museum, Jewish museums in Prague, Berlin, and Vienna, the Terezín Ghetto Museum, the Bibliotheca Rosenthaliana, and the Warsaw Ghetto Museum (under construction), among numerous other venues and private collections. In gathering my art to partner with Robert Jan's illuminating texts, I'm delighted to say that, without question, I've chosen the right path.

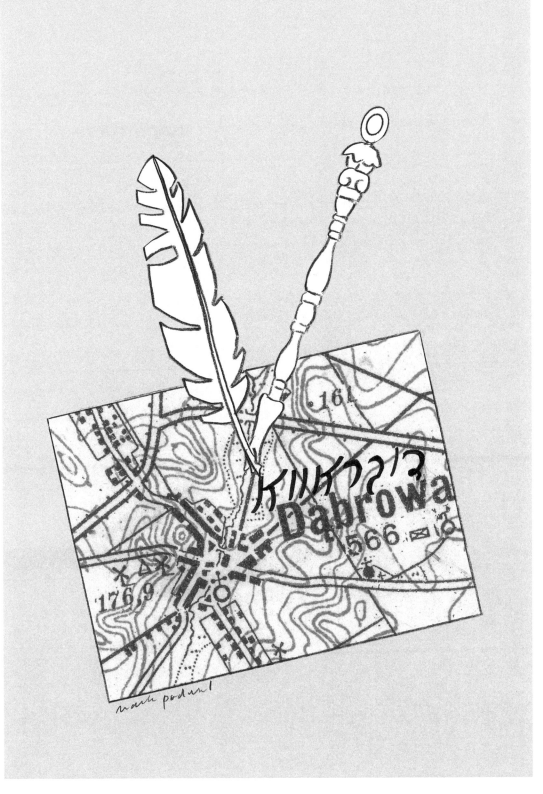

Yiddish Dąbrowa (2016)

Prologue:
On Jewish Habitations

Tents of Jacob (1990)

Mah tovu ohalekha Yaakov, mishkenotekha Yisrael. "How beautiful are your tents, Jacob, your dwelling places, Israel!" These words are traditionally spoken upon entering a synagogue, words that give thanks for one's entry into a holy place. These words, which echo through the ages, are found in the Torah and were first spoken not by the high priest Aaron upon entering the Tabernacle in the desert but by the Moabite soothsayer Balaam. Sent by King Balak to curse the migrant Hebrews who had pitched their tents in Moabite territory east of the Dead Sea, Balaam had a change of heart when he saw the encampment of the strangers in the desert. Instead, he composed this beautiful blessing on the people he was told to fear and hate.

To many, the spaces and places of the Jews, both material and conceptual, appear at first sight strange and even uncanny. Synagogue services and the liturgical practices observed at Ha-Kotel Ha-Maʿaravi (the Western Wall), a part of the original retaining wall of the Temple of Jerusalem, and derogatorily referred to by Christians as the "Wailing Wall," seem chaotic to an observer used to orderly forms of Christian worship. When Samuel Pepys, who was not ill disposed to Jews, visited a Simchat Torah (Rejoicing with the Torah) celebration in the Sephardic synagogue in London on October 14, 1663 / 23 Tishri 5424, he was both spellbound and horrified. "But, Lord!" he noted in his diary, "to see the disorder, laughing, sporting, and no attention, but confusion in all their service, more like brutes than people knowing the true God, would make a man forswear ever seeing them more and indeed I never did see so much, or could have imagined there had been any religion in the whole world so absurdly performed as this." Pepys's view is also embodied in the German custom to refer to a disorderly crowd as a *Judenschule* (synagogue). Talmudic reasoning appears absurd to those schooled in the traditions of logic pioneered by Aristotle. And in the case of many, confusion is also framed by prejudice. Exploiting a long lineage of Christian anti-Judaism, modern antisemites spin tales of a sinister global conspiracy directed by Jewish financiers lurking in the shadows. Indeed, the way Jews occupy a place in the imagination of non-Jews has a direct lineage to Balak's panic when he saw the twelve tribes, led by Moses and Joshua, enter his land as they made their way to Canaan. Yet, closer consideration of the facts may bring the change of heart that killed the curse and brought the word "beautiful" to Balaam's lips.

Philosophers refer to beauty as a mystery, the *mysterium fascinans*, the mystery that attracts. Yet they have also noted that it is closely related to the *mysterium tremendum*, the dreadful mystery that repels, that makes one tremble. The God of the Jews is a deity who has both qualities, and so has Jewish history, and so has Jewish space. This space not only encompasses the order of the camp of the Hebrews in the desert, which made Balaam say a blessing instead of a curse, but also the Temple of Jerusalem, with its inner Holy of Holies, or the medieval Altneuschul in Prague—a building that most perfectly embodies Jewish liturgical space—or the Jewish cemetery located close to that synagogue, or the dining table in a Jewish home on Friday evening, when the candles are lit. Identity is a relationship: between the person I think I am and the person others think I am; between the deeds I do and the deeds that are done to me. Therefore, the space of Jews and Jewish space also includes the Roman Arch of Titus, which celebrates the destruction of the Temple, the wall that enclosed the Kraków ghetto, and the mass graves at Babyn Yar and elsewhere that received the bodies of those who had welcomed each Friday evening the Shabbat as a princess bride.

The purpose of this book is to provide a portrait of a current understanding—or, to be more precise, my current understanding—of Jewish space and the space of Jews, both material and mental, conscious and repressed. It does so in a spirit articulated by Polish Jewish writer Bruno Schulz, who had trained as an architect: "We are building our houses with broken pieces of sculptures and ruined statues of gods as the barbarians did." Yet for Schulz, this was a source not of despair but of wonder: "Even the soberest of our notions and categories are remote derivatives of myths and ancient oral epics. Not one scrap of an idea of ours does not originate in myth, isn't transformed, mutilated, denatured mythology." This applies to all civilizations, but especially to that of the Jewish people, because of its continuity in discontinuity.

An Atlas of Jewish Space traces a chronological trajectory that spans 3,000 years and is divided into three major periods. The first one begins in the early urban cultures of the Middle East that are the context of the stories of the Bible and ends with the destruction of an independent Jewish state in 70 CE. The second period covers the simultaneous development of Rabbinic Judaism and Christian doctrine; it describes the formation of a Jewish culture that is the basis of current Jewish traditions and practices, and ends with the beginning of Jewish emancipation in the late eighteenth century. The third one deals with the opportunities and conflicts that accompany the encounter between Judaism, Jews, and the modern world.

The first part covers much biblical material but does not seek to recount the well-known history of the ancient Hebrews, their descendants who were to live as Israelites and Judahites in the rival states of Israel and Judah, and the descendants of the Judahites who came to be known as Jews, as it is taught in Hebrew school to Jewish children or Sunday school to Christians. Instead, it seeks to present an account of the dialectic between space, place, territory, and architecture that derives its insights from the work of biblical scholars who have attempted to understand the historical Israel (used in this case as a shorthand for the civilization founded by the Hebrews) that produced the biblical Israel. This is an essentially political history. My account rests on scholarly foundations laid by George Mendenhall, Frank Moore Cross, Richard Elliott Friedman, and Baruch Halpern. "To say that Israel's was an historical religion, a cliche so worn that it might clothe any emperor, is to say, too, that politics were Israel's religion. History, for the Israelite, was politics, and so was theology," Halpern observed forty years ago. He believed that biblical scholarship had ignored the political heart of biblical history. "The history of religion must rest on the prior basis of socio-political history. To investigate the latter on the basis of the former is to contaminate it. Simply, one cannot proceed from a theological history to an historical theology." In the first part I seek to follow Halpern's advice, providing a sense of the political foundations of the Jewish understanding of space and of Jewish spaces—which were all the result of political facts, even if they were at times dressed up in religious apparel. For some readers the spirit of this first part, which is an attempt to tell the story of what actually came to pass, may offer a fresh perspective on the origins of the Jews. For others it might be heresy. Whatever may be the case, I hope that even when you might not agree with my views, you will still be able to enjoy Mark's images.

The second part of this book centers on Judaism, as it evolved both on earlier biblical foundations and, as important, in a dialectic with Christianity and the conditions of life imposed by the Christian majority society on the Jews. It does not consider the influence of Islam on specific Jewish understandings of space and the evolution of Jewish spaces within the Muslim world. In contrast with Christianity, the polemic with Judaism never acquired a central role in Muslim theology. In addition, restrictions within the Muslim world imposed on Jews were also imposed on Christians. And, perhaps most important, the specific form of antisemitism that led to Babyn Yar and Auschwitz did not have roots in Islam or the Muslim world but evolved from Christian anti-Judaism and the particular assumptions that shaped the ideology of the nation-state as it evolved in nineteenth-century Europe. This second part provides a close look at the unique spatial practices of Judaism, embodied in the design of traditional synagogues, the textual space of the Talmud, the ritual significance of the Jewish home, and the weekly takeover of the public sphere by the private domain by means of the *eruv*. In this part the question of politics recedes, a necessary outcome of the destruction of Jewish political space during the many centuries of exile, which led to the contraction of the Jewish public sphere into the communal, personal, and private spheres.

The third part covers a period of widening horizons and a deep abyss of utter perdition in the nineteenth and twentieth centuries. The question can be asked, of course: May the gas chambers of German death camps or the execution pits be labeled as Jewish spaces? When in 1965 a number of famous German authors were invited to contribute an essay on an important place to a literary atlas, the German Jewish writer Peter Weiss, who had spent the Holocaust years in the relative safety of Swedish exile, considered the place where he was born, and all those towns and cities where he had lived for longer or shorter times, merely as places of transit. "The cities I lived in, in whose houses I dwelled, whose streets I walked on, whose inhabitants I spoke with, have no particular contours, they flow into one another, they are parts of a single earthly external world in continual flux, have a harbor to show here, a park there, here a work of art, there a fairground, here a room, there a gateway, they are present in the basic pattern of my wanderings, in a fraction of a second they can be reached and left again, and each time their characteristics have to be invented anew." Yet there was one place that was radically different, one place he never saw until late middle age, but a place that had been set apart since he was a young man. "It is a place for which I was destined and which I evaded. I myself learned nothing in this place. I have no other connection to it beyond the fact that my name stood on the list of those meant to be relocated there forever." Of all the places in the world, Auschwitz was the only place that existed *within* Peter Weiss—it had existed there since he first learned about it in 1945 and was to persist there until his death. And Auschwitz and the other places of Jewish martyrdom such as Belzec, Sobibor, Treblinka, and Babyn Yar inhabit the souls of so many Jews, and not only those who witnessed their horrors at the time but also their children, grandchildren, and great-grandchildren: *l'dor v'dor* (from generation to generation).

> The three-part journey through Jewish history is preceded by a short orientation in a terrain that will be for many both very familiar and quite strange at the same time. This introductory section touches on the sense of Jewish space presented in the musical *Fiddler on the Roof* and its literary origin, the Yiddish-language stories written by Solomon Naumovich Rabinovich, better known under his pen name Sholem Aleichem. An expression of American popular culture at its most impactful, *Fiddler* shaped, and continues to shape, the perception of both non-Jews and at least assimilated Jews alike as to what Jewish culture was like in the heartland of the Jewish world before World War I: eastern Europe. It was the center not only because as late as the year 1900, even after two decades of emigration to the New World, two-thirds of the world's 10 million Jews lived in the western part of the Russian Empire and adjacent area of the Austro-Hungarian Empire. It was also a stronghold because here the difficult conditions of Jewish existence, with its continuing restrictions, had made Jews grow inwardly in their own small communities, which were deeply rooted in each particular location and, thanks to regularly returning pogroms, also proved a very unstable ground. However, at the same time, these communities were connected to each other, allowing for a rich traffic of, if not ideas, then at least care and devotion. "In this period our people attained the highest degree of inwardness," Abraham Joshua Heschel observed. "I feel justified in saying that it was a golden period in Jewish history, in the history of the Jewish soul." It is that very tenderness of the soul, so well embodied in the writing of Sholem Aleichem and brought on the stage and screen by *Fiddler*, that provides not only a good point of departure but, given the way eastern European Jewish history came to a close, also the only right one.

The narrative shows not only an evolution of a range of important concepts but also, simultaneously, a persistence of earlier understandings alongside newer ones. The Temple Mount in Jerusalem preserves not only the original Jebusite identification of that place with Mount Zaphon (today Jebel Aqra) on the Syrian-Turkish border, or the Jewish temples that stood on the site, or a Roman temple dedicated to Jupiter, or a dung heap, or today's Dome of the Rock, but also all the messianic projects for that place that were never realized, all the fragments that have been scattered by means of prayers, stories, and depictions—both high-brow and low-brow—to the ends of the world, and all the apocalyptic dreams that are being spun, even today, by zealots of Jewish, Christian, and Muslim religious denominations. In addition, it makes space for the countless Jewish households where, on Friday evening, women blessed the candles to welcome the Shabbat; as the wax combusted, it produced particles of smoke that traveled to the sky to find their way to the center of gravity of the Jewish imagination. And, in the same manner, Jerusalem gathered the specks of dust that arose not only from pyres that burned Jewish bodies at Babyn Yar, at thousands of other mass-execution sites in eastern Europe, and at the Chelmno, Belzec, Sobibor, and Treblinka extermination camps but also from the chimneys of the Majdanek and Auschwitz crematoria.

> Few of the (mostly) men who set out to destroy Jewish institutions, Jewish homes, and Jewish lives ever experienced the change of heart ascribed to Balaam when he first set eyes on the camp of the Hebrews. Even as the shooting pits and the gas chambers filled with women and children, these men never stopped to see what was in front of them and consider on the basis of their observations that they might be wrong. Thoughtlessness, Hannah Arendt postulated, and not monstrosity, was an essential part of the Nazi mind, and this thoughtlessness was based on an inability and unwillingness to see reality from the standpoint of somebody else, which is the beginning of all thinking.

Why did Balaam speak a blessing instead of a curse? The Bible suggests an answer: because for once he had not searched for obscure signs that would reveal to him, the trained diviner, a hidden reality, but instead trusted the evidence in front of him, and because he had learned to see the camp of the Hebrews not from the perspective of King Balak but from that of the King of Kings. "Now when Balaam saw that it pleased the Lord to bless Israel, he did not resort to divination as at other times, but turned his face toward the wilderness. When

Balaam looked out and saw Israel encamped tribe by tribe, the Spirit of God came on him and he spoke his message: 'The prophecy of Balaam son of Beor, the prophecy of one whose eye sees clearly, the prophecy of one who hears the words of God, who sees a vision from the Almighty, who falls prostrate, and whose eyes are opened: How beautiful are your tents, Jacob, your dwelling places, Israel!'"

An Atlas of Jewish Space

TRADITION ON EDGE

For many American and European non-Jews, the stage musical *Fiddler on the Roof* (1964), or its film version (1971), is the gateway to pre-Holocaust Jewish life in eastern Europe. Sunrise, somewhere in the Russian Empire: the camera sweeps over the roofline of a village, until it focuses on a man, sitting on the ridge of a farmhouse, playing a simple tune on a violin. "A fiddler on the roof. Sounds crazy, no?" And with these words, the protagonist of the story, Tevye the Milkman, enters our world. He explains that in the village of Anatevka, "every one of us is a fiddler on the roof, trying to scratch out a pleasant, simple tune without breaking his neck. It isn't easy. You may ask, why do we stay up there if it's so dangerous? Well, we stay because Anatevka is our home. And how do we keep our balance? That I can tell you in one word: Tradition!" And as the chorus line of dancers takes over the stage in the musical, and Tevye begins to deliver the milk in the film version, we can leave the pleasant Broadway and Hollywood productions, which were mercilessly criticized as misrepresentations of the stories written by Solomon Naumovich Rabinovich, also known as Sholem Aleichem, which in turn have been accused of providing a sentimental misrepresentation of life in the *shtetl* (a Yiddish noun derived from the Middle High German *stetlin*, "small town"). But yet, *Fiddler on the Roof* did make history by bringing to mind, for the first time since 1945, the tragic fate of eastern European Jewry, and it did also bring back the memory of that uniquely eastern European Jewish character, known in Yiddish as *luftmentsh* (air man) and in German as *Luftmensch*, the impractical, apparently rootless person who survives as a fiddler playing on the roof in a world that doesn't allow him to be at home—an artist who looks at the sky so he doesn't have to face the wretchedness in the yard below.

Fiddlers on Roofs (1995)

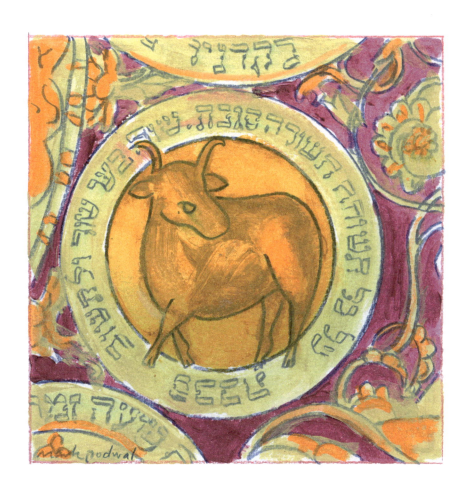

Fragment of Wooden Synagogue Interior (2021)

A WORLD LOST

When in 1970, Norman Jewison decided to make a film version of *Fiddler on the Roof*, Auschwitz survivor Branko Lustig, who had been hired as the European location manager, suggested the Croatian village of Lekenik might do as Anatevka: it had the required wooden houses and muddy streets the American public associated with a Ukrainian shtetl. Yet it lacked a wooden synagogue, which had been the heart of each Jewish community in the Cherta Postoyannoy Yevreyskoy Osedlosti (Boundary of a Settled Area for Jews—better known in English as the Pale of Settlement). Lekenik never had such a synagogue, and in the parts of eastern Europe where hundreds had existed, none were left by 1970: pogroms, secularization, and finally the Germans had taken care of a building type unique in Jewish history—the only one that had no counterpart in the architecture of the Gentiles but emerged uniquely from a Jewish sense of space and the traditions of Jewish folk art. Architect Robert Boyle, who was the movie's production designer and had made a reputation in making the replicas of Mount Rushmore for Hitchcock's *North by Northwest*, researched the now-lost building type and constructed a replica, with beautiful painted murals showing animals, the zodiac, and texts of the most common prayers, which were traditional in these buildings. In the final cut of the film, Anatevka's synagogue got only minimal exposure in a few close-up shots of the decorations, and at the end when, at the time of the expulsion of the Jews of Anatevka, the rabbi and his son take the two scrolls of the Torah from the ark, to carry them into exile—making the synagogue into a symbol of a lost world. Perhaps because of this, Jewison sought a future home for the building, which he believed to be a unique representation of a crucial link in the history of Jewish architecture. When Mayor Teddy Kollek of Jerusalem refused to find a place for a movie-set piece in a city that has authenticity as its brand, and a plan to reconstruct it on the campus of Bar Ilan University fell through, the production team turned its back on the building, and it subsequently disappeared from the face of the earth.

POPPY-SEED LOAF

Anatevka is based on the setting of many of Sholem Aleichem's stories: the fictional shtetl Kasrilevka. The name of the town derives from *kasril* or *kasrilik*, which the writer suggests is a pauper and a failure who, nevertheless, will not be beaten down by circumstances—a small joke because, in fact, the Hebrew name *Kasril* or *Katriel* means exactly the opposite of a failure: "God surrounds and supports me." Kasrilevka was a settlement distant from the highways and byways of progress and civilization. Stuck away in the countryside, it was, as its chronicler recorded, "orphaned, dreaming, bewitched, and immersed in itself." And the Kasrilevkites are different from the people who inhabit the larger towns and cities, people with high ambitions and great affairs. None of the inhabitants of Kasrilevka seem worried about such concerns; they are a cheerful and lighthearted breed of *luftmentshen*, who live if not from day to day, then at least from week to week. The Kasrilevka that Sholem Aleichem described is an itsy-bitsy small town that appears to the traveler that approaches it, "like a loaf of bread thickly studded with poppy seed." There are no streets or squares to speak of because the houses are not built according to any plan, and besides, where would be room for such a thing as a street or a square? Why should there be vacant space when you can build something on it? At the center is a market square with some stores and market stalls, and "the synagogues, the meeting houses, the chapels and schools of the town where Jewish children study the Holy Writ. The noise they and the rabbis make with their chanting is enough to deafen one. The baths where the women go to bathe are also there, and the poorhouse where the old men die, and other public institutions." Yet none of these buildings deserves the honor of a description—not even the synagogues.

Yiddish Typewriter (2018)

Dąbrowa Białostocka Synagogue in Shape of Tzedakah (Charity) Box (2016)

BACKBONE OF THE SHTETL

"… and the poorhouse where the old men die, and other public institutions." Sholem Aleichem did not need to articulate the nature of those "other public institutions," because his readers would know what they were about, given the fact that the phrase followed the mention of the poorhouse. The scriptwriters of *Fiddler on the Roof* did not include any of them in their depiction of Anatevka, not because the audience would not know them but more likely because they anticipated that even a cursory list would hinder the dramatic development of the plot, which centered on generational conflict and struggle for women's emancipation in the home of Tevye, his wife, and three strong-headed daughters—an issue relevant both in the shtetl before 1914 and, of course, again in 1960s America. Yet, suppressed in literature and on the stage, these "other institutions" deserve a mention: they provided a backbone for what was, by all means, an extremely self-sufficient society that did not expect anything from the non-Jewish world—except trouble, of course. These institutions were all the charitable organizations, paid for by the kopecks the poor and the rubles the somewhat less poor dropped in the many charity boxes placed in the synagogue, funding the society to provide poor brides with a dowry, the society to pay for circumcisions, the society to take care of orphans, the society to provide a little extra for Shabbat, the society to provide bread to the poor, the society to provide night lodgings to weary travelers, the society to help prisoners, the society to visit the sick, and, in some special places, the society to provide an education to girls. The most important society was the one dedicated to the *mitzvah* (commandment) of participating in the burial of the dead.

WAY OF WALKING

In the early 1920s, the British Jewish writer Israel Zangwill summarized the paradox that is at the basis of Judaism—and is a source of confusion for many non-Jews—in a story that talks about an eastern European Jewish young man who is drafted into the army. When he is asked to list his religion, he replies in astonishment: "I have no religion—after all, I am a Jew." Zangwill judged this anecdote "far more pregnant than all the learned scribblings about Judaism," because "this equivalence of Judaism and life is a central characteristic of the religion. It led necessarily to religion pervading the home, to a domestic ritual, with the father for priest and the mother to bless the Sabbath candles." Indeed, while the world recognizes the historical significance of biblical Judaism to be the articulation of monotheism, the unique character of Rabbinic Judaism is not to be found in a postulate of faith but in a continuous debate and decision making on the ethics of everyday life known as Halakhah (the way of walking). The most burning issue is not, "What should I believe?" but "What ought I do next?" And this is difficult, because it assumes that one first takes the measure of the situation in which one finds oneself—and, as George Orwell famously observed, "to see what is in front of one's nose needs a constant struggle." Guidance is provided by *mitzvoth* (plural of *mitzvah*), ten of which are said to have been revealed to Moses on Mount Sinai. Halakhah expanded these into no fewer than 613. A mitzvah also refers to a deed that fulfills a commandment and to an individual act of human kindness and solidarity that is conducted in the spirit of the commandments. As in all human relations, a mitzvah may be seen as the first part of a transaction, to be reciprocated by the recipient in the future. However, one mitzvah cannot be returned: the act of burial. Therefore, helping to lay the body of a deceased to rest is the greatest of mitzvoth—and it is also the most urgent one, as Jewish tradition demands that it must be done without delay.

Carrying the Deceased to the Cemetery (2019)   36

Ancestors (2008)

THE PEOPLE'S FIELD

"Everywhere people die the same death, and they are placed in the same earth, and are beaten down with the same spades," the chronicler of Kasrilevka tells the reader, adding the qualification that this was the opinion of his rabbi, "when he was happiest, at a wedding or other celebration, after he had had a few glasses of wine and was ready to lift up the skirts of his long coat and dance a kazatsky." The fundamentally egalitarian character of Jewish society in the shtetl was expressed in the fact that the most important site was the graveyard—in the case of Kasrilevka, two cemeteries. "This old cemetery, though it is overgrown with grass and with bushes and has practically no upright headstones, they still value as they might a treasure, a rare gem, a piece of wealth, and guard it like the apple of their eye. For this is not only the place where their ancestors lie, the rabbis, men of piety, learned ones, scholars and famous people, including the dead from the ancient massacres of Chmelnitski's time—but also the only piece of earth of which they are the masters, the only bit of earth they own where a blade of grass can sprout and a tree can grow and the air is fresh and one can breathe freely. […] 'Have you been in our field yet?' a Kasrilevkite will ask you cheerfully, as though he were asking if you had been in his father's vineyard. If you haven't been there, do him a kindness, and go down to 'the field,' read the old, half-obliterated inscriptions on the leaning tombstones and you will find in them the story of a whole people. And if you happen to be a man of feeling and imagination, then you will look upon this poor little town with its rich cemeteries and repeat the old verses: 'How beautiful are your tents, O Jacob; how good are your dwelling places, O Israel.'"

COVENANT

"I will establish my covenant as an everlasting covenant between me and you and your descendants after you for the generations to come, to be your God and the God of your descendants after you." These words mark the beginning of Jewish history, and they help us understand the importance of the cemetery in the Jewish tradition as a place where the chain of generations is present and visible. Judaism, the German Jewish philosopher Franz Rosenzweig proposed in 1918, is a religion that knows everlasting life not in the promise of an existence in the beyond but in the community. "Blessed art thou, O Lord our God, King of the universe, who hast given us the Law of truth, and hast planted everlasting life in our midst." This blessing is said after the reading of a part of the Torah, and refers both to the Torah itself, the law of truth, and to community gathered around it, the everlasting life, embodied in the succession of generations, "each producing the generation to come, and bearing witness to those gone by. Bearing witness takes place in bearing—two meanings but one act, in which eternal life is realized. Elsewhere, past and future are divorced, the one sinking back, the other coming on; here they grow into one. The bearing of the future is a direct bearing witness to the past. The son is born so that he may bear witness to his father's father. The grandson renews the name of the forebear. The patriarchs of old call upon their last descendant by his name—which is theirs. Above the darkness of the future burns the star-strewn heaven of the promise: 'So shall thy seed be.'" Thus Rosenzweig reflected on his Jewish heritage while defending his German fatherland during World War I.

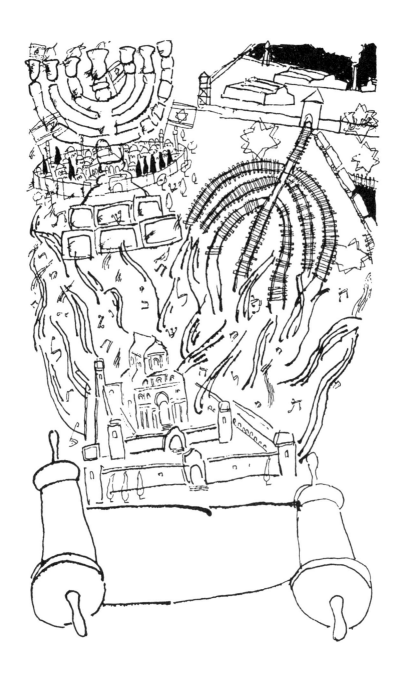

A History (1988)

Giftschrank (2021)

DARK STAMMERINGS

In early 1933, weeks after his party had come to power, Hitler invited a few senior Nazis, including Hermann Rauschning, for tea and cookies in the Reich Chancellery. The conversation turned to the baleful influence of religion, as Rauschning reported in some detail after his break with Hitler and his move to the United States. "We are fighting against the perversion of our soundest instincts," Hitler said. "Ah, the God of the deserts, that crazed, stupid, vengeful Asiatic despot with his powers to make laws! That slavekeeper's whip! That devilish 'Thou shalt, thou shalt!' And that stupid 'Thou shalt not.' […] 'I am the Lord thy God! Who? That Asiatic tyrant? No! The day will come when I shall hold up against these commandments the tables of a new law. And history will recognize our movement as the great battle for humanity's liberation, a liberation from the curse of Mount Sinai, from the dark stammerings of nomads who could no more trust their own sound instincts, who could understand the divine only in the form of a tyrant who orders one to do the very things one doesn't like. This is what we are fighting against: the masochistic spirit of self-torment, the curse of so-called morals, idolized to protect the weak from the strong in face of the immortal law of battle, the great law of divine nature. Against the so-called ten commandments, against them we are fighting." There was more to Hitler's antisemitism than his desire to unchain what Friedrich Nietzsche had labeled "the beast within"—one that had been shackled by a wicked, archaic morality. But at the core of Hitler's vision for a new and better future for the German people was a New Order with libraries in which Bibles would be locked up in the librarian's *Giftschrank* (poison cabinet)—a New Order without Jews and without any Jewish legacy.

MAH TOVU OHALEKHA, YAAKOV

Around 1940 the Austrian writer Gertrud Fussenegger visited the old Jewish cemetery in the center of Prague. "I found myself displaced in a dissolute maze, in an ominous and ugly labyrinth of countless tombstones which arise on top of each other, tombs that occupy like so many seeds of discord the grassless, black dirt soil—erratic masses, lopsided and straight, still standing and fallen over, just as it comes. It is said that the dead lie here in seven layers; seven times has the narrow patch been crammed with corpses." Frau Fussenegger was ignorant of the causes of this overcrowding—the fact that until the emancipation of the Jews in the modern age, most European societies that tolerated their presence forced Jews to live in the confinement of special neighborhoods with small cemeteries and denied them an opportunity to increase the size of their ghettos or graveyards as the population of the living and the number of dead increased. The houses could go upward, and the graves downward, but only so much. And as Halakhah forbade the clearing of graves, Jewish graveyards became congested with tombstones. Ignoring causes, Frau Fussenegger considered only the most apparent effect. An enthusiastic Nazi, she believed in the unity of *Blut und Boden* (blood and soil), and she perceived the Jewish cemetery as an ecological disaster that affected anything that tried to eke out a living at that spot. "Poisoned by this dreadful thronging, the earth seems here to have lost its ability to dissolve the corpses that are entrusted to her into their own, pure and original form, and thus it has lost its power to conciliate that which has expired with itself. As she cannot produce even one more flower, the earth lifts herself only in crippled, bent trees, with branches that creep in all directions closely to the ground, covering the throng of the old funeral monuments with gloomy-green, shadowy twilight." To Frau Fussenegger, the uncanny space of the Prague cemetery was a judgment on the Jewish people.

Ghetto Cemetery (2001)

IT'S JUST A PLACE

The destruction of Jewish life that is already unfolding in Poland at the time of Frau Fussenegger's visit to Prague, an annihilation that will overwhelm the rest of European Jewry in the next five years, is obviously beyond the capacity of Broadway to present in song and dance. And so, when in the 1960s, the destruction of Jewish life in eastern Europe must be brought on the stage in *Fiddler*, it is touched on only lightly. Instead of SS men with machine guns, the end of Jewish life in Anatevka is announced by a somewhat embarrassed policeman, who—justifying an edict of expulsion with the general statement, "There's trouble in the world, troublemakers"—gives Tevye the Milkman, his family, and his neighbors three days to clear out. The community tries to put its loss in perspective: "Yente: 'Well, Anatevka hasn't exactly been the Garden of Eden.' Tevye: 'That's true.' Golde: 'After all, what have we got here? A little bit of this, a little bit of that ...' Yente: 'a pot ...' Mordcha: 'a pan ...' Mendel: 'a broom ...' Lazar: 'a hat.' Tevye: "Someone should have set a match to this place years ago ...' Avram: 'a bench ...' Lazar: 'a tree—what's a house?' Golde: 'or a stove?' Mendel: 'People who pass through Anatevka don't even know they've been here ...' Golde: 'a stick of wood ...' Yente: 'a piece of cloth ...'" Anatevka, the neighbors acknowledge, wasn't much: an underfed, overworked, intimate, obstinate, tumbledown, workaday little town. Yet there everyone knew everyone else; there people were not a strangers. But, pushing the all-too-human attachment to their hometown aside, the Jews of Anatevka settle on a final judgment that Jews have been forced to make in every generation: "Golde: 'Eh, it's just a place.' Mendel: 'Our forefathers have been forced out of many, many places at a moment's notice.' Tevye: 'Maybe that's why we always wear our hats.'" And so, the Jews of Anatevka closed the book on their shtetl, moved on, and opened another one somewhere else.

CATASTROPHIC DESTRUCTION

"Our forefathers have been forced out of many, many places at a moment's notice." This line in *Fiddler* refers to an understanding of Jewish history as one that is shaped by a rhythm of destruction and persecution over a 2,600-year period. Orthodox Jews refer to the Holocaust that unfolded between 1933 and 1945 as a *Churban*, Hebrew for "catastrophic destruction." This term is also associated with the Roman destruction of the Temple of the Jews in 70 CE. This temple was constructed in Jerusalem by King Herod to replace an earlier Temple, constructed by Zerubbabel after the return of a group of Jews from Babylonian captivity. The annual commemoration of this Churban on the ninth day of the month of Av is an important date in the Hebrew calendar—in part because tradition tells that, in 597 BCE, on that very same date, the Babylonians destroyed the First Temple, built by King Solomon. To remember the Churban marked by the destruction of Solomon's Temple and the Churban marked by the destruction of Herod's Temple is to remember also the rebeginnings that the survivors of expulsions, pogroms, massacres, and the Holocaust made in the ruins of their former lives—rebeginnings that imitated our common father and mother, Adam and Eve, who, after the expulsion from the Garden of Eden, decided to begin again by giving birth to Cain and Abel, and after the catastrophe that resulted in the death of Abel and the departure of Cain for the Land of Nod, had enough faith in the future and trust in the world to begin once again. "Adam made love to his wife again, and she gave birth to a son and named him Seth, saying, 'God has granted me another child in place of Abel, since Cain killed him.' Seth also had a son, and he named him Enosh. At that time people began to call on the name of the Lord."

Ninth of Av (2012)

Come and Read (1997)

DIVINELY REVEALED

The tale of Adam and Eve and their two families and three sons belongs to a library of stories, songs, sayings, and visions that the Jews know as the Tanakh, which is an acronym of the three major divisions in that library: Torah (Teaching), which consists of five books that tell a largely mythical history that begins with the creation of the world and ends with Moses's death; Nevi'im (Prophets), which consists of seven major books and twelve smaller texts that are rooted in both legendary and actual history of the Hebrews and the Jews from around 1100 BCE to 500 BCE; and Ketuvim (Writings), a miscellany of eleven books that includes the Psalms, Proverbs, Song of Songs, and so on. Originally the creation and inheritance of a small nation that emerged some 3,000 years ago in the land between the Jordan River and the Mediterranean, this library became a universal heritage when a Jewish sect, following the teachings of Yeshua, son of Josef, and believing that he had been the anointed one to overcome the perdition brought about by Adam and Eve's disobedience in paradise, included this library as a preliminary part of the collection of its own sacred literature, consisting of four Gospels, the Acts of the Apostles, various letters, and a revelation about the end of times. This preliminary part the Christians labeled as the Old Testament. The following pages present a reading of the development of Hebrew and Jewish conceptions of territory and space that is largely based on Nevi'im but which was framed by a legendary prehistory found in Torah—the key books of the Jewish canon, believed by many Jews and Christians to be divinely revealed, books that include legendary tales about the founding parents of humanity, Adam and Eve; the founding fathers and mothers of the Jewish nation, Abraham and Sarah, Isaac and Rebecca, Jacob (also known as Israel), and Leah and Rachel; and the leaders who forged a mass of refugees into a nation, Moses, Miriam, Aaron, and Joshua.

THE LOFTY DWELLING

In many different ways, the five books of the Torah turn against common assumptions about the relationship between the human and the divine worlds in the ancient Middle East. Beginning with the White Temple, erected some 5,600 years ago on an elevated platform in the center of Uruk, sanctuaries were all assumed to connect heaven and earth. This junction was made possible by locating a shrine at a holy place where such a bond was already in place. A tablet describes the Sumerian city of Nibru (also known as Nippur) as "the lofty bond between heaven and earth." In its middle arose the temple of Enlil, "the shining temple, the lofty dwelling. Its fearsomeness and radiance reach up to heaven, its shadow stretches over all the foreign lands, and its crenellation reaches up to the midst of heaven." The ideology of the temple as a building that knots heaven, earth, and underworld led to the construction of ziggurats (from the Akkadian *zaqāru*, "to build high"), stepped temple-towers that articulated the idea of reaching the heavens by elevating the sanctuary where the god or goddess lived high into the sky. The most famous one was the ninety-meter-high Etemenanki (House of the Foundation of Heaven on Earth), constructed in Babylon. Yet, the Torah judges the ambition to create such buildings that seem to storm heaven as an imposition on the domain of the divine. "Now the whole world had one language and a common speech. As people moved eastward, they found a plain in Shinar and settled there. They said to each other, 'Come, let's make bricks and bake them thoroughly.' They used brick instead of stone, and tar for mortar. Then they said, 'Come, let us build ourselves a city, with a tower that reaches to the heavens, so that we may make a name for ourselves; otherwise we will be scattered over the face of the whole earth.' But the Lord came down to see the city and the tower the people were building. The Lord said, 'If as one people speaking the same language they have begun to do this, then nothing they plan to do will be impossible for them. Come, let us go down and confuse their language so they will not understand each other.'" And so he did, and construction stopped.

Tower of Babel (1994)

Abraham Smashes the Idols (1994)

THE LAND I WILL SHOW YOU

The best preserved, or perhaps most ambitiously reconstructed, ziggurat is in Tell el-Muqayyar in Iraq, a site that once hosted the city referred to in the Torah as Ur Kaśdim (Ur of the Chaldeans). It was the birthplace of the mythical Abram, the man who decided to abandon a life in the shadow of a temple that offered a direct stair to heaven and seek a new destiny in a faraway land named Canaan. The Lord had said to Abram, "Go from your country, your people and your father's household to the land I will show you. I will make you into a great nation, and I will bless you; I will make your name great, and you will be a blessing." So, Abram went, as the Lord had told him. A later elaboration of the story of his departure for a new life elsewhere mentions that Abram's father, Terah, had been a manufacturer of idols, and that Abram, in rebellion, smashed the idols before his departure with his wife, Sarai, his nephew Lot, and their slaves. The literature of the ancient Middle East has tales in which the protagonist goes on an adventure—the epic of Gilgamesh provides a splendid example. But permanent separation from one's native soil typically meant catastrophe worse than death. This is the plot of the most famous Egyptian story, the tale of Sinuhe. It tells that when the courtier Sinuhe fears for his life as a result of intrigues, he flees to Canaan, where he raises a family and becomes wealthy. Yet, despite his success in Canaan, Sinuhe cannot be at home in any place but his land of origin. "Whatever God fated this flight—be gracious, and bring me home! Surely You will let me see the place where my heart still stays! What matters more than my being buried in the land where I was born?" Shortly before his death he returns to Egypt. The pharaoh forgives his disloyalty and grants him proper burial in his native land. Sinuhe represents the norm. Abram, to be renamed Abraham after his arrival in Canaan, is the exception.

FOUNDING FATHERS AND MOTHERS

The land of Canaan provided a land bridge between Mesopotamia and Egypt; it was bordered by the Mediterranean Sea in the west, Anatolia in the north, the desert in the east and south. For most of history, the region acted as a buffer between the more advanced states that arose along the Euphrates and the Nile; at times, it was a direct vassal of its northeastern and southwestern neighbors. Throughout the Bronze Age, Canaanite civilization centered on city-states, including Megiddo, Hazor, and Jebus in the southern part—the region of Canaan that is the focus of biblical history. Around 1400 BCE, Canaan began to decline, as it became a battleground between Assyria, Egypt, the Aramaeans, and sea peoples including the Philistines. Many cities were abandoned, and within the slow collapse of urban civilization settled groups of onetime city dwellers arriving from elsewhere, peasants who had fallen on hard times, traditional outlaws, and wanderers and nomads. Egyptian texts typically referred to them as *Habiri*—Hebrews. By 1300 these Hebrews began to coalesce into more formal but still egalitarian communities, and the biblical books of Judges and Samuel, which contain a largely legendary account of this period, suggest that these Hebrews were led by charismatic leaders who emerged from the people. These "judges" included men like Gideon, Samson, Eli, and Samuel, and the formidable Deborah: "Villagers in Israel would not fight; they held back until I, Deborah, arose, until I arose, a mother in Israel." The Hebrews also treasured tales about mythical immigrant ancestors—symbolic types who never existed: Abraham, his son Isaac, and his grandson Jacob, also known as Israel (meaning "wrestles with God"). When, around 1200 BCE, civilization in the Levant collapsed, taking down all the remaining Canaanite cities but one, the Hebrews proved very resilient: by 1100 BCE they controlled the Jordan Valley and all the hill country of biblical Canaan, with the exception of the strongly fortified Canaanite city of Jebus, which was protected by the chief of the Canaanite pantheon: El-Elyon (God the Most Highest).

Canaanite City in Ruins (2020)

Shtetl Synagogue (1993)

THE TENT OF MEETING

The great majority of the Hebrews lived north of Jerusalem in a loose confederation of some ten tribes and clans, the two largest of which were Ephraim and Manassah. Hebrew priests, many of whom belonged to the Levi clan, attended the larger shrines at Shiloh, Dan, Shechem, Gibeon, Gilgal, and Beth-El. These sanctuaries were of Canaanite origin and were dedicated to the Canaanite god El (the Lord), and this area of Hebrew settlement was henceforth known as Israel—a name that means "he wrestles with El" or "he retains El." The Israelites had a sacred object unique in the ancient world: the so-called Tent of Meeting, in which the elders of the Israelite confederation met in counsel. This structure was associated with the mythical Moses, believed by the Israelites to have pulled the Hebrew communities in the territory north of Jebus together into a confederation. "The Lord said to Moses: 'Bring me seventy of Israel's elders who are known to you as leaders and officials among the people. Have them come to the tent of meeting, that they may stand there with you. I will come down and speak with you there, and I will take some of the power of the Spirit that is on you and put it on them. They will share the burden of the people with you so that you will not have to carry it alone.'" Judah was a politically and culturally isolated Hebrew territory south of Jebus. In addition to ordinary holy places dedicated to El, the Judahites, a largely pastoral and warlike clan, had a portable sacred object known as the Ark of the Covenant, dedicated to the Hebrew warrior god Yahweh. This god was believed to live in the Sinai, from where he came in times of crisis to lead the Judahites in battle. The mythical ancestor of Judah was a man named Aaron. While Israel and Judah were to be politically unified between around 1040 BCE and 930 BCE, it took another few centuries for the Israelite and Judahite narratives of origin to merge into a single myth, in which Moses and Aaron, with the help of their sister Miriam, led the descendants of the twelve sons of Abraham's grandson Jacob from Egypt, creating a nation in the desert.

SAUL AND DAVID

The Hebrews were sandwiched between a people of partly Achaean origin, the Philistines, who occupied the coastal plain between Mount Carmel and Gaza, and the Ammonites and Moabites, Semitic peoples who lived east of the Jordan River. When the Philistines began to push eastward, and the Ammonites westward, the Hebrews, divided into the Israelite confederacy in the north and the Judahite clan in the south, found themselves in peril. Samuel, a judge and priest at Shiloh, got the Israelites and Judahites to accept a greater level of unity under the kingship of Saul, a scion of a prominent family from the Israelite tribe of Benjamin, which was geographically close to Judah. Hence Saul appeared to be a wise choice as the unifier of all Hebrews. Yet, while he was able to have some success on the battlefield, the manic-depressive Saul proved unable to create a solid political or social foundation for a single Hebrew state. When Saul got in conflict with Samuel, the latter anointed a young man from Judah, David, as counter king. Subsequently, David became Saul's courtier and healer. "Whenever the spirit from God came on Saul, David would take up his lyre and play. Then relief would come to Saul; he would feel better, and the evil spirit would leave him." David also made a reputation as a brave warrior against the Philistines. When Saul died, his son Ishbaal succeeded him as king of all the Hebrews, but Judah seceded. "Then the men of Judah came to Hebron, and there they anointed David king over the tribe of Judah." Two years later Ishbaal was assassinated, and the Israelites decided to also accept David as their ruler. "When all the elders of Israel had come to King David at Hebron, the king made a covenant with them at Hebron before the Lord, and they anointed David king over Israel." While the biblical account of the lives of Saul, David, and even David's son Solomon has mythical elements, with the attending narrative amplification, there appears to be a factual kernel within those stories that allows our narration to proceed as legend—that is, as stories that have a connection to facts as they actually occurred and places as they actually exist.

Tower of David as a Spice Box (2021)

Fortified City (1997)

A BOND IS SEALED

David now unified Judah and Israel, and he ruled both states, which, however, kept their own institutions. Having witnessed Saul's failure to overcome the divergence between the constituent parts of the new state, David decided that it was necessary to create a contiguous territory and to establish a capital for the federated monarchy of Judah and Israel that could be seen as acceptable to all Hebrews. The conquest of the city of Jebus and the establishment of a royal court in that city, which was now to be known as Jerusalem, was to tie the north and the south together. "The king and his men marched to Jerusalem to attack the Jebusites, who lived there. The Jebusites said to David, 'You will not get in here; even the blind and the lame can ward you off.' They thought, 'David cannot get in here.' Nevertheless, David captured the fortress of Zion—which is the City of David. [...] David then took up residence in the fortress and called it the City of David. He built up the area around it, from the terraces inward. And he became more and more powerful, because the Lord God Almighty was with him. Now Hiram king of Tyre sent messengers to David, along with cedar logs and carpenters and stonemasons, and they built a palace for David." With the inclusion of Jerusalem within the united monarchy of Judah and Israel, the Hebrew state got in fact a third constituent part, with its Jebusite aristocracy and Canaanite traditions. Through his marriage with the Jebusite Bathsheba, David sealed the bond between the Hebrews and Jerusalem. David recognized that his own elevation had been the result of historical contingency. If he was to prevail as king, he had to create a more permanent claim to supremacy. The Israelite god El, the Canaanite god El-Elyon, and the Judahite god Yahweh were to provide the necessary support.

SOLOMON'S TEMPLE

After the conquest of Jerusalem, David failed to integrate the Israelite, Jerusalemite, and Judahite religious establishments. His inability to expand the Jebusite shrine located on Mount Zion immediately north of the city into a royal sanctuary that supported the federated monarchy left a stain on his legacy. After his death, his son Solomon boldly and forcibly moved ahead to create a united monarchy that centered on an alliance of Judahite muscle and Jebusite brains, while suppressing Israelite particularism. Without regard for older shrines in Shiloh, Shechem, and Beth-El, he commissioned the construction of a royal temple on Mount Zion, a sacred place associated with the Canaanite god El-Elyon. Solomon's architect was to find a framework that would also allow the Israelite god El and the Judahite god Yahweh to share that site with El-Elyon. The solution was straightforward: both the description of Solomon's Temple in the book of Kings, which is part of Nevi'im, and in the text of Psalm 29, and a reference in the first book of Chronicles that conflates the Temple of Jerusalem and the Tent of Meeting, suggest that an inner room separated from the main sanctuary contained sacred Israelite, Jebusite, and Judahite symbols. The first was the Tent of Meeting. The second were two winged guardian beings with the head of a human being and body of a lion or bull that protect deities in the ancient Middle East. The third was the Ark of the Covenant. Considering the precise description of Solomon's Temple, it appears that this inner room, *Debir* (West), was in fact a throne platform raised ten cubits (5.2 meters) from the floor. The Israelite Tent of Meeting was pitched below the platform, while the two Canaanite guardian beings, known to the Hebrews as cherubim, stood on top of the platform, creating a protective enclosure for El, El-Elyon, and Yahweh, while the Judahite Ark of the Covenant was placed between the cherubim, serving as a footstool for the three-in-one and one-in-three protector of Solomon's monarchy.

Holy of Holies (2020)

The Golden Calf (2020)

DOMAIN AS THRONE

After the death of Solomon, the united monarchy fell apart after the secession of Israel, which had been excluded from its proper share of power. Judah and Jerusalem, which had been tightly integrated during Solomon's reign, remained united. The leader of the Israelite secession, Jeroboam, became king of Israel. He realized that the success of his dynasty would depend on severing Israelite ties to the Temple of Jerusalem, which was associated with the Davidic dynasty. A royal shrine adjacent to Jeroboam's residence in Shechem was problematic, because Shechem was associated with the older charismatic religious traditions that Solomon had tried to suppress when he created the Temple in Jerusalem. Jeroboam and priests from the Levite clan agreed to designate two old Israelite shrines as royal sanctuaries: the first in Gad, at the northern border of the country, and the second in Beth-El, at the southern border. In each of these towns, the king erected a golden statue of young bull in honor of El. These more earthly parallels to the cherubim were obviously intended to serve as the pedestals of a new throne for the god of Israel, which was not simply located at some place within Israel, as the throne of El, El-Elyon, and Yahweh had been located on Mount Zion—rather, this concept of two pedestals at the boundaries of the kingdom designated the whole of Israel as the throne. Given the earlier importance of the Tent of Meeting, which most likely remained in Jerusalem, this can be seen as a literal "big tent" approach to the concept of sanctuary. However, the tent may have been too big. Older fertility rituals, related to a Canaanite deity known as Ba-El, were revived. Ba-El was a perfectly benign deity, but he proved a useful straw man when Levite priests, who had been associated with the cult of El and feared a loss of influence, began to criticize Ba-El as an "idol." It did not do the Levites much good to insult a popular deity, and they were banned from serving in the royal shrines of Israel.

CONCENTRATION CITY

After the dissolution of Solomon's kingdom, the Tent of Meeting, symbol of the Israelite El cult, ceased to be an important relic in the Jerusalem temple. It is likely that it was effectively forgotten and at one time or another removed. In the Judahite imagination, the remaining artifacts on the throne dais, the Jebusite cherubim and the Judahite Ark of the Covenant, merged into a single object, in which smaller cherubim came to sit on top of the ark. For two centuries, Israel and Judah, which included Jerusalem, were rivals, each claiming to be the true heir of the Hebrew legacy. However, Assyria's conquest of Israel in 721 BCE successfully enticed the elite of the Israelite population—priests, scribes, and craftsmen—to turn their backs to a life at the periphery and be a part of the economic upswing in the big cities at the heart of the mighty empire. The rural majority of the Israelite population, meanwhile, remained in the ancestral land, which later became known as Samaria. This formerly Israelite peasant population preserved many Hebrew customs and beliefs but lost its connection to what proved to be the more vital Hebrew lineage, which centered on Jerusalem. Thanks to a policy of accommodation with Assyria, the kingdom of Judah escaped the fate of Israel. Yet Judah's continued existence was difficult: Assyrians tempted Judahite elites to voluntarily move to Nineveh and other cities in Mesopotamia. "Each of you will eat fruit from your own vine and fig tree and drink water from your own cistern." In addition, they regularly conducted raids into Judah to force peasants to resettle in Assyria. In order to preserve the population base of Judah, the Judahite king, Hezekiah, decided to transfer much of the rural population into Jerusalem and a couple of other fortified cities. To sever the relationship between the peasants and the land, Hezekiah initiated a policy to destroy village sanctuaries; this led to a centralization of all sacrifices at the Temple of Jerusalem. While many must have mourned the loss of their local sanctuaries, others might have enjoyed what Philo of Alexandria centuries later identified as the "brief breathing-space in scenes of genial cheerfulness" offered by a pilgrimage to Jerusalem.

Praise (2013)

I AM WHO I AM

During the time of the federated monarchy under David and the united monarchy under Solomon, the priesthood in Jerusalem consisted of Israelite Levites, Jebusite Zadokites, and Judahite Aaronites. After the split of the kingdom, few Levites had chosen to remain in Jerusalem. But when the Assyrians erased the kingdom of Israel, Levites who had attended local Israelite shrines returned to Jerusalem—not as members of the establishment, like their ancestors, but as destitute refugees. In order to appeal to a sense of solidarity among the well-entrenched Jerusalem priesthood, these Levites fashioned a common history that transcended any messy reality under David and Solomon. They wove various old legends into a coherent story of an exodus from Egypt of the descendants of the patriarchs Abraham, Isaac, and Jacob, who, having been welcomed in Egypt generations earlier, had been enslaved. These refugees from Egypt had become a nation with the support of a deity, whose name is אֶהְיֶה אֲשֶׁר אֶהְיֶה, Ehyeh Asher Ehyeh (I Am Who I Am), under leadership of Moses, Aaron, and Miriam, all Levites themselves; and both Israelites and Judahites had descended from this new nation wrought in the desert. If this story was to remind the good people in Jerusalem of a common ancestry and a debt to be paid, the Levite refugees also fashioned a new beginning to the prehistory of the Exodus—one that spoke of that single, universal god who had aided the Hebrews in their flight from Egypt and was also the single creator of the world: "In the beginning God created the heavens and the earth." The concept of a universal God who is the creator of everything and hence also the king of all that exists also brought a sense of the unity of all of God's creation, a unity that is rooted in its common beginning, and which is embodied in the Hebrew letter *aleph*, the first of the twenty-two letters of the Aleph-Bet, and the first letter of both Ehyeh and Asher.

EVERYWHERE AND NOWHERE

The Levite articulation of this new concept of a universal, all-powerful deity made the mythic notion of a specific holy place, where the gods reside at the center of the world, obsolete. If God resided everywhere, then it ought to be possible to encounter him anywhere—for example in a burning bush in the middle of nowhere. This was a revolutionary concept and led to a most significant innovation in the history of architectural thought: a sanctuary does not need to be associated with a particular preexisting sacred place; it can be built even amid the void. Thus the Levites provided a theological justification for King Hezekiah's policy to destroy local shrines in order to force the Judahite peasants into fortified cities. They now began to create a historical foundation for this new concept of a shrine that is independent of a preexisting holy place by writing such a placeless sanctuary into the new history of the Hebrew people while they had sojourned in the desert between the Exodus and the return to Canaan. As to the practical problems associated with surviving in a no-place: God would take care of that. "In the desert the whole community grumbled against Moses and Aaron. The Israelites said to them, 'If only we had died by the Lord's hand in Egypt! There we sat around pots of meat and ate all the food we wanted, but you have brought us out into this desert to starve this entire assembly to death.' Then the Lord said to Moses, 'I will rain down bread from heaven for you. The people are to go out each day and gather enough for that day. In this way I will test them and see whether they will follow my instructions.'" And thus daily loaves of bread dropped from the sky and confirmed the effective power of the Tabernacle as a link to the divine—despite the fact it was a placeless sanctuary.

Manna (1998)

Manna (1977)

SANCTITUDE BY DESIGN

The Levites named that no-place sanctuary *Mishkan* (dwelling place), but it is referred to in English as the Tabernacle ("tent," in Latin). Because the Tabernacle could be erected anywhere, the question of its form, execution, and furnishings—which included an altar for burning animal sacrifices, an altar for burning incense, a basin for washing, a golden table to hold the bread of presence, a golden lampstand with seven lights, and the Ark of the Covenant—acquired a precise ideological and theological significance that had no parallel in earlier architectural traditions. Indeed: precision of the design of the structure and its parts had to compensate for the lack of a sacred location. As the basis of their design, the Levite priests took the arrangement of the Temple of Jerusalem, with its main room, which the book of Kings labels as *Hekal* (Great Hall), in which was located an inner room, *Debir* (West). They reduced the dimensions of the desert sanctuary to 50 percent of those of the Temple. In addition, they reduced the somewhat complex relationship between Hekal and Debir by articulating a simple sequence: a Holy Place that gave access to the *Kodesh HaKodeshim* (Holy of Holies). In the Temple, the Debir is a cube, measuring twenty by twenty by twenty cubits, that is *inserted into* the Hekal, which measured twenty by sixty by thirty cubits; in the Tabernacle, the Holy of Holies, a cube measuring ten by ten by ten cubits, *follows* the Holy Place, which measures ten by twenty by ten cubits. The Tabernacle not only reinterpreted the architecture of the Temple of Jerusalem but also revived the Israelite tradition of the Tent of Meeting, which had been attended by the Levites. The Tent of Meeting had been absorbed into the Temple of Jerusalem and forgotten after the separation of the unitary monarchy into Israel and Judah. It goes without saying that in this Levite utopia, Levites had a significant role in the management of the Tabernacle—an invented past that might have served a useful purpose for refugee Levites seeking to find a job in the Temple complex in Jerusalem during Hezekiah's reign.

TWELVE PRECIOUS STONES

The Levites imagined the Hebrew nation sojourning in a tented city in the desert during a time of national emergency in Judah. This becomes clear in Bemidbar (In the Wilderness), the fourth book of the Torah, known in English as Numbers. It describes how, after Moses had established the Tabernacle, God instructed him to take a census of the twelve tribes, counting "all the men in Israel who are twenty years old or more and able to serve in the army." Levites were to be exempt from military service. "The Lord had said to Moses: 'You must not count the tribe of Levi or include them in the census of the other Israelites. Instead, appoint the Levites to be in charge of the tabernacle of the Testimony.'" Then God gave instructions as to the arrangement of the camp. In the breastplate of the high priest Aaron, the twelve tribes, symbolically represented by twelve precious stones, were aligned in three vertical columns of four. Now the camps were to be symmetrically arranged around the Tabernacle, "each of them under their standard": three tribes to the east, three to the south, three to the west, and three to the north. The section in the east, associated with sunrise and commanded by Judah, was ranked highest and also was to provide the avant-garde in battle. This was the arrangement that made Balaam, who was hostile to the Hebrews, utter the words "How beautiful are your tents, Jacob, your dwelling places, Israel!" The beauty, to be sure, was rooted in the appearance of combat readiness the camp projected. "God brought them out of Egypt; they have the strength of a wild ox. They devour hostile nations and break their bones in pieces; with their arrows they pierce them. Like a lion they crouch and lie down, like a lioness—who dares to rouse them? May those who bless you be blessed and those who curse you be cursed!" A model society for a troubled age—not much different from the well-armed Jewish nation-state envisioned by Zionists a century ago.

Twelve Tribes (2011)

Moses (1990s)

A FORBIDDEN PLACE

In suppressing the importance of the concept of a sanctuary that is associated with a preexisting sacred place, the Levites reversed an understanding of the meaning and experience of space. True, in a bow to traditional sensibilities, the Torah maintains that the core principles of the moral life, the Ten Commandments, were given to Moses on Mount Sinai. Yet, it also made clear that God did not live on Mount Sinai but chose to appear there to Moses only because the latter happened to be there—as God had appeared elsewhere to Moses when he spoke in a burning bush. And for the duration of God's presence at Sinai, the mountain was forbidden to all except Moses. "Put limits for the people around the mountain and tell them, 'Be careful that you do not approach the mountain or touch the foot of it. Whoever touches the mountain is to be put to death. They are to be stoned or shot with arrows; not a hand is to be laid on them. No person or animal shall be permitted to live.' Only when the ram's horn sounds a long blast may they approach the mountain." Thus Mount Sinai was off-limits during the Hebrews' sojourn in the desert. It represented an otherworldly reality that ordinary mortals found difficult to negotiate. For example, it had given such a radiance to Moses's face that he inspired fear among the Hebrews, a reaction that prompted him to wear a veil over his face. As a forbidden, numinous place, Mount Sinai, unlike Mount Zion, never acquired importance afterward as a place that legitimized sanctuaries in Judah or as a destination for pilgrimages. This abandonment of Mount Sinai as a focus of the Judahite and subsequent Jewish religious imagination occurred, it must be understood, not only because it was ethereal but also because the revelation at Mount Sinai was a myth exclusively located in a faraway and almost inaccessible territory in the past, while Mount Zion was a powerful reality in the present and, during the long periods of exile that shaped the Jewish worldview, a promise for the future.

BOUNDARIES

The spatial practice of the Levites focused on boundary. In their writings, which are embodied in the narrative strand in the Torah that is known as *P* (for "priestly writings"), one finds an obsession with a huge and increasingly intricate system of boundaries that begins with Moses's instructions to the Hebrews not to approach Mount Sinai and quickly reveals its core message: "I am the Lord your God, who brought you out of Egypt, out of the land of slavery. You shall have no other gods before me. You shall not make for yourself an image in the form of anything in heaven above or on the earth beneath or in the waters below. You shall not bow down to them or worship them." The prohibition against the worship of images is a major boundary between past and future, between the Hebrews and the other nations. It sets the Hebrews apart, because it commands them not to get tied up with any fixed notion, with a particular embodiment of an idea. "Everything in Judaism must remain fluid—streaming, changeable, on the running board of history," the Yiddish writer Abraham Golomb observed in his interpretation of the second commandment. This call to remain flexible and creative suggests that the Hebrews participated in the creation of the world, that they are partners of God. "Remember the Sabbath day by keeping it holy. Six days you shall labor and do all your work, but the seventh day is a Sabbath to the Lord your God. On it you shall not do any work, neither you, nor your son or daughter, nor your male or female servant, nor your animals, nor any foreigner residing in your towns. For in six days the Lord made the heavens and the earth, the sea, and all that is in them, but he rested on the seventh day. Therefore the Lord blessed the Sabbath day and made it holy." These boundaries were meant to set the Hebrews apart from other people, a separation that was to create a unique *esprit de corps* that was to hold them together, through a partnership with God, in a dangerous and unpredictable world in which, as the history of the kingdom of Israel had shown, one military defeat could mean extinction as a recognizable nation.

Sinai (2011)

THE SEVENTH DAY

The commandment concerning the Shabbat is the hinge between the commandments that apply to the people's relationship to God and those that apply to the relationship among themselves. "Therefore the Lord blessed the Sabbath day and made it holy." This sentence invites comparison with the account of God's creation of the world, which was also composed by the Levites. The account begins with the well-known, "In the beginning God created the heavens and the earth," moves through the six days in which God creates and creates, and finally ends with two concluding sentences: "By the seventh day God had finished the work he had been doing; so on the seventh day he rested from all his work. Then God blessed the seventh day and made it holy, because on it he rested from all the work of creating that he had done." This is the first use in the Torah of the word *holy*, which means that the day is consecrated—not a place, like the heavens, nor a creature. It is a moment in time: the seventh day. "This is a radical departure from accustomed religion," the great teacher of Judaism and social activist Abraham Joshua Heschel wrote in *The Sabbath*. Other cultures celebrated holiness in space, yet the Levites, in creating the no-place sanctuary in the desert and composing the account of creation, declared Shabbat as the first in holiness. "Judaism teaches us to be attached to holiness in time, to be attached to sacred events, to learn how to consecrate sanctuaries that emerge from the magnificent stream of the year. The Sabbaths are our great cathedrals; and our Holy of Holies is a shrine that neither the Romans nor the Greeks were able to burn; a shrine that even apostasy cannot easily obliterate: the Day of Atonement." It was a holiness of time that, over time, became the object of a profound love, a love of the Shabbat that carried the descendants of Abraham through the most difficult of times. "It was if the whole people were in love with the seventh day," Heschel concluded. "Much of its spirit can only be understood as an example of love carried to the extreme."

COVENANT OF THE HEART AND SOUL

In 612 BCE the Assyrian Empire collapsed after decades of pressure by the Babylonians. The king of Judah, Josiah, made use of the resulting power vacuum on its northern frontier by conquering the territory that had been the home of the Israelites. An important new ideology created by the Levite Jeremiah at Josiah's court in Jerusalem aimed to justify what seemed to be a restoration of the federated monarchy established by David, except that it was now all part of Judah. It stressed Josiah's descent from David and the special covenant between David and God. An unexpected "discovery" of a hitherto unknown text hidden in the Temple of Jerusalem, which was to become known as the biblical book of Devarim (Words), or Deuteronomy (Second Law), created the justification of a new ideology of a conditional covenant between God and the people of Judah and Israel—conditional on the good behavior of the people (and this new text suggested that because the Israelites had broken the covenant, Israel had disappeared as a nation, leaving only the remnant population of the Samaritans). This book was read, on instructions of King Josiah, to the people assembled in the court of the Temple. "The king stood by the pillar and renewed the covenant in the presence of the Lord—to follow the Lord and keep his commands, statutes and decrees with all his heart and all his soul, thus confirming the words of the covenant written in this book. Then all the people pledged themselves to the covenant." This public act shows that a shift had taken place in the understanding of the proper nature of the people's relationship with God: the Temple, with its sacrifices conducted by priests on behalf of the people at the main altar in the forecourt, did not really matter. What counted was the covenant of the heart.

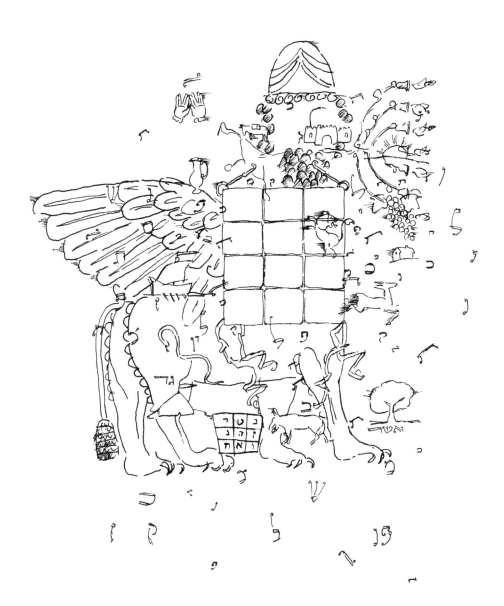

Exile of the Tribes (1990s)

THE LORD WILL SCATTER YOU

This covenant came with the promise of great rewards: "If you fully obey the Lord your God and carefully follow all his commands I give you today, the Lord your God will set you high above all the nations on earth." A short list of particular blessings followed. Yet it also came with the certainty of punishment if the Judahites were to err in their ways: "However, if you do not obey the Lord your God and do not carefully follow all his commands and decrees I am giving you today, all these curses will come on you and overtake you." This list was long and terrifying. A couple of samples will suffice: Failure in every enterprise, war, crushing defeat, plague, illness, infertility, bad harvest, hunger, even cannibalism. And above all, the end of nationhood—exile. "Then the Lord will scatter you among all nations, from one end of the earth to the other. There you will worship other gods—gods of wood and stone, which neither you nor your ancestors have known. Among those nations you will find no repose, no resting place for the sole of your foot. There the Lord will give you an anxious mind, eyes weary with longing, and a despairing heart. You will live in constant suspense, filled with dread both night and day, never sure of your life. In the morning you will say, 'If only it were evening!' and in the evening, 'If only it were morning!'—because of the terror that will fill your hearts and the sights that your eyes will see." Deuteronomy erected a terrifying horizon around Judah—a horizon that was also shaped by the memory of the fate of the kingdom of Israel. Deuteronomy created fear, but like a vaccine, it also prepared the people for the worst—for this to happen in some future.

PASSOVER CLEANSING

Subsequent to the adoption of the new covenant, Josiah decided to clean house. First of all, he removed all vestiges of idol worship that had encroached on the Temple. "He took the Asherah pole from the temple of the Lord to the Kidron Valley outside Jerusalem and burned it there. [...] He also tore down the quarters of the male shrine prostitutes, which were in the temple of the Lord." Subsequently, he erased all the traces of the older Ba-El cults that had remained popular in the newly annexed parts of his kingdom—territories that had been part of the defunct kingdom of Israel and now also defunct Assyrian Empire. In Josiah's view, Ba-El was an idol, and the eradication of Ba-El cults was nothing less than a battle of good versus evil, with no prisoners taken. "Just as he had done at Beth-El, Josiah removed all the shrines at the high places that the kings of Israel had built in the towns of Samaria and that had aroused the Lord's anger. Josiah slaughtered all the priests of those high places on the altars and burned human bones on them. Then he went back to Jerusalem." Upon his return, Josiah established a new festival, which was based on the Levite history of the Exodus from Egypt, a historic event that had become official history during the reign of Hezekiah and now deserved its own festival. "The king gave this order to all the people: 'Celebrate the Passover to the Lord your God, as it is written in this Book of the Covenant.' Neither in the days of the judges who led Israel nor in the days of the kings of Israel and the kings of Judah had any such Passover been observed. But in the eighteenth year of King Josiah, this Passover was celebrated to the Lord in Jerusalem." Immediately thereafter, Josiah resumed the cleansing of his kingdom from all that violated the covenant, getting rid of "the mediums and spiritists, the household gods, the idols and all the other detestable things seen in Judah and Jerusalem." Yes, it proved to be too little too late: a bill was due for the many transgressions during the years that separated the reigns of Hezekiah and Josiah. "I will remove Judah also from my presence as I removed Israel," God announced.

Matzoh Moon (2004)

RHYTHMS AND TRUTHS

The ideology that shaped the books of Exodus and Deuteronomy presented a powerful nexus that connected an understanding of grand history with liturgical precision. It was the product of those connected to the Temple in Jerusalem. But at the same time, there was a different reality in the countryside of Judah, where life unfolded in a timeless manner, with the regular rhythms of sowing, waiting, tending, and harvesting crops and birthing, tending, and slaughtering animals—rhythms sometimes interrupted by calamities such as droughts, floods, and diseases, which provide a horizon of uncertainty around the stable core of peasant life. In the villages, Judahite elders steered the life of the community and instructed the young with the usual admonitions to look beyond the needs of the day: "Go to the ant, you sluggard; consider its ways and be wise! It has no commander, no overseer or ruler, yet it stores its provisions in summer and gathers its food at harvest. How long will you lie there, you sluggard? When will you get up from your sleep? A little sleep, a little slumber, a little folding of the hands to rest—and poverty will come on you like a thief and scarcity like an armed man." Pithy proverbs also arose, simple messages meant to provide guidance in social life: "When pride comes, then comes disgrace, but with humility comes wisdom." "Better to be a nobody and yet have a servant than pretend to be somebody and have no food." "The Lord tears down the house of the proud, but he sets the widow's boundary stones in place." These messages show that, in the final analysis, all the tales about that originally egalitarian society of refugees in the desert were, for the majority of the Judahite population, just tales. They also show that if in some ways the Judahites and their descendants, the Jews, stand apart from other people, they are also the same—especially when facing the question of how to live a life of practical righteousness amid their neighbors. Hence the enduring popularity of the book that collected all of them: Mishle (Proverbs).

YOUR BELOVED IS KNOCKING

If life in the Judahite countryside resembled that of peasants everywhere, the concerns of young aristocrats in Jerusalem were like those of the young and restless of all ages. While the priests attended to their God of the covenant in the Holy of Holies of the Temple, young men and women celebrated their covenants, both imagined and experienced, in the Song of Songs. "He: 'I have come into my garden, my sister, my bride; I have gathered my myrrh with my spice. I have eaten my honeycomb and my honey; I have drunk my wine and my milk.' Friends: 'Eat, friends, and drink; drink your fill of love.' She: 'I slept but my heart was awake. Listen! My beloved is knocking […] I arose to open for my beloved, and my hands dripped with myrrh, my fingers with flowing myrrh, on the handles of the bolt. I opened for my beloved, but my beloved had left; he was gone. My heart sank at his departure. I looked for him but did not find him. I called him but he did not answer. The watchmen found me as they made their rounds in the city. They beat me, they bruised me; they took away my cloak, those watchmen of the walls! Daughters of Jerusalem, I charge you—if you find my beloved, what will you tell him? Tell him I am faint with love.'" It remains a credit to the sages who decided on the final compilation of the Tanakh that they included the Song of Songs in the literary canon of the Jewish people. Of course, the justification was not to be found in the sexual longings the text was able to engender. *He* was read as an allegory of God, and *She* as a symbol of the Jewish people. As to the watchmen: there are too many candidates. And having become the story of the love affair between God and the Jews, it acquired a central place in the Jewish imagination. "For all of eternity in its entirety is not as worthy as the day on which Song of Songs was given to Israel," Rabbi Akiva ben Yosef declared not long after the destruction of King Herod's Temple. "All the Writings are holy, but Song of Songs is the Holy of Holies."

Song of Songs: The Watchmen Found Me (2016)

Nebuchadnezzar (1980s)

EXILED BUT NOT ABANDONED

"In the ninth year of Zedekiah's reign, on the tenth day of the tenth month, Nebuchadnezzar king of Babylon marched against Jerusalem with his whole army. He encamped outside the city and built siege works all around it." After a long siege the Babylonians were able to break through the walls; they destroyed the Temple and the city. "Nebuzaradan the commander of the guard carried into exile the people who remained in the city." In this exile, which began in 597 BCE, enough Judahites knew that they had been exiled because of their disobedience to God, and they also had the certainty that exile did not mean separation from God. While most Judahites likely assimilated into the Babylonian population, enough decided to stand apart, nurturing memories of past happiness in Jerusalem. "By the rivers of Babylon we sat and wept when we remembered Zion. [...] 'If I forget you, Jerusalem, may my right hand forget its skill. May my tongue cling to the roof of my mouth if I do not remember you, if I do not consider Jerusalem my highest joy.'" Jeremiah, the author of the ideology of a conditional covenant, told the exiles not to lose hope: God had not abandoned them, and a return to Jerusalem was assured. "This is what the Lord says: 'I will restore the fortunes of Jacob's tents and have compassion on his dwellings; the city will be rebuilt on her ruins, and the palace will stand in its proper place. From them will come songs of thanksgiving and the sound of rejoicing. I will add to their numbers, and they will not be decreased; I will bring them honor, and they will not be disdained. Their children will be as in days of old, and their community will be established before me; I will punish all who oppress them. Their leader will be one of their own; their ruler will arise from among them. I will bring him near and he will come close to me—for who is he who will devote himself to be close to me?' declares the Lord. 'So you will be my people, and I will be your God.'"

THE CRUCIBLE OF CAPTIVITY

"It was during the troubled interval between the destruction of the Temple by Nebuchadnezzar and the beginning of the reconstruction under Cyrus, it was when Israel sat down by the rivers of Babylon and wept when he remembered Zion, that his soul, quickened as never before, produced the major Prophets and the Psalmists that are his peculiar glory." Thus Israel Zangwill summarized the importance of the Babylonian exile in the history of the Jewish people. Everything that had happened before was only prehistory, raw material to be used in the creation of a new nation, known as the Children of Israel, in memory of the patriarch Jacob, who had been given the name Israel (wrestles with God) after his fight with the angel. The exiles forged a new national identity, and a new individual identity, in memory of Judah: Jew. "It was when he hanged his harps on the willow-trees and asked how could he sing the songs of the Lord in a strange land that, in fact, he sang them most sincerely and passionately. It was then that he, for the first time, preferred Jerusalem above his chief joy. It was then that the ethical messages of the older prophets first found their real response, and that the tender mysticism by which Amos had expressed the peculiar bond between Israel and his God penetrated sweetly into the soul of the exiled captives. For this was the birth-period of Judaism proper, and of the bulk of that self-conscious literature, which first inspired and then enswathed. The very 'Book of the Law of Moses' seems scarcely known before Ezra brought it from Babylon. It was too in the sixth century B.C. that the historical books were written, re-edited or re-coloured to constitute the epic which was to console and resurrect the people that was its theme."

Sefer (1980)

Ezekiel 41:1 And He Brought Me to the Temple (2013)

ARCHITECTURE OF PROMISE

One characteristic aspect of the Hebrew religious tradition that had persisted throughout the history of both Israel and Judah was the appearance of prophets, who held rulers and peoples to account and sketched the catastrophic futures that might arise if they did not change their ways. During the Babylonian captivity, a prophet named Ezekiel spoke within the catastrophe itself and, like Jeremiah, sketched a happy future for the exiles on the condition that they did not abandon their faith in God. This vision included a detailed description of a new temple that the Jews, after the end of their exile and return to Jerusalem, might build. "I saw a man whose appearance was like bronze; he was standing in the gateway with a linen cord and a measuring rod in his hand. The man said to me: 'Son of man, look carefully and listen closely and pay attention to everything I am going to show you, for that is why you have been brought here. Tell the people of Israel everything you see.'" The man began surveying the temple in all its details. As the prophecy unfolds, it becomes clear that the new temple is both an enlarged and above all perfected version of the destroyed temple constructed during Solomon's reign. When the surveyor finished measuring the inside, "He measured the east side with the measuring rod; it was five hundred cubits. He measured the north side; it was five hundred cubits by the measuring rod. He measured the south side; it was five hundred cubits by the measuring rod. Then he turned to the west side and measured; it was five hundred cubits by the measuring rod. So he measured the area on all four sides. It had a wall around it, five hundred cubits long and five hundred cubits wide, to separate the holy from the common." A comparison between the description of the Temple of Solomon in 1 Kings and the visionary temple of Ezekiel shows the new obsession with establishing clear boundaries between spaces of increasing sanctity. Did this mean a return to the sanctity of space?

BOUNDLESS REDEMPTION

Semper in absentes felicior aestus amantes, wrote the Roman poet Sextus Propertius. "Passion is often greater in absent lovers." This ancient knowledge certainly applies to the Jews' exile. Among them arose a prophet named Isaiah, who spoke about Jerusalem—which he referred to as Zion—the absent lover, in a language never heard before. "Listen to me, you who pursue righteousness and who seek the Lord: Look to the rock from which you were cut and to the quarry from which you were hewn; look to Abraham, your father, and to Sarah, who gave you birth. When I called him he was only one man, and I blessed him and made him many. The Lord will surely comfort Zion and will look with compassion on all her ruins; he will make her deserts like Eden, her wastelands like the garden of the Lord. Joy and gladness will be found in her, thanksgiving and the sound of singing." The new Jerusalem, to be rebuilt by the exiles after their return from Babylon, became in the prophet's supercharged language a city like none before, a vision of history justified and suffering redeemed. "The children of your oppressors will come bowing before you; all who despise you will bow down at your feet and will call you the City of the Lord, Zion of the Holy One of Israel. Although you have been forsaken and hated, with no one traveling through, I will make you the everlasting pride and the joy of all generations. You will drink the milk of nations and be nursed at royal breasts. Then you will know that I, the Lord, am your Savior, your Redeemer, the Mighty One of Jacob. Instead of bronze I will bring you gold, and silver in place of iron. Instead of wood I will bring you bronze, and iron in place of stones. I will make peace your governor and well-being your ruler. No longer will violence be heard in your land, nor ruin or destruction within your borders, but you will call your walls Salvation and your gates Praise." A sacred space to be sure, but one that hardly met older notions of holiness.

The Four Holy Cities (2011)

Temple in Ruins (1998)

PERIPHERAL SANCTUARY

In 539 BCE the Persians, led by King Kurus (Cyrus), conquered Babylon. A delegation of exiled Jews requested permission to return to their ancient homeland. Kurus allowed them to do so. However, a significant number of the exiles decided that a return to the land between the Jordan and the Mediterranean, now a Persian province, known at that time as Yehud Medinata and later as Judaea, was not necessary. While they had not assimilated into the general population, they decided to remain in Babylon as Jews—the beginning of the Jewish diaspora. A minority of Jews returned to their ancient homeland—a journey that came to resemble, in the memory of the Jewish people, the journey of Abraham from Ur to Canaan. In Jerusalem the exiles began the reconstruction of the city. Initially there was little interest in reconstructing the Temple: the Jews had lived in Babylonia without a sanctuary constructed from stone and mortar, and for a whole generation the site of the former Temple remained a ruin. Then, after a failed harvest, the Lord's word was heard through the prophet Haggai: "'Is it a time for you yourselves to be living in your paneled houses, while this house remains a ruin? […] You expected much, but see, it turned out to be little. What you brought home, I blew away. Why?' declared the Lord Almighty. 'Because of my house, which remains a ruin, while each of you is busy with your own house.'" And thus, decades after their return to Jerusalem, the Jews commenced with the construction of a new sanctuary without the support of a royal house—after all, Judaea was far away from the Persian capital. As a sanctuary of a small people in a peripheral province, the Second Temple was for many centuries to remain a very poor imitation of the original, at least if one assumed the description in the biblical book of Kings to be true. But it did not really matter, as the Jews had ceased to believe that God really lived in a building made by hands.

TEXT AS TEMPLE

Around a hundred years after the return from Babylon, a scribe named Ezra put the final nail in the coffin of monumental architecture—at least as far as the Jews were concerned. For a decade Ezra had been compiling and redacting the various sacred writings of the Jews. The result became the Torah. With the Torah, which included the stories about the Tower of Babel, Abraham's journey from Ur to Canaan, the Exodus from Egypt, the revelation of the Ten Commandments at Mount Sinai, and the Tabernacle in the desert, Ezra had created the ultimate portable sanctuary that celebrated the covenant—both unconditional and also conditional—between God and his people. It was a covenant that had been tested during the period of exile—and it had held. "All the people came together as one in the square before the Water Gate. They told Ezra the teacher of the Law to bring out the Book of the Law of Moses, which the Lord had commanded for Israel. So on the first day of the seventh month Ezra the priest brought the Law before the assembly, which was made up of men and women and all who were able to understand. He read it aloud from daybreak till noon as he faced the square before the Water Gate in the presence of the men, women and others who could understand. And all the people listened attentively to the Book of the Law." Imitating King Josiah's public reading of Deuteronomy, which was included in the Torah, Ezra had made the temple effectively obsolete, a development that had been initiated by King Hezekiah and the Levites during the time of the Assyrian domination and completed during the Babylonian captivity. Thus Ezra honored the second commandment, which forbade Jews to worship graven images, and gave life to the idea that the Jewish past is not a fixed point of reference but a partner as one lives one's life in the present, with an eye to the future. "Then all the people went away to eat and drink, to send portions of food and to celebrate with great joy, because they now understood the words that had been made known to them."

This Is the Law of Moses (2008)

Wooden Synagogue of Zabludow (1999)

HOUSE OF ASSEMBLY

The Torah, and the idea of a *minyan* (number) of at least ten adult Jewish men (and today also women in progressive congregations) who share the reading of the Torah, completed the liberation from the tyranny of sacred site and sacred building. The Torah marked a radical new understanding of the world that departed from existing religious practices anywhere. True, sacrifice of animals, which went back on Mount Zion to Canaanite times, continued as long as the Temple of Jerusalem stood. Yet, as there was only one temple, most Jews interacted with it only occasionally. The increasing primacy of text over sacrifice and time over space in the Jewish religion gave rise to a specific architectural type that came to occupy a central place in the ordinary lives of Jews, and that was built wherever Jews lived: the *Bet Knesset* (House of Assembly), known in Greek, the common language at the time, as *sunagoge* (assembly). The synagogue was not considered a rival to the Temple; it was not sacred space and did not demand liturgical purity. In fact, it was not only constructed everywhere but also could be located anywhere; one of the best preserved synagogues from antiquity, in Sardes (today's Turkey), was located in the compound of the city's bathhouse. While the synagogue was not a sacred place, it did contain, however, one or more special places for a sacred object: the Torah. But apart from the requirement that it should offer a place to store the Torah safely when not in use, and a place where it could be opened and read, there were no other requirements. While the Temple of Jerusalem stood, it claimed, of course, preeminence on the basis of its ancient prestige. But the text of King Solomon's prayer of dedication, composed during the Deuteronomic Reform during King Josiah's reign, made clear that this prestige rested on a narrow base: "But will God really dwell on earth? The heavens, even the highest heaven, cannot contain you. How much less this temple I have built!" The synagogue represented the future.

ASPIRATION VERSUS OBLIGATION

The culture of the Hebrews, since their origins as a set of semi-outlaw communities that survived in the ruins of Canaanite civilization, had stood in a tension with the customs of the urban civilizations around them. Tensions increased with the emergence of monotheism following the articulation of the convergence of El, El-Elyon, and Yahweh into the I Am Who I Am who confronted Moses in the burning bush. Judahite culture developed an either/or character, rejecting other peoples' and/and way of living. This saved and shaped the Jews during the Babylonian exile but also created enormous tensions centuries later, when Judaea became part of the pluralistic, multiethnic Hellenistic commonwealth created by Alexander the Great. Hellenism was based on the Greek polis and offered the possibility of a citizenship that was disconnected from a person's ethnic or religious identity. Now Jews, especially urban Jews, faced the temptation of assimilating as citizens into a new, exciting, and universalizing cosmopolitan world, while at the same time preserving a particular Jewish religious identity. Yet, it proved difficult to negotiate the tensions between the universality of Greek aspirations and the particularity of Jewish obligations. Around 180 BCE, Seleucid ruler Antiochus IV Epiphanes decided on a policy of forced Hellenization in his realm, which included the province of Judaea. He outlawed the Shabbat and circumcision, commissioned a statue of Zeus to be erected in the Temple of Jerusalem, and told priests to sacrifice pigs at its altar. Now the space of accommodation that had existed in Judaea, between full assimilation into Hellenism and total refusal of the ideal of the polis, disappeared.

Zeus Defiling the Temple (1997)

Hanukkah Menorah (2011)

COME, LIGHT THE MENORAH

Jewish collective memory has chosen to remember with pride Judah Maccabee, who despised the ways of the Greeks and their insistence that the Jews widen their horizons and adjust some of their customs and traditions to accommodate the demands of citizenship in a well-ordered city based on the ideal of the Greek polis. Judah Maccabee's mind did not move easily in the and/and universe framed by intercultural encounter but held fast to either/or choices implied by a strict adherence to Jewish laws of purity. His revolt against Greek rule and intelligent compromise, happily commemorated in the Jewish festival of Hanukkah, certainly delights children and Jewish schoolteachers, but it also represents one of those episodes in Jewish history in which the continuing dialectic of intellectual expansion and contraction pulled the Jewish mind into a self-imposed ghetto. Certainly, without this revolt, Judaism might have become so diluted that it might not have survived the end of antiquity. The Maccabees created an independent Jewish state known in Aramaic as Mamleket Yehuda (Kingdom of Judaea) that postponed a final reckoning between the demands of assimilation and the desire for separation for over a century. Yet, at the same time, the revolt of the Maccabees led to the tragic and ongoing split between Jews—that is, Judaeans, who saw themselves as descendants of the Judahites—and the descendants of the Israelites who had not been deported by the Assyrians and had maintained traditions of their ancestors. Until the Maccabee revolt, these Samaritans (named so because the former territory of Israel was now named Samaria) and Jews had mixed. But when the Samaritans, who were culturally more flexible, refused to support the Maccabees, they became in the view of the Jews who joined the revolt a nation of traitors. The rift remains to this day.

FOLIE DE GRANDEUR

"The lady doth protest too much, methinks," Queen Gertrude wittily comments in Shakespeare's *Hamlet*, when she observes the insincere overacting of a character in a play within the play, written by Hamlet to indict his uncle for the murder of the king of Denmark. Gertrude's quip would be a good title for a history of architecture that presents the architecturally most accomplished examples of any building type, from abbey, acropolis, and agora to yurt, ziggurat, and zoo. When in the fifth century the Athenians created in the Parthenon the most perfect example of the Greek temple, in fact the heart of their community had already shifted to the agora, and the Parthenon, embodiment of the ideal city, served at best as a source of legitimacy for the workings of the actual city below. The same applied to the Temple of Jerusalem. When the Romans incorporated Judaea as a protectorate within their empire, they were initially not interested in the future of the Temple. However, when they appointed Herod as a client-king of Judaea, the Temple became an important piece in the three-dimensional chess game Herod played with the Roman overlords and his Jewish, Samaritan, and other non-Jewish subjects. An Edomite by birth, Herod was a parvenu, and as a typical example of one, he tried to prove his worthiness through megalomaniac building projects, such as large palaces constructed in the desert, including one that was the setting of his tomb, and three temples in honor of Emperor Augustus—all in cities other than Jerusalem. Distrusted by the Jewish majority population, Herod tried to prove his Jewish credentials by pulling down the four-centuries-old Temple, built with so much delay and with so few resources after the exiles' return from Babylon, and covering Mount Zion with an enormous trapezoidal platform that still exists and is known as the Haram al-Sharif (Noble Sanctuary), and building on this new base the magnificent Temple, which surpassed in size any other sanctuary in the Roman Empire. Nevertheless, as in the building's earlier and more modest incarnation, the Holy of Holies was empty: the Ark, taken by the Babylonians, was never recovered.

High Priest (1997)

TABERNACLE AS DECLARATION

Philosophy has always been alien to the Jews: Who needs metaphysics with that God of theirs? Nevertheless, philosophers emerged from time to time, first—and most famous—Philo of Alexandria. "Among the other nations the priests are accustomed to offer prayers and sacrifices for their kinsmen and friends and fellow-countrymen only, but the high priest of the Jews makes prayers and gives thanks not only on behalf of the whole human race but also for the parts of nature, earth, water, air, fire." Philo wrote at the time that a certain Yeshua born in Nazareth talked about an all-inclusive Kingdom of God, and Philo also argued that Judaism was essentially a universal religion—even if its rites were performed by a particular people. Philo's cosmological interpretation of the temple liturgy was a direct reply to the Roman accusation that Jews were a backward people who offered a political and social challenge to the underlying principles of the Pax Romana by showing contempt for the Roman gods. After the destruction of the King Herod's Temple, the Roman Jewish historian Yosef ben Matityahu, better known as Flavius Josephus, also considered the Tabernacle in the desert as a means to prove that the Jews were not a backward provincial people, as many Romans believed, but an open-minded, cosmopolitan nation worthy of an honored place in a global empire. "But one may well be astonished at the hatred which men have for us and which they have so persistently maintained, from an idea that we slight the divinity whom they themselves profess to venerate. For if one reflects on the construction of the tabernacle and looks at the vestments of the priests and the vessels which we use for the sacred ministry, he will discover that our lawgiver was a man of God and that these blasphemous charges brought against us by the rest of men are idle. In fact, every one of these objects is intended to recall and represent the universe, as he will find if he will but consent to examine them without prejudice and with understanding."

STAIRWAY TO UNDERSTANDING

The cosmic symbolism of the Tabernacle/Temple was reflected not only in its general structure but also in its details. For Philo, a thoughtful consideration of the Tabernacle offered the mind a stairway up to an understanding of God. The basin with water in the forecourt symbolized a need for self-knowledge, the altar a need for boldness. Within the Holy Place one could see the altar of incense, representing gratitude; the table with the twelve loaves, symbolic of earth's fertility; and the menorah, symbol of the perfection of the heavens. Then followed the Holy of Holies, with the Ark of the Covenant, guarded by cherubim. "Some hold that, since they are set facing each other, they are symbols of the two hemispheres, one above the earth and one under it, for the whole heaven has wings. I should say myself that they are allegorical representations of the two most august and highest potencies of Him that is, the creative and the kingly. His creative potency is called God, because through it He placed and made and ordered the universe, and the kingly is called Lord, being that with which He governs what has come into being and rules it steadfastly with justice. For, as He alone really is, He is undoubtedly also the Maker, since He brought into being what was not, and He is in the nature of things King, since none could more justly govern what has been made than the Maker." In Philo's philosophy, the allegorical reading of the Tabernacle proved to be an inexhaustible source of insight, and he carefully calibrated his interpretations for two different audiences: the educated layperson who sought to understand the harmony between the teachings of Judaism and Hellenism, and the philosopher who was rooted in the Platonic tradition. In his own time, Philo's reading had a limited impact, but long after his death, when Christian theologians noted that Matthew reported that at the moment of Christ's death the veil that separated the Holy Place from the Holy of Holies had parted in two, Philo's allegorical interpretations of the Tabernacle and its parts—including the veil—acquired enormous importance as an underpinning of a Christian theology that understood the Tabernacle and Temple as foreshadowing Christ's physical and symbolic body.

Holy Ark (1997)

The Burning Bush (1997)

SHINE OUT IN GLORY

Philo was a Jew who was fully assimilated into Hellenistic culture, and he lived in the most cosmopolitan and multicultural city of antiquity: Alexandria. Greeks, Jews, and Egyptians made up almost equal parts of the half million inhabitants. Yet, despite the generally favorable cultural climate and the size of their community, Jews did not always feel safe. In 38 CE anti-Jewish riots broke out, and Jewish houses of assembly, or synagogues, were burned. As part of a Jewish delegation that traveled to Rome to petition the emperor to intervene, Philo expressed his increasing sense of the vulnerability of the many Jewish communities that had arisen outside of the ancient homeland between the Mediterranean and the Jordan, and also his confidence in their ability to survive, in an allegorical interpretation of the burning bush. "Moses saw that though the bush was on fire it did not burn up. So Moses thought, 'I will go over and see this strange sight—why the bush does not burn up.' When he had gone over to look, God called to him from within the bush, 'Moses! Moses!' And Moses said, 'Here I am.'" Philo interpreted this episode as a message to a small nation surrounded by mighty and often hostile neighbors: "All this is a description of the nation's condition as it then stood, and we may think of it as a voice to the sufferers: 'Do not lose heart; your weakness is your strength, which can prick, and thousands will suffer from its wounds. Those who desire to consume you will be your unwilling saviours instead of your destroyers. Your ills will work you no ill. Nay, just when the enemy is surest of ravaging you, your fame will shine forth most gloriously.'" Specifically, of course, the nation that sought to destroy the Hebrews in Moses' time was Egypt—a fact that was not lost on the Jewish community of Alexandria. Philo also made the allegory speak to the non-Jews of his own time. "Again fire, the element which works destruction, convicts the cruel-hearted. 'Exult not in your own strength' it says. 'Behold your invincible might brought low, and learn wisdom. The property of flame is to consume, yet it is consumed, like wood. The nature of wood is to be consumed yet it is manifested as the consumer, as though it were the fire.'"

MELTING-POT KINGDOM

The inclusion of Judaea within the Roman Empire deepened the sense of uprootedness within the Jewish world that had been initiated by Alexander the Great's conquest of the land of the Jews. People of different backgrounds, each with their own language, traditions, and religions, ended up cheek by jowl in Judaea, especially in the region of Galilee. Hellenistic values that focused on human individuality, Jewish traditions that stressed the importance of community, and Roman values that praised service to the state stood against each other. A charismatic Jewish teacher from the town of Nazareth, Yeshua, son of Josef, who was to become famous as Jesus of Nazareth, attempted to create a new synthesis between Athens and Jerusalem: he engaged in a social critique that appealed to individuals to change their personal lives and thus make possible a new kind of community. Yeshua lab led this new community the Kingdom of God. Not only did it offer a place for every single individual but in fact its meaning was in the coming together of different peoples formerly separated by prejudice, custom, and tradition. Thus a charitable Samaritan—member of a people despised since their support for Antiochus IV—could become a model citizen. Yeshua was not afraid to mix with those who were seen to be religiously impure and socially beyond the pale. "While Jesus was having dinner at Matthew's house, many tax collectors and sinners came and ate with him and his disciples. When the Pharisees saw this, they asked his disciples, 'Why does your teacher eat with tax collectors and sinners?' On hearing this, Jesus said, 'It is not the healthy who need a doctor, but the sick.'" Indeed, as a teacher and social visionary, Yeshua thought outside the box: "You have heard that it was said, 'Eye for eye, and tooth for tooth.' But I tell you, do not resist an evil person. If anyone slaps you on the right cheek, turn to them the other cheek also."

Samaritan Alphabet (2020)

THE JERUSALEM SYNDROME

The reform movement that Yeshua began had great promise, but in the end led to a schism within the Jewish community when, in the view of the majority, followers of this Yeshua overreached. The attempt by Yeshua, son of Josef, to widen the Jewish horizon in terms of the Kingdom of God reached a crisis when he and his movement came to Jerusalem. The open debate about the limits of the community that had been possible in the multiethnic backwater of Galilee was immediately politicized in a city in which the Jewish religious and social establishments, the common people, and other groups lived in friction among themselves and in an uneasy compromise with the Roman administration. And then there was the very genius loci of the city, a kind of curse that remains alive today. "My own childhood in Jerusalem rendered me an expert in comparative fanaticism," Israeli author Amos Oz observed in 2002. It was a city full of "self-proclaimed prophets, redeemers, and messiahs. Even today, every other Jerusalemite has his or her personal formula for instant salvation. […] There is an established mental disorder, a recognized mental illness known as the 'Jerusalem syndrome': People come to Jerusalem, they inhale the wonderful lucid mountain air, and then they suddenly get up and set fire to a mosque or a church or a synagogue. Or else, they simply take off their clothes, climb onto a rock and start prophesying. No one ever listens." Yet enough listened to Yeshua, for they had been told that a descendant from King David would herald a redemption from all foreign oppression and internal contradiction.

MAN OR MESSIAH?

Prophecies concerning the arrival of this *mashiach* (anointed), or messiah, appeared in many texts but perhaps most explicitly in the book of Daniel, a text that was written at the time of the Maccabee uprising against Greek rule. Writing about the end-time, Daniel pronounces: "At that time Michael, the great prince who protects your people, will arise. There will be a time of distress such as has not happened from the beginning of nations until then. But at that time your people—everyone whose name is found written in the book—will be delivered. Multitudes who sleep in the dust of the earth will awake: some to everlasting life, others to shame and everlasting contempt. Those who are wise will shine like the brightness of the heavens, and those who lead many to righteousness, like the stars for ever and ever." For Daniel, the messiah was a charismatic leader but also an ordinary mortal. In the book of Enoch, which dates from the same period, the prophet Enoch has a vision in which he sees God accompanied by someone with the appearance of a man. When asked his identity, an angel responds: "This is the son of man who has righteousness, with whom dwells righteousness, and who reveals all the treasures of that which is hidden, because the Lord of the spirits has chosen him, and whose lot has the pre-eminence before the Lord of the spirits in uprightness for ever. This son of man whom you have seen shall raise up the kings and the mighty from their seats and the strong from their thrones, and shall loosen the reins of the strong and break the teeth of the sinners." Some identified Yeshua as the Messiah, and as the Romans did not tolerate a challenge to their power, Yeshua was indicted for high treason, convicted, and executed.

Elijah Leading the Messiah at the Golden Gate (1990s)

Tyrants Sought to Destroy Us (1971)

EMBRACING TRADITION

In 66 CE, Jews in Judaea, inspired by both a memory of Maccabee success and messianic speculations, rose up against Roman rule. It took the Romans four years to suppress the uprising. After the conquest of Jerusalem, they destroyed King Herod's Temple, moved its treasures to Rome, and sent the surviving population of Jerusalem into exile. But they also allowed Rabbi Johanan ben Zakkai and his disciples to establish a religious academy in the village of Yavne. "In Yavne the foundation was laid for a pyramid whose completion would remain a task and opportunity of the future," the young Abraham Joshua Heschel observed in 1936 in Berlin. "In laying this foundation, Rabbi Johanan was not only a molder of Jewish history, but comparable to, say, Ezra the Scribe: he showed how a definitive political catastrophe could be transformed into a moral and spiritual recovery." Between 1933 and 1941, many Jews living in Germany and German-ruled Europe believed that the Nazis might offer the increasingly isolated Jews some contemporary version of Yavne, and with that, a possibility of spiritual renewal. According to Heschel, the historical Yavne marked the point where the Jews turned their back to revelation and the outward trappings of the liturgy to embrace tradition and learning. "For the people, the sanctuary in Jerusalem was the visual manifestation of the Beyond, an enduring miracle. Its destruction was a theft from the imagination of the believer. The destruction of the Temple was the destruction of a magnificent legend. To what concrete symbol should the energy that stemmed from devotion and wonder now turn? Through Rabbi Johanan ben Zakkai *the myth of learnedness* came into being. From here on, teaching, knowledge, and wisdom became the themes around which the tales of the people are woven." However the Temple was not completely forgotten. While tradition and learning took center stage in Judaism, the Temple was to remain present as an idealized object of both nostalgia and longing—a spiritual presence that would remain ever fresh and that could be mobilized at a moment's notice to give life in exile both meaning and purpose.

ALCHEMY OF MEMORY

Jerusalem remained a ruin until the reign of Emperor Hadrian, when the decision was taken to construct it as a Roman city, with a temple dedicated to Jupiter on the site where King Herod's Temple had stood. This decision awakened a dormant messianic fervor, and the most important Jewish religious leader in Palestine, Rabbi Akiva ben Yosef, recognized Simon ben Kosevah (better known as Bar Kokhba) as messiah. An ensuing rebellion led to a short-lived independent Jewish state in Judaea, followed by a crushing defeat, the execution of many, the exile of the remaining Jews, and a prohibition on teaching the Torah. Jewish education occurred now in secret. A rabbi in Galilee, however, insisted on teaching in public, which led to his arrest. "The Romans brought Rabbi Hanina ben Teradyon for judgment, and they said to him: 'Why did you occupy yourself with the Torah?' Rabbi Hanina ben Teradyon said to them, citing a verse: 'As the Lord my God commanded me.' They immediately sentenced him to death by means of burning. […] They brought him to be sentenced, and wrapped him in the Torah scroll, and encircled him with bundles of branches, and they set fire to it. […] His students said to him, 'Our teacher what do you see?' Rabbi Hanina ben Teradyon said to them: 'I see the parchment burning, but its letters are flying to the heavens.'" When a scribe writes on the parchment of the Torah, the ink is not absorbed, and the letters dry on top of the surface. This is the cause of the phenomenon observed by Rabbi Hanina ben Teradyon in his agony. As such, alchemy of a nation's collective memory transforms individual tragedy into martyrdom, which in turn becomes the foundation of community. This foundation held for 2,000 years, but the question is whether it has a future in a secular world. "Unhappy the land that has no heroes," the title character's pupil Andrea Sarti observes at the end of Bertolt Brecht's play *Galileo*, furious at his teacher's recantation of his own teachings. "No" Galileo replies. "Unhappy the land where heroes are needed."

Flying Letters (2006)

Holy Opening (2004)

WINDOW OF HEAVEN

The Romans made a concerted effort to erase the Jewish past. They not only forbade Jewish education and Jewish religious observances but also renamed Judaea as Palaestina, in memory of the Philistines, the Hebrews' ancient foes, and constructed on the ruins of Jerusalem the provincial city of Aelia Capitolina—a "fact on the ground" that was to extinguish the hopes of Jews that a Jewish Jerusalem might be rebuilt. A Byzantine-era floor mosaic of the Holy Land preserved in Madaba, Jordan, presents a rather accurate view of the Roman city, if considered only from the terrestrial perspective. Yet Jews who were able to temporarily sojourn in the city, when allowed by its successive Roman, Byzantine, Arab, and Ottoman rulers, also saw something else. Rabbi Abraham Azulai, who spent some time in Jerusalem in the seventeenth century, noted that when the twelve tribes were sojourned in the desert after their exodus from Egypt, God created a window in heaven, so that he could be with his people. "And by the merits of our ancestors and the mercy of the Almighty, blessed be He, and through the rights of our holy fathers, a gap was opened in heaven, and all the spheres were pierced, that the holiness might pass through the opening ... and this opening hovered over the tents of Israel's tribes while they wandered in the desert, and it followed them from above until it reached the land of Israel. [...] Let it be known to you that when it is said that the land of Israel is placed under the gate of heaven, that means under the opening in the 'window' which is in the firmament of the size of the Holy City of Jerusalem, and the divine Emanation came from above through the 'royal channel' and descended on the Temple and from its own strength spread over all the Holy Land." Thus an ancient tradition, going back to Sumerian ideas of temples creating a knot that ties earth and heaven together, remained alive to an exiled people. What happened at Mount Zion mattered to the world at large. One of the most concise descriptions of this fact was given by the fourth-century sage Samuel ben Nahman: "Before the Temple was built the world stood on a throne of two legs; but when the Temple was built, the world became firmly founded and stood solidly."

CENTER OF THE EARTH

Learned rabbis and ordinary storytellers spun countless myths that centered on the memory of the Temple. Many of them evoked the idea, common in antiquity, that a sacred location identifies the navel of the earth. The common characteristics of such a navel were: it was a place exalted above the surrounding territories; it was the origin of the earth, in the same way that the human navel is the origin of the embryo; it was the center of the earth; it was the place where the lower world, the earth, and the upper world communicate; it was the medium by which food was distributed over the earth. "The navel is the seat of natural and civil order, a symbol of the divine throne, the place where the order of the universe is regulated," Arent Jan Wensinck concluded a century ago in a pathbreaking essay on the concept of the navel in Semitic cultures. Jerusalem in general, more particularly Mount Zion, and very specifically the remarkable rock formation that was the base of the Debir of the Temple of Solomon and the Holy of Holies of the Temple constructed after the return from exile and King Herod's Temple, and that has been crowned since the seventh century by the Dome of the Rock, is such a navel. All the different legends within the Jewish tradition that speak about Jerusalem, Mount Zion, and that rock as the center of the earth—the Foundation Stone, where God began the creation of the world by placing a solid thing into the boundless fluidity of the primordial waters, the place where the lower, middle, and upper worlds come together—explore one or more implications of the cosmic navel and umbilical cord, a concept that, while not unique to Judaism, received under the conditions of exile a uniquely nostalgic and hence existential significance.

Hebrew Zodiac (2001)

Jacob's Ladder over Jerusalem (2004)

FOUNDATION STONE

The Jewish tradition of Jerusalem as the navel of the earth differs from the concept in other cultures, because the main emphasis of Jewish belief systems had moved, since the Babylonian captivity, from an obsession with the sanctity of particular places to one of the sanctity of particular events. The rock that was the center of Mount Zion, which, in turn, was the center of Jerusalem, became in the legends the very location where crucial events of the history had taken place. There God scraped some dust from the Eben Shetiyah (Foundation Stone of the World) and with that dust he created Adam. And there Adam, Qayin (Cain), and Hevel (Abel) offered their sacrifices. And there Sheyt (Seth) buried his father, Adam. And there, in the time of Noah, rose the waters from the abyss below, flooding the whole world. And there they receded again. And there Noah made his sacrifice in celebration of a new covenant between the world and God. And there Abraham circumcised himself. And there the father of all the Hebrews shared a meal with Melchizedek, the Canaanite priest-king of Jerusalem. And there Abraham bound Isaac. And there Jacob dreamt of the heavenly ladder that links heaven and earth. And from there God recalled the plagues from Egypt. And there the Messiah will announce, at the end of history, the redemption of the Jews and all the world. Such assertions were not stories for entertainment; in a condition of exile in which the many communities of the diaspora might have drifted apart, the continuing invocation of the centrality of Jerusalem in history provided a commons for Jews wherever they lived—even if it was unavailable in the present. That commons had been forged during the Babylonian exile. "By the rivers of Babylon we sat and wept when we remembered Zion. There on the poplars we hung our harps, for there our captors asked us for songs, our tormentors demanded songs of joy; they said, 'Sing us one of the songs of Zion!' How can we sing the songs of the Lord while in a foreign land?" But they had learned to do so, and thus kept the memory of Zion alive.

GOOD NEWS

After his death, the movement that Yeshua had created did not disappear—despite the fact that he had not turned out to be the powerful messiah described in the books of Daniel and Enoch. To the contrary: his disciples pushed for an ever more radical agenda to universalize basic elements of the Jewish social and religious code. They began to describe their own movement as an alternative to that of the Pharisees, a sect that was particularly concerned with purity. The Pharisees were not in power, and the followers of Yeshua found in this group a convenient straw man to use to sharpen their arguments in favor of discarding concerns of purity. What began as a polemic within Judaism between two marginal groups that were not representative of mainline Jewish thought was to be interpreted, in the centuries to come, as a polemic between Yeshua and "the Jews." In addition, stories began to circulate about Yeshua in which he was first interpreted as a prophet, then as a new Moses, a man of miracles who feeds multitudes. Now he was given the epithet *Christ* (Greek for "anointed"). Finally, after the destruction of the Temple of Jerusalem in 70 CE, Yeshua became an alternative to the Temple. "I will destroy this temple made with human hands and in three days will build another, not made with hands." Executed on Friday and resurrected on the third day, Yeshua's body now became the New Temple, not built by human hands. Now the meaning of his life ceased to be in his teachings but was located in his death and resurrection. As both God incarnate and the New Adam, Yeshua repaired the Fall triggered by the first Adam and thus saved humanity. This was the Good News to be preached to the world.

A Wondrous Star Announced the News of Jesus's Birth (2004)

The Scapegoat (2003)

BLOOD OF CHRIST

The evolving narrative around Yeshua, from teacher to Christ to God, did not impress the great majority of Jews. How to persuade them? The writer of the Epistle to the Hebrews, often assumed to be Paul of Tarsus, developed an argument of foreshadowing and fulfillment. In the Jewish liturgy, the high priest had sacrificed animals on behalf of the Jewish people while he officiated in the Tabernacle and the Temple made by hands. In the Christian liturgy, Christ sacrificed himself on behalf of the whole of humanity in the Temple of Heaven. Paul also took into account the story from the Gospel of Matthew that, at the time of Yeshua's death, the veil that separated the Holy Place from the Holy of Holies (or Most Holy Place) had parted—suggesting that, while in the Jewish cult the main activity took place in the Holy Place (or outer room), in the Christian cult the focus was on the Most Holy Place (or inner room). In Paul's words: "When everything had been arranged like this, the priests entered regularly into the outer room to carry on their ministry. But only the high priest entered the inner room, and that only once a year, and never without blood, which he offered for himself and for the sins the people had committed in ignorance. The Holy Spirit was showing by this that the way into the Most Holy Place had not yet been disclosed. [...] But when Christ came as high priest of the good things that are now already here, he went through the greater and more perfect tabernacle that is not made with human hands, that is to say, is not a part of this creation. He did not enter by means of the blood of goats and calves; but he entered the Most Holy Place once for all by his own blood, thus obtaining eternal redemption. [...] He entered heaven itself, now to appear for us in God's presence." The allegory was composed to show Jews that Christ was the true high priest—but history shows that few Jews were willing to jettison their special and above all intimate covenant with God, maintained in good and bad times, for a new and untested one.

A NEW JERUSALEM

By the end of history, when all the world was to have accepted the implications of the Good News, a new city would arise around the New Temple, which was Christ's symbolic body, also known as the Ecclesia (Church, understood as the community of faithful that includes both those who are baptized on earth and those who have passed on to their reward in heaven). Thus, we have Saint John's vision in Revelation: "Then I saw 'a new heaven and a new earth,' for the first heaven and the first earth had passed away, and there was no longer any sea. I saw the Holy City, the new Jerusalem, coming down out of heaven from God, prepared as a bride beautifully dressed for her husband. And I heard a loud voice from the throne saying, 'Look! God's dwelling place is now among the people, and he will dwell with them.'" Further on, he clarifies: "I did not see a temple in the city, because the Lord God Almighty and the Lamb are its temple." The Lamb was, of course, Christ, the New Temple. "The city does not need the sun or the moon to shine on it, for the glory of God gives it light, and the Lamb is its lamp." However, it was not a city for all: "Nothing impure will ever enter it, nor will anyone who does what is shameful or deceitful, but only those whose names are written in the Lamb's book of life." The New Jerusalem was only to house those who had accepted Christ as the Savior and Lord. It goes without saying that such a vision explicitly condemned the attitude of the Jews, once again living in exile, who dreamed of a reconstruction of a limited earthly and Jewish Jerusalem with a physical temple, a fourth one, at its center. Because it had appropriated the New Jerusalem as a symbol of its promise of universal redemption, the Church had a vested and vital interest in preventing a return of Jews to the site of the old Jerusalem. While the Jewish reconstruction of Jerusalem after the Babylonian captivity had been of no interest to anyone except Jews, a Jewish reconstruction of Jerusalem was a theological impossibility in the Christian era.

Earthly and Heavenly Jerusalem (2004)

Destruction of the Temple (1980)

CONSOLE, O LORD,
THE MOURNERS OF ZION

Christian theology was based on the notion that Christ's death on the cross and his resurrection had fulfilled Judaism, and that the destruction of the Temple of Jerusalem in 70 CE proved that Judaism was no longer needed in God's plan for the world. Ecclesia was triumphant; Synagoga defeated for all time. Many gnostic Christians, who believed in a world in which good and evil were radically opposed to each other, espoused utter rejection of the Jews: If the old covenant killed and the new covenant gave life, as Saint Paul had claimed, then Jews were agents of the devil. Mainline theologians, however, preached a more inclusive position that reflected the ideology of the Epistle to the Hebrews, which described Moses and Christ as connected. "Moses was faithful as a servant in all God's house, bearing witness to what would be spoken by God in the future. But Christ is faithful as the Son over God's house." The old and new covenants were not distinct and separate but part of one story of salvation, theologians like Irenaeus and Tertullian maintained. While it was true that Christ had initiated a new era, the old one was not totally obsolete: it had been "a shadow of things to come." Furthermore, the Old Testament, which encompassed almost all of the Jewish Tanakh, confirmed the validity of the New Testament. "Behold," Jeremiah had prophesied, "the days are coming, says the Lord, when I will make a new covenant with the house of Israel and the house of Judah, not like the covenant which I made with their fathers." The history of the Jews, in short, testified to the history of both the old and the new covenants, and by having some Jews around as witnesses of the veracity of that earlier covenant, the Ecclesia built a firm foundation. So Jews were to be preserved, the fifth-century church father Saint Augustine admonished, but to demonstrate that they were the rejects of history, they should be preserved in misery.

IN WITH THE NEW, OUT WITH THE OLD

Like the Romans after the Bar Kokhba revolt, the Church, after becoming in the fourth century first a recognized denomination and finally the official state religion of the Roman Empire, had a vested interest in severing the ties between Jews and Jerusalem, above all Mount Zion—the place where the Temple had stood. While during the rule of Constantine the Great, Aelia Capitolina was renamed Jerusalem, this was in memory not of the Jewish city but of the city of the Gospels. Sites associated with Christ's life, death, and resurrection were identified, cleared from existing structures, and preserved within new shrines. "On the very spot which witnessed the Saviour's sufferings, a new Jerusalem was constructed, over against the one so celebrated of old, which, since the foul stain of guilt brought on it by the murder of the Lord, had experienced the last extremity of desolation, the effect of Divine judgment on its impious people," Bishop Eusebius of Caesarea wrote. "It was opposite this city that the emperor now began to rear a monument to the Saviour's victory over death, with rich and lavish magnificence. And it may be that this was that second and new Jerusalem spoken of in the predictions of the prophets, concerning which such abundant testimony is given in the divinely inspired records." Monumentalized with magnificent shrines, these sites, above all the Holy Sepulchre, were conceived as physical proofs of the veracity of a body of writings that had been consolidated in the New Testament. To emphasize the point that, in their refusal to acknowledge Yeshua as Christ and Lord, the Jews had lost their role in God's plan for humanity, the now Christian Romans didn't touch the site where the Temple of the Jews had stood. It quickly became the city's garbage dump and dung heap. And while filth accumulated on Mount Zion, the Christians forgot that Yeshua had been executed by Romans but remembered the calls of the Jerusalem crowd, which when offered the opportunity to pardon either Barabbas or Yeshua, elected to save the former and abandon the latter. "His blood is on us and on our children!"

Now Crowned by a Great Church (2004)

Some Believe That Halfway Between Heaven and Earth (2004)

APPOINTED TIME FOR DELIVERANCE

While Jews were not allowed to live in Jerusalem, they did live in other parts of their ancient homeland—especially in Galilee. They were permitted to make an annual pilgrimage to the city on the occasion of the ninth of Av, to commemorate the destruction of the Temple. In addition, Jews in neighboring countries adopted the custom of transporting the remains of the deceased to be buried as close to Jerusalem as possible. This was also the time that the whole body of literature concerning the Foundation Stone of the World and the central location of the Temple acquired its final form. The persistence of Jews to remain focused on the Temple both as memory and future appeared to pay off when, in 363 CE, Emperor Julian, who hated Christianity and was nostalgic about the older dispensation in which many different pagan cults operated side by side, announced that the Jews would be allowed to reconstruct the Temple on its original site. Preventing this became a matter of life and death for the Christian community, and fortunately for them Julian died in battle after a two-year reign. His successor, Emperor Jovian, reestablished the Church as the state religion of the Roman Empire. A second opportunity to rebuild the Temple arrived in the early seventh century, when the Sasanians (Persians) conquered Jerusalem. Adherents of the Zoroastrian religion, the Sasanians did not care about Christian ownership of Jerusalem. A Jewish text from the time, the book of Zerubbabel, described the immanence of the end-time, which included, on the ninth of Av, the gathering of exiles, those alive and the resurrected dead, in the Promised Land. "Then the Lord will lower the celestial Temple which had been previously built to earth, and a column of fire and a cloud of smoke will rise to heaven. The Messiah and all of Israel will follow them to the gates of Jerusalem."

ROCK AT THE END OF THE MOSQUE

The Sasanian capture of Jerusalem was a theological disaster for Christendom. Luckily for the Christians, a new Temple of the Jews never materialized. When in 634 CE, the Muslims led by Caliph Umar ibn al-Chattab laid siege to the city, the Christian patriarch of Jerusalem, Sophronius, engaged in an act of realpolitik. He would support Umar's takeover of Jerusalem if he were to offer the Christians many special privileges—and, in addition, join the fight against the messianic dreams of the Jews. A Christian text written a few centuries later records that after the conquest, Caliph Umar decided not to appropriate any of the churches, as an acknowledgment of Sophronius's support. "Then Umar said to him, 'There is however one duty and obligation on your part. You must show me a place where I might build a mosque.' The Patriarch said, 'I will give you a place where you can build a mosque, a place where the emperors of Rome would not allow anything to be built. At this place can be found the rock where God spoke to Jacob and which Jacob called the gate of heaven. Jews called it the Holy of Holies and it is the middle of the earth. The temple of the Jews once stood there and Jews venerated it.' [...] Then Sophronius the patriarch took Umar ibn al-Chattab by the hand and led him directly to the dung heap. Umar took hold of the edge of his garment, filled it with dirt and threw it into the valley of Gehenna. When the Muslims saw Umar ibn al-Chattab carrying dirt in his lap, each one hurried to carry dirt in their laps and in their cloaks and shields, as well as in baskets and jars, until the place was cleared and cleansed and the rock was visible. Then someone said, 'Let us build the mosque and let the rock serve as the *qibla* facing south.' But Umar said, 'No. We will build a mosque and put the rock at the end of the mosque.' And Umar built the mosque with the rock at the end of the mosque." And thus a splendid Muslim sanctuary came to occupy the site of the Temple.

A Dome Of Gold Shining Like A Second Sun (2004)

Disputation (2021)

YOUR SPEECHES ARE MADE IN VAIN

The Christian-Jewish conflict in seventh-century Jerusalem was unusual. From around 300 CE to 1000 CE, the Church had many more important things on its agenda than persecuting Jews and libeling Judaism. For seven centuries the Church was involved in the Herculean task to sort out its theology, agree on the text of the creed, deal with the fallout of schisms, and above all convert the many different heathen peoples that populated the continent: Anglo-Saxons, Frisians, Saxons, Danes, West Slavs, Poles, Hungarians, Russians, Prussians, Lithuanians, and so on. Given these enormous undertakings, made urgent by the intermittent arrival of new and mostly warrior-like peoples who also needed to be saved by the Gospel of the Lamb, the Church had little time for the Jews, a scattered minority. The very low level of education of the clergy contributed to the fact that almost all Christians forgot why they were supposed to despise the Jews. In that sense, the Dark Ages allowed Jews and Judaism to survive as just another group with another religion, not much different from the other heathens. However, Christians began to dust off their prejudices after the year 1000 CE. By then Jews were the only non-Christian minority left in most of Europe, and with the revivals of urban life and theological learning in the monasteries and, later, in the cathedral schools and universities, and the increasing need of the Church to combat heresies among the faithful, the Jews and Judaism became of increasing interest. One of the manifestations of this were public disputations, organized by Christian rulers on advice of theologians, between a representative of the Church and a rabbi to debate, on the basis of evidence from the scriptures, and at times from rabbinical writings, whether the Messiah had appeared or not, whether the Messiah is a divine or a human being, and whether Christianity had superseded Judaism. Such debates, forced upon the Jews, proved at times to be triggers for anti-Jewish riots, expulsions, and worse.

GOD DOES NOT REPENT OF
THE GIFTS HE MAKES

By the year 1000 CE, Judaism had survived at the margins of Christendom. In the 700 years that had passed, and in the 700 years that were to follow, it lived a quiet if not mute existence, without interference in the grand affairs of the world. Yet it was not disconnected to that world: Christians often paired Ecclesia (the Church), symbolized as a bright-eyed, crowned woman holding a cross as a scepter, looking confidently into the world, with Synagoga (synagogue, or the Jews), a defeated, blindfolded woman holding a broken staff while the Ten Commandments are slipping from her left hand. Pairing the two implied not only an opposition but also a strange codependency: Ecclesia needed the presence Synagoga and not only as a dejected witness to its glory. Christian theology claimed that the Church was *in* the world and at the same time not *of* the world. Yet the gigantic task to convert the pagans at the frontiers of Christendom and to maintain a proper Christian order within it often swallowed up all the energies of the Church, leading to the forgetfulness about its also supernatural essence. Because she was blinded, Synagoga, like the blind bards of Greek lore, could perceive a truth beyond the urgency of the here and now. Having lost responsibility for the salvation of the world, Synagoga may have lived from a human perspective in humiliation, but from God's perspective she already dwelt at the point where history touches eternity, which was still a goal for Ecclesia. As such, the Jews, in their small, scattered, and powerless communities, provided for Christians, pilgrims on the road to salvation, a living testimony that not only is there purpose in history but also that history as such is not that purpose.

WHY DID THE STARS NOT WITHDRAW THEIR BRIGHTNESS?

The decisive turning point in Christian-Jewish relations was the First Crusade. When in 1096, Christian Germans got ready to depart for the Holy Land, with the aim to crush the Muslim infidels and return Jerusalem to Christian control, anti-Jewish lynch mobs formed in the Rhineland, which was at that time the center of Jewish life in Europe. Why only kill Muslims over there when there were also Jews over here? Thus the Jewish communities in the towns of Speyer, Worms, and Mainz were destroyed, an event that contemporaries identified with the destruction of the Temple. Utter desperation reigned in the Jewish communities. Besieged by mobs in their synagogues, many Jews killed their children before committing suicide, believing that it was better for their children to die as Jews than to live as Christians. It appears that these acts of desperation provided Jew-haters with the raw material from which arose the tale of the blood libel—the accusation that Jews killed Christian children at Passover and used their blood in baking unleavened bread. The possibility of sudden massacre framed the Jewish horizon, as did the experience of an equally sudden expulsion into the unknown. However, in the same way that the Crusades expanded the world for Christians, they did so also for Jews. First of all, the destruction of any sense of security within Roman Catholic societies provided European Jews with a greater motivation to seek to establish contact with Jewish communities in the Orthodox and Muslim worlds. After all, departure for these less hostile regions might become urgent at some future date. In addition, the creation of regular ship routes between Genoa, Venice, and Acre in the Regnum Hierosolymitanum (Kingdom of Jerusalem) meant that the Holy Land also became accessible to Jewish pilgrims. Some of these pilgrims decided to stay, creating the foundation of a new Jewish community in Palestine.

The Christian church had established itself in late antiquity as a militant institution in a fallen world, and hence it required that all its members remain committed to a core set of dogmatic principles articulated in the creed. At the same time the Jews, who actually lived in an increasingly dangerous world as the might of the Christians increased, had been living for many centuries without a clearly articulated dogma, without a definitive creed. Indeed, Judaism does not offer an equivalent to the Christian creed—except perhaps the simple statement, "Hear, O Israel: the Lord our God, the Lord is one." And Judaism has no real theology, that is, a body of speculations on the nature of God. And it has no dogma. Instead of adopting a clear set of shared beliefs as a means of survival, Jews engaged in endless debate, one that was never closed. It is counterintuitive to celebrate debate while rowing a lifeboat and seeking shelter as a storm of destruction rages. But that was the choice Jews made after the destruction of the Temple, and it might have been the very secret of their survival. This debate is embodied in the Babylonian Talmud (Instruction), the central text—or better, library—of Rabbinic Judaism. The Talmud arose because the many commandments, as they are written in the Torah, offer a lack of detail that makes it impossible to execute them properly; at times they might even be in contradiction with other commandments. These problems were, however, addressed in a tradition that went back to Moses. This was the so-called Oral Torah, which was taught from generation to generation and was under the stewardship of scholars. "You must act according to the decisions they give you at the place the Lord will choose. Be careful to do everything they instruct you to do. Act according to whatever they teach you and the decisions they give you. Do not turn aside from what they tell you, to the right or to the left." The Oral Torah is summarized in a written compendium known as the Mishnah (Study by Repetition), a fragment of which is present at the center of every page of the Talmud.

Boskovice Synagogue and Castle (2017)

Sea of Talmud (1992)

THE TALMUD SAYS ...

At the core of the Talmud, and hence at the core of Judaism in the past 1,500 years, is the dynamic interaction between the Torah and the Mishnah as they acquire shape in the teachings and opinions of many rabbis on a variety of subjects, including Halakhah, Jewish ethics, philosophy, customs, history, lore, and many other themes. These discussions, known as Gemara (Completion), together with the Mishnah, make up the Talmud, which became the basis for all codes of Jewish law and continues to be widely quoted in rabbinic literature. If from its very beginnings the Christian tradition aimed to offer a final statement on all matters relating to humankind's state and destiny, the Talmud was content to present constellations of different opinions about a myriad of very particular questions without defining any final conclusion on any topic. The Talmud, in other words, is the record of an ongoing debate. Hence it represents a textual labyrinth in which the outsider gets lost, or a deep water in which those who do not know how to swim drown. Almost anything can be found in the Talmud, and hence a hostile outsider who seeks to libel Jews and Judaism for this or that will always find in the Talmud a sentence or clause that, taken out of context, will seem to "prove" their case. The antisemite's favorite phrase is: "The Talmud says ..." While the Talmud became the center of mainstream Judaism, it was not without its Jewish detractors. The Karaite sect rejected the legitimacy of the Oral Torah and hence had no need for the Talmud. In the past 200 years, religious Jews who belong to the Reform and Conservative denominations and secular Jews alike have turned their backs to the Talmud, judging its discussions to be casuistic and irrelevant for the dilemmas of modern life.

ARCHITECTURE OF THE TALMUD

The first page of the Talmud shows this clash of opinions very clearly. Considered from the standpoint of typography alone, the printed page of the Talmud is an amazingly complex text with many intertextual connections representing fifteen centuries of discussion. The text of the Mishnah is in the middle, written in square Hebrew letters. This text is surrounded by commentaries. The most important commentary is that of Rashi (Rabbi Solomon bar Isaac), always found on the side of the page closest to the binding. The Tosafists, who provided a supercommentary on Rashi's commentary, appear on the opposing side of the Talmud. The first Tosafists were Rashi's sons-in-law and grandsons. If the theologies developed by the Christian church can be compared to a coherent, well-integrated system that has a clearly defined boundary of what is accepted and what is not accepted, or heretical, the discourse within Judaism is not linear and decisive but fluid, and results in multidirectional constellations of meanings. The text of the Talmud reads like an architectural plan that shows a powerful centrifugal force from the center to the periphery. While, of course, the Mishnah at the center is the most important part, and as such comparable to a traditional sanctuary, the energy of the debate and the very life of the text are located at the periphery. It is there that the ongoing debate about the Talmud, known as *pilpul*, has its proper place, continuing today, at times circling out of control but always engaging, always utterly vital.

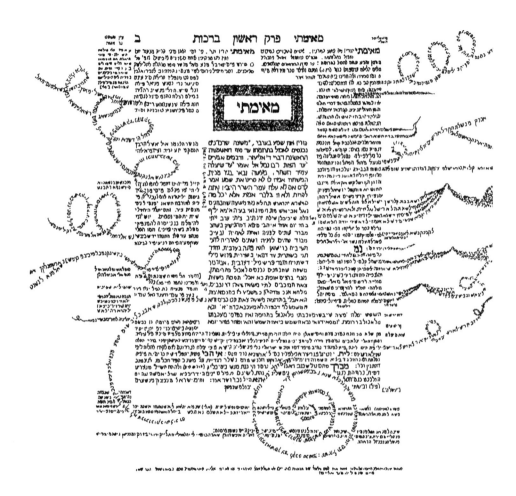

Pilpul ("Dialectical Exegesis") (1977)

Two Panels of a Triptych (2020)

IN SCORN OF CHRIST OUR SAVIOUR

The very existence of the Talmud threatened Christian doctrine. In late antiquity, theologians like Augustine had assigned those Jews who were their contemporaries their proper place in history: fossil remains of the Old Testament Hebrews; their historical task in the plan of God had been fulfilled. For the rest of history, they were to remain in place until the end of time, and then they were to accept Christ, upon his return to earth, as the Messiah, and thus herald the final reckoning. The existence of the Talmud, however, made clear that Judaism was not a fossil. To the contrary: it was alive and well. The Christians responded with a polemic that included not only the relatively tame iconography that pitted Ecclesia against Synagoga but also particularly obscene images of Jews both suckling and having intercourse with a large sow, an unclean animal according to Jewish dietary law. Now Jews were forced to wear a special sign on their garments, and throughout much of Europe, Jewish men had to wear a special yellow or white hat, as if they were lepers to be avoided. And the Christian imagination went into overdrive when it accused Jews of the murder of Christian children around Passover, so that they could use their blood to bake their unleavened bread. Most notorious was the case of Simon of Trent, allegedly murdered by Jews on March 21, 1475. "When the Jews residing in this city were about to celebrate Easter (the Passover) according to their customs, but lacked Christian blood with which to prepare their unleavened bread, they took this child, which they had stolen, to the house of Samuel the Jew"—thus goes the account in the *Nuremberg Chronicle*. After a lengthy description of the gruesome murder, the text notes: "The Jews hurried to their evening meal, and ate of unleavened bread made with the blood, in scorn of Christ our Saviour. They threw the corpse into the river flowing by their house, and celebrated their Passover with joy." Thus Jews became in Christian eyes not only a theologically vanquished people but also the representatives of the devil among humanity, with Judaism acquiring the reputation of a satanic cult.

ENDURANCE IN FEARFUL SITUATIONS

"To every six hundred Germans there was one Jew," Lion Feuchtwanger wrote in his magisterial historical novel *Jud Süss* (Süss the Jew). "Under the refined extortions of the people and the authorities, they lived anxious, straitened, obscure, at the mercy of every caprice. Handwork and every free vocation was interdicted to them, and the official regulations drove them into the most complicated and difficult forms of chaffering and usury, restricted their purchase of necessaries, did not let them shave their beards, confined them to ridiculous and shameful garb, pressed them into narrow quarters, barred the gates of their Ghettos, locked it up, evening after evening, and guarded their going in and coming out. Pressed close together they sat: they multiplied, but they were granted no more space. And because they could not expand their buildings horizontally, they piled them on high, story upon story. Ever narrower, darker, more winding, became their streets. Neither tree nor grass nor flower had room; they stood in each other's light, without sun, without air, in thick disease-bearing dirt. They were separated from the fruitful earth, from heaven, from verdure. The wandering wind was trapped in their drab, stinking streets, the high toppling houses barred their view of the drifting clouds, the blue sky. [...] They were like dead brackish water, cut off from the freely-flowing life outside, dammed off from language, the art, the spirit of others." Yet, at the same time, the conditions of the ghetto conspired to create an increasing sense of community, a sense of family life that had a greater intimacy between the generations than could be found in non-Jewish households. And the ghetto proved a crucible that shaped a remarkable resilience. "In Europe [...] they have gone through an eighteen-century schooling such as no other nation on this continent can boast of," German philosopher Friedrich Nietzsche observed in the late nineteenth century. "Every Jew possesses in the history of his fathers and grandfathers a great fund of examples of the coldest self-possession and endurance in fearful situations, of the subtlest outwitting and exploitation of chance and misfortune; their courage beneath the cloak of miserable submission, their heroism in *spernere si sperni* [despise that one is despised], surpasses the virtue of all the saints."

Outside the Ghetto Wall Sat the Drummer (2020)

Murdered in Those Days (2020)

WIPING OUT THE DEBTOR

Jewish life in Christian Europe was difficult at best, and on its horizon was always the likelihood of random violence by outside mobs with its destruction of property, injuries, and death. The annual reenactment of Christ's Passion around Easter was enough to whip up anti-Jewish hatred. "'What shall I do, then, with Jesus who is called the Messiah?' Pilate asked. They all answered, 'Crucify him!' 'Why? What crime has he committed?' asked Pilate. But they shouted all the louder, 'Crucify him!' When Pilate saw that he was getting nowhere, but that instead an uproar was starting, he took water and washed his hands in front of the crowd. 'I am innocent of this man's blood,' he said. 'It is your responsibility!' All the people answered, 'His blood is on us and on our children!'" And when this was combined with the rumor that Jews abducted and killed Christian children to use their blood as an ingredient for matzoh eaten at Passover, one child missing around Easter was enough to incite a slaughter of local Jews. More practical considerations also created a strong motivation to get rid of them from time to time. Jews could not become tradespeople because the trades were organized in guilds, and admission to those organizations demanded an oath to be sworn on the Trinity. Thus Jews were forced into the only activity that was forbidden to Christians: lending money against interest. This made the presence of Jews important to many Christian monarchs, who were always in need of cash. However, Christian theology taught that usury constituted violence against God, as it made fertile what was supposed to be sterile—and as such it was the inverse of sodomy, which made sterile what ought to be fertile. Hence usurers and sodomites end up next to each other in the seventh circle of Dante's Hell. But there was the prospect of perdition not only in the afterlife but also in this one. "Being a Jew was thus a dangerous occupation from which there was no escape," Israel Zangwill observed. "It was dangerous because there is no bigotry like that of defalcating creditors, whose debts can be wiped out by wiping out the debtor."

WHAT REMAINED WAS THE WORD

But yet, but yet ... The walls of the ghetto created not only a virtual prison but also protection. And they provided conditions within the community that allowed for a concentration of purpose—survival—and a concentration of identity, based on a sense of time embodied in the sequence of generations and on the key treasure of the community: the Tanakh and the Talmud. "They had no state, holding them together, no country, no soil, no king, no form of life in common," Feuchtwanger observed in his *Jud Süss*. "If, in spite of this, they were one, more one than all the other peoples of the world, it was the Book that sweated them into unity. Brown, white, black, yellow Jews, large and small, splendid and in rags, godless and pious, they crouch and dream all their lives in a quiet room, or fare splendidly in a radiant, golden whirlwind over the earth, but sunk deep in all of them was the lesson of the Book. Manifold is the world, but it is vain and fleeting as the wind; but one and only is the God of Israel, the ever-lasting, the infinite, Jehovah. Sometimes the Book was overgrown by the weeds of life, but it stuck fast in each of them, and in the hours when they were most themselves, at the highest points of their lives, it was there, and when they died it was there, and what flowed out from one to the other was this Word. They bound it with phylacteries round heart and head; they fastened it to their doors; they opened and closed the day with it; as sucklings they learned the Word; and they died with the Word on their lips. From the Word they drew the strength to endure the piled-up afflictions of their way. Pale and secretive they smiled over the might of Edom, over its fury and the madness of its past works and its future plans. All that would pass; what remained was the Word."

Ghetto Wall (1997)

The Altneuschul (2008)

THE CENTER HOLDS

The alleyways in the crowded ghettos were mean and dark, and building codes imposed by town authorities forbade the creation of synagogues that would challenge, in height, even the lowliest Christian chapel. But despite the lack of space and the height limit, the small synagogues that allowed the community to meet around the book, that allowed them to pray together and to study and debate the Talmud, are small miracles of intensely Jewish architecture, even when they adopted the architectural language of the Christians. The synagogues may borrow their garments from churches and chapels, but their spaces reflect the very centrifugal principles that became central in first Judahite and then Jewish thought and that can be found on each page of the Talmud. Instead of a clearly organized service and a linearly organized space that offers a central progression from sin to redemption, the center is occupied. In the Altneuschul (Old-New Synagogue) in Prague, constructed in 1270 and the oldest still-active synagogue in Europe, two columns and the bimah occupy the central axis, and the entry is off to one side. The members of the community face each other, which means that half of the community sits with its back to the bimah, from which the Torah is read. In fact, both the layout of the synagogue and its use, with many different activities happening simultaneously—creating in the eyes of Christian observers, who expect a synagogue to operate like a church without Christ, a sense of utter chaos—have an order not dissimilar to that of a page of the Talmud. It is an order apparent only to those who belong, an order based on the strict adherence to the unchanging sequence of prayers and the unchanging sequence of readings from the Torah, with an annual cycle that commences on one year's holiday of Simchat Torah with the beginning of Bereshit (Genesis), to end at next year's Simchat Torah with the end of Devarim (Deuteronomy), to immediately begin again with the solemn announcement of God's authorship of all that is: "In the beginning God created the heavens and the earth."

FROM OLDEST TO YOUNGEST

As one attempts to understand the difference between Jewish and Christian liturgical space, it is important to remember that in the synagogue service, all adult men (and in Reform and Conservative synagogues, also all adult women) are considered to be equal and equally able to conduct the service. There is no distinction between priesthood and laity. The rabbi is not a priest, and neither is the cantor. In the Christian service, there is a spatial hierarchy between the priest who administers the sacraments and the ordinary faithful who receive the sacraments. In the synagogue, the only hierarchy is in time. Franz Rosenzweig identified Judaism as a covenant between scion and ancestor. "Descendant and ancestor are thus the true incarnation of the eternal people, both of them for each other, and both together for whom stands between them, just as the fellow-man become brother is the Church incarnate for the Christian. We experience our Judaism with immediacy in elders and children. The Christian experiences his Christianity in the sensation of that moment which leads the brother to him at the height of the eternal way. For him, all of Christianity seems to crowd together there. It stands where he stands, he stands where it stands; at the middle of time between eternity and eternity. We too are shown eternity by the moment, but differently: not in the brother who stands closest to us, but rather in those who stand furthest from us in time, in the oldest and the youngest, in the elder who admonishes, in the lad who asks, in the ancestor who blesses and in the grandson who receives the blessing."

Began His Education with the Holy Book, the Torah (2017)

THOUGHT IS FLUID, EVER-CONTINUING

Until the nineteenth century, when assimilated Jews tried to make synagogues respectable in the eyes of both Christians and themselves (in that order) by creating synagogues, which they named temples, that sought to rival churches in their monumental architecture, synagogues were deliberately modest. Sometimes known as *Batei Tefila* (Houses of Prayer), they were more commonly known as *Batei Midrash* (Houses of Study), which led to the common Yiddish term for synagogue, *shul* (school). "One of the most striking features in Jewish traditional culture is its lack of big, massive architectural art forms," Yiddishist teacher and writer Abraham Golomb observed. "No enormous novels, no great symphonies, no tremendous canvases. It is a source of annoyance to many Jewish nationalists. Viewing Jewish life as they do through foreign spectacles, measuring it by other people's standards, it looks miserably poor to them." However, for those within the Jewish tradition, this judgment did not touch the core of Judaism and Jewish values: the fact that thinking and life in general are processes of becoming—unfinished business in short. "The Jew prefers to express his thought in short, laconic formulations—in a parable, a proverb, a witticism, an epigram, a hint, rather than a complete statement, a lifting of an eyebrow, a pursing of the lips—it is alive. [...] That is how the Jew wants it—flashes of insight, brief formulations which make you think and make you carry the thought further in your own mind. Those other, completely worked-out systems appear to him dull, they blunt the intellect. They confront you with a closed finished construction. And his mind rebels against the thought being finished and complete, even in the mind of the writer. Thought is fluid, ever-continuing." And thus the place where Jews assemble to pray is a like a school, a modest place to be sure, but with an open horizon.

NEIGHBOR OR PILGRIM?

Many synagogues are *shtiblekh* (Yiddish for "small rooms"), intimate places, not as intimate as the private domain of the living room but about as familiar as the front porches of older times, where neighbor spends some time with neighbor. The shtibl and the synagogue are in that sense personal spaces, where all present know one another, often a bit too well, and they are together with their God, who is like a special neighbor. In that sense of the personal they are different from churches. While churches come in smaller and larger sizes, they are in principle public spaces, places where the faithful are together with people they know and people they don't know, people who might already belong to the faith but also those who do not yet. The shtibl and the shul are places where a community meets and into which its members are born. These Jewish places of gathering, study, and worship do not assume to be crucibles of spiritual transformation but seek only to gather and confirm what already exists. Church buildings are tools of transformation: the house of a community into which its members are admitted, by means of the sacrament of baptism, and in which this admission is confirmed and reconfirmed by six other sacraments, with the aim to turn sinner into saint. As such, the path that leads from the church entrance in the west to its altar in the east is a pilgrim's road, from darkness to light, from the profane to the sacred, from Adam and Eve's fall to the final consummation in the heavenly Jerusalem. Those who are gathered in the church are not neighbors but fellow pilgrims.

Fallen Angels (2006)

A PLEBIAN GOD

"Then God said, 'Let us make mankind in our image, in our likeness, so that they may rule over the fish in the sea and the birds in the sky, over the livestock and all the wild animals, and over all the creatures that move along the ground.'" Thus is the biblical account of God's creation of humankind. As to humankind's creation of God: since the German Jewish political philosopher Ludwig Feuerbach articulated, in 1841, the thesis that God is our alienated self, many, including Feuerbach's friend Karl Marx, have come to the conclusion that we had better liberate ourselves, sending God into a well-deserved retirement. Those of a more scholarly disposition preferred to honor Feuerbach's legacy through investigations into how each culture creates its gods in its own image and likeness. They notice, for example, that it was unavoidable that, in the Middle Ages, Christians imagined God to be a fusion of a heavenly pope and an emperor, enthroned and surrounded by an enormous court of angels, in a cathedral-like heavenly palace. He was to be approached only through intermediaries: priests, saints, Mary, Christ. As to the God worshipped in the shtiblekh and the shtetls: he was, as Irving Howe phrased it, "a plebian God, perhaps immanent but hardly transcendent. Towards Him the Jews could feel a peculiar sense of intimacy: had they not suffered enough in His behalf? In prayer His name could not be spoken, yet in or out of prayer he could always be spoken to. Because the east European Jew felt so close to God he could complain to him freely, and complain about Him too. The relation between God and man was social, intimate, critical, seeming at times to follow like a series of rationalistic deductions from the premise of the Chosen People."

ACCEPT THE YOKE OF HIS KINGDOM

In 1913, Franz Rosenzweig decided, after a yearlong philosophical debate on the world-historical purpose of both Judaism and Christianity with his professor Eugen Rosenstock-Huessy, a German Jew who had converted to Christianity a decade earlier, that he also would undergo baptism. However, Rosenzweig determined that before his official conversion he would attend one more Yom Kippur service—this time not in one of the grand synagogues of the German Jewish elites but in a small shtibl that served poor eastern European Jews. For one day, he would pray like a Jew and fast like a Jew seeking atonement for his sins against God. At the end of that day, Rosenzweig had found his way back to the community of his ancestors. "The Day of Atonement, which climaxes the ten-day period of redemption, is quite properly called the Sabbath of Sabbaths," he wrote, four years later, while serving as a German soldier at the front. "The congregation now rises to the feeling of God's nearness as it sees in memory the Temple service of old, and visualizes especially the moment when the priest, this once in all the year, pronounced the ineffable name of God that was expressed by a circumlocution on all other occasions, and the people fell on their knees. And the congregation participates directly in the feeling of God's nearness when it says the prayer that is bound up with the promise of a future time, 'when every knee shall bow before God, when the idols will be utterly cut off, when the world will be perfected under the kingdom of the Almighty, and all the children of flesh will call upon his name, when he will turn unto himself all the wicked of the earth, and all will accept the yoke of his kingdom.'"

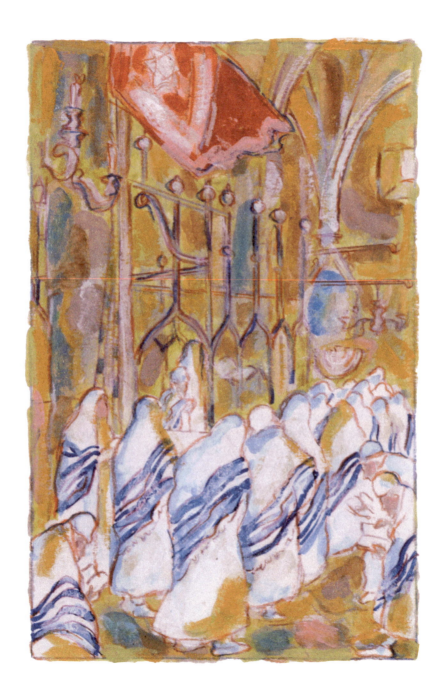

Yom Kippur in the Altneuschul (2008)

Accept the Prayers of Your People (2008)

PROVIDE FOR THE REDEMPTION
OF THE LAND

From 70 CE, when the Romans destroyed King Herod's Temple, until 1948, when Jews proclaimed the State of Israel in the ancient homeland between the Mediterranean and the River Jordan, Jews lived in an awareness that home did not mean a homeland in which one is rooted in the land itself, as a tree. Instead, they always realized that they were strangers. Even when they dreamt of a return to the land of the ancestors, it would not be their land. "The land must not be sold permanently, because the land is mine and you reside in my land as foreigners and strangers": thus God told the Jews during their forty years in the desert that even if they were to settle in the land that was to become a Jewish kingdom centered on Jerusalem, it would at best be a temporary tenancy, and the rights of its previous inhabitants were never to be annulled. "Throughout the land that you hold as a possession, you must provide for the redemption of the land." This was in line with the biblical idea that God had given Adam and Eve a stewardship over the Garden of Eden, but that he had reserved ownership to himself. "In a most profound sense possible, this people has a land of its own only in that it has a land it yearns for—a holy land," Franz Rosenzweig observed at the time when the British government announced its resolve to support the Zionist cause to establish a Jewish national home in Palestine. Over a century after the Balfour Declaration, and seventy years after the establishment of the State of Israel, it appears that Rosenzweig may have been right.

IT TAKES TEN

The longing and yearning for the Holy Land, which is but a longing and yearning for God, acquired form in the vessel of daily life in the act of waiting, understood as an act of preparation, of becoming present to what is about to happen. Because Christians believe that the great battle for redemption has already been fought and won in Christ's Passion and resurrection, waiting does not play an important role in the Christian experience. Only during the days of Advent, the twenty-four days that precede Christmas, do Christians ritually observe a time of waiting. In Judaism, waiting is central, but not in the way Christians assume, in a centuries'-long wait for the Messiah, an epochal waiting that encompasses the whole of history. Waiting, in Jewish practice, is not a world-historical event but a daily occurrence that unfolds in the nearness of the synagogue. Services can be held only with a minyan—a quorum of ten adult men (in the Orthodox communities) or ten adult men and women (in many non-Orthodox communities)—which represents the community that can hold a service. Ten boys of thirteen who have done their bar mitzvah constitute a minyan, while nine learned rabbis do not. Thus, each service is preceded by a period of waiting, which intensifies with the arrival of the seventh, eighth, and ninth man (or woman, depending on the congregation), to culminate in the appearance of the tenth man (or woman)—a person who, when the waiting has been long, may be welcomed with the enthusiasm and affection that foreshadows a greater encounter.

Mezuzah (2021)

ON THE DOORFRAMES OF YOUR HOUSES

If synagogues are, compared to churches, secular in nature, Jewish homes are, compared to Christian homes, more sacred in nature. In fact, the argument can be made, and has been made, that the Jewish home has a greater foundational value in the preservation of the Jewish people than the synagogue. God's promise to Abraham was not salvation in heaven but a great nation on earth. The house is the home where that nation is born and raised. The *mezuzah* at the threshold of the house marks it as a place of the covenant between God and his people. A small container, the mezuzah holds an extract from the Torah that obliges Jews to observe the mitzvoth in their daily lives: "Hear, O Israel: the Lord our God, the Lord is one. Love the Lord your God with all your heart and with all your soul and with all your strength. These commandments that I give you today are to be on your hearts. Impress them on your children. Talk about them when you sit at home and when you walk along the road, when you lie down and when you get up. Tie them as symbols on your hands and bind them on your foreheads. Write them on the doorframes of your houses and on your gates." The Torah does not command Jews to write the commandments on the doorframes of their sanctuaries or to remember them when they bring their sacrifices to the altar. Instead, they are to frame the rhythms and customs of the habitual until they have become an almost unconscious part of human existence. If Christianity calls on people to emerge from the cycles of the quotidian to embrace a transcendent, threefold deity, Judaism urges them to immerse in the day-to-day, where they will find an immanent and unitary God.

TEMPORARY SHELTERS

Sukkoth, the Feast of Tabernacles, underlines the special status of the home in the Jewish tradition. For seven days in the fall, Jews are obliged to live in a temporary dwelling, a *sukkah* (booth), covered in branches, that recalls the makeshift shelters in which their ancestors lived during their forty-year sojourn in the desert. There the family invites seven *ushpizin* (guests): Abraham, Isaac, Jacob, Moses, Aaron, Joseph, and David. Thus the booth completes the House of Israel both in space and in time. As is said in Leviticus 23: "So beginning with the fifteenth day of the seventh month, after you have gathered the crops of the land, celebrate the festival to the Lord for seven days; the first day is a day of sabbath rest, and the eighth day also is a day of sabbath rest. […] Live in temporary shelters for seven days: All native-born Israelites are to live in such shelters so your descendants will know that I had the Israelites live in temporary shelters when I brought them out of Egypt. I am the Lord your God." On the first day of Sukkoth, Jews read the closing chapter of the book of Zechariah, which tells of the Day of the Lord, at the end of time: "On that day there will be neither sunlight nor cold, frosty darkness. It will be a unique day—a day known only to the Lord—with no distinction between day and night. When evening comes, there will be light. On that day living water will flow out from Jerusalem, half of it east to the Dead Sea and half of it west to the Mediterranean Sea, in summer and in winter. The Lord will be king over the whole earth. On that day there will be one Lord, and his name the only name. […] Jerusalem will be raised up high from the Benjamin Gate to the site of the First Gate, to the Corner Gate, and from the Tower of Hananel to the royal winepresses, and will remain in its place. It will be inhabited; never again will it be destroyed. Jerusalem will be secure."

Seder (1991)

ON THIS NIGHT

The main Jewish festival, which recalls the Exodus from Egypt, is celebrated in the home, around the table. It begins with a blessing over the wine, which every person at the table, man, woman and child, is to drink, and then the person leading the ceremony raises the platter with unleavened bread, the matzoh. "Behold the bread of affliction which our ancestors ate in the land of Egypt! Let any who hungers come and eat, any in need come and celebrate with us. This year we are here; next year may we be in the land of Israel. This year Israel is not yet free; next year may Israel be free." In the Passover meal, which involves ancient ritual, a fine meal, many stories, and popular songs that speak to both the old and the young, all the generations participate, stressing the importance of Judaism as a religion of a people that recognizes its core in the sequence of generations: *l'dor v'dor*. And the youngest person at the table is given the honor to ask the four questions, which begin with: *Mah nishtanah halailah hazeh mikol haleilot?* "How different is this night from all other nights? On all other nights we eat leavened or unleavened bread; on this night only unleavened bread. On all other nights we eat herbs of any kind; on this night only bitter herbs. On all other nights we do not dip our herbs even once; on this night we dip them twice. On all other nights we eat and drink either sitting or reclining; on this night we all recline." Thus the ritual of the Passover meal, known as *seder* (order), is set within the context of meals eaten on other days, stressing its place within the rhythms of domestic life. When Christians reinterpreted the Passover meal Yeshua shared with his disciples into an announcement of his self-sacrifice on behalf of humanity, they quickly moved its liturgy to the sanctuary of the church building and in the exclusive control of the priests. Among Jews, Passover always remained a home-based and homespun affair.

IN EVERY GENERATION

The Passover meal is one without illusions about either Jewish history, past or present. With the words "In the beginning our ancestors were idolaters," the narrative begins, granting that Abraham's father, Terah, served other gods. Then it quickly summarizes how God led Abraham to Canaan, "and multiplied his seed through giving him Isaac," and in turn Jacob, who went with his sons to Egypt, where they and their descendants sojourned, first as guests and finally as slaves—but with the assurance, made by God to Abraham, of ultimate deliverance. "This promise made to our fathers holds true also for us in every generation. Not one alone has risen against us, but in every generation there are those who rise against us to destroy us; but the Holy One, blessed be He, rescues us from their hand." This is the English translation of the Hebrew- and Aramaic-language ritual as made available to Jewish soldiers in the United States Army for use during the Passover of 5703, or 1943 in the Gregorian calendar. "May it bring to them together with sweet associations of home and hearth, the renewed thrill and the indomitable strength born out of that ideal of liberty which lives so intensely in every fibre of the American Jew," the publishers of the army Haggadah wrote in the dedication. As Allied soldiers celebrated Passover in their barracks, tents, and billets, and their families did so in their homes; Jews did so in hiding in German-occupied Europe, secretly in the concentration camps and in the last remaining ghettos; and the Germans launched their final assault on the Warsaw ghetto, the remnant of what had been the largest Jewish community in Europe. Its inmates put up a heroic fight.

Every Generation (2013)

Seder Plate (2011)

NEXT YEAR IN JERUSALEM

Twenty years before the Warsaw ghetto uprising, a Jewish resident of Prague described the present as a moment of crisis located in the temporal gap between the past as a force that presses us from behind and a future as a force that blocks the road ahead. Franz Kafka aptly describes the space of the Jews, a space that is symbolically concentrated in the Passover meal, which in turns centers on the seder plate, a domestic version of the Holy of Holies in space. The first such meal was eaten in haste when, beaten down by ten plagues, pharaoh allowed the enslaved Hebrews to leave Egypt. Ahead lay a sea to be traversed without boats. The plate reflects the meaning of the seder as an ordered meal, and it contains a special place for all the ritual foods eaten on Passover, including the bitter herbs, in memory of Hebrew servitude in Egypt. Just before these are eaten, the leader of the ceremony lifts them up for all to see and says: "In every generation one must look upon oneself as if he personally had come forth from Egypt." But not only the past encroaches on the present; so does the future. Cups of wine are supplied for every participant and emptied three times with the usual blessings. However, when the cups are filled for the fourth and last time, wine is also poured in an extra cup, readied to be drunk by the prophet Elijah, who heralds the messianic age. In expectation of his arrival and participation in the seder, the meal was eaten with the door of the house open. The meal ends with blessings, and the hopeful exhortation: "Next year in Jerusalem."

MAY IT GIVE YOU HEALTH

Before the beginning of the Shabbat, many pious Jewish men will go to a ritual bath to cleanse themselves by submerging three times in the water of a stream or the groundwater below—water that the Talmudic sages say is part of the Great Sea created on the third day. Women will have gone the day before, because on Friday they are too busy, as they are preparing the Shabbat dinner. In 1905 in Vitebsk, then Russia, now Belarus, ten-year-old Bella Rosenfeld accompanied her mother, Alta, to the Jewish bathhouse, located on the bank of the Western Dvina. First they get scrubbed, soaped, and rinsed by an attendant, and then Bella and Alta proceed through the steam room to the *mikvah*. "I stumble into the black chamber like a prison," Bella recalled a quarter century later. "On a staircase stands the old attendant. In one hand she holds the burning candle, from her other arm dangles a large white sheet. Mother—I have been so fearful about her—quietly descends the four slippery steps and goes into the water up to her neck. When the old Jewess cries out a blessing, mother is frightened. Like one condemned, she holds her nose, closes her eyes, and plunges into the water as though forever—God forbid! 'Ko-o-o-sher!' cries the attendant, with the voice of a prophet." Alta's head emerges, and then submerges two more times. Finally, she rises from the bath, smiling. "Contentment spreads over her whole body. She walks from the water as from a fire, clean and purified. 'May it do you good, may it give you health,' the attendant says, smiling too. Her long, thin arms lift the sheet up high. Mother wraps herself in it as in a pair of huge white wings, and smiles on me like a white angel." The bathhouse was an important, if not the most important, institution in a Jewish community. While prayers could be said by ten men gathered in a private room, or even outside, a visit to the communal bathhouse was a religious obligation for a woman after she had her period. Only after a ritual cleansing could she again act in obedience to the very first commandment: "So God created mankind in his own image, in the image of God he created them; male and female he created them. God blessed them and said to them, 'Be fruitful and increase in number.'"

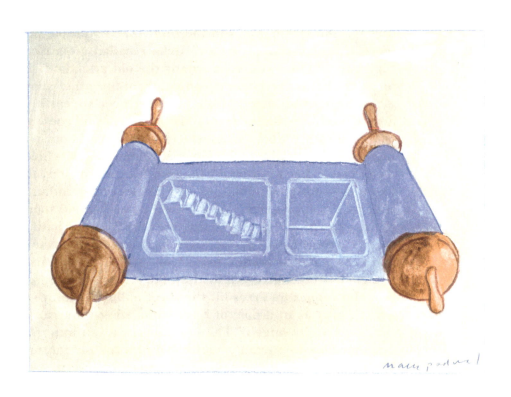

Becomes a Human Again (2017)

HEAD AND HEART ALIKE UPLIFTED

When the Levites in the time of King Hezekiah articulated the commandment to keep the Shabbat, they introduced a revolutionary idea that changed human consciousness. First, it reversed the relationship between work and rest: rest ceased to be a precondition for work and became the goal of work. As important, the Shabbat applied to all: master and mistress, servant and slave alike, no distinction was made. In relation to the Shabbat, all were equal, symbolizing the essential equality and unity of all humans in the face of God. The capacity of the Shabbat to transform even the lowest slave into a person with dignity acquired vital importance during the period of exile. In the mid-nineteenth century, Heinrich Heine wrote the poem "Princess Shabbat," in which he compared the life of a Jew during the weekdays with that of a dog. "In Arabia's book of fable, / we behold enchanted princes / Who at times their form recover, / fair as first they were created. // The uncouth and shaggy monster / Has again a king for father; / Pipes his amorous ditties sweetly/ On the flute in jewelled raiment. // Yet the respite from enchantment / Is but brief, and, without warning, / Lo! we see his Royal Highness / Shuffled back into a monster. // Of a prince by fate thus treated / Is my song. His name is Israel, / And a witch's spell has changed him / To the likeness of a dog. // As a dog, with dog's ideas, / All the week, a cur, he noses / Through life's filthy mire and sweepings, / Butt of mocking city Arabs; // But on every Friday evening, / On a sudden, in the twilight, / The enchantment weakens, ceases, / And the dog once more is human. // And his father's halls he enters / As a man, with man's emotions, / Head and heart alike uplifted, / Clad in pure and festal raiment. // 'Be ye greeted, halls beloved, / Of my high and royal father! / Lo! I kiss your holy door-posts, / Tents of Jacob, with my mouth!'" Heine wrote his poem on the eve of the emancipation of the German Jews. For him the Shabbat was both a regular experience and a foreshadowing of what life might be like as a German citizen.

LIGHT ONE CANDLE AFTER ANOTHER

The act of waiting crystallizes a sense of time that has a very special and invasive quality; it is clear why the Jewish practice of having the new day begin at sunset provides a special character to each Shabbat, to each festival. With exception of the Midnight Mass celebrated at the beginning of Christmas, Christians awaken into the days of their festivals, into their Sundays. Jews await them consciously and ritually welcome them, as princess brides. And this welcome occurs at home, not in the public sphere. In Vitebsk, around 1905, on a Friday evening, Alta Rosenfeld is about to welcome the Shabbat. "She quickly washes her face and hands, puts on a clean lace collar that she always wears on this night, and approaches the candlesticks like a quite new mother. With a match in her hand she lights one candle after another. All the seven candles begin to quiver. The flames blaze into mother's face. As though an enchantment were falling upon her, she lowers her eyes. Slowly, three times in succession. She encircles the candles with both her arms, she seems to be taking them into her heart. And with the candles her weekday worries melt away. She blesses the candles. She whispers quiet benedictions through her fingers and they add heat to the flames. Mother's hands over the candle shine like the tablets of the Decalogue over the holy ark." Now Alta mentions in her benediction the names of her husband, her children, and her parents. "'May the Highest One give them his blessing!' concludes mother, dropping her hands at last. 'Amen,' I say in a choking voice, behind my fingers. 'Good shabbes!' mother calls out loudly. Her face, all opened, looks purified. I think she has absorbed the illumination of the Sabbath candles." Once the men have left for the synagogue, mother and daughter share a moment of quiet reflection. "The white table with the candles is illuminated for us alone. It seems to me that the sky too has been warmed by the candles and is peeping in at the window. Mother is sitting under the twinkling overhead lamp and is praying quietly." A moment for the women, before the men return from the service, expecting a feast. They are not disappointed.

Shabbat Lamp (2017)

Shabbat (2002)

SPACE SO BOUNTIFUL

"We looked up at each other from our reading / quite simultaneously. And through our eyes / there passed the very same serene surprise / that everything could be so good and pleasing." Thus reads the first stanza of the poem "Sjabbath" (Shabbat), written by nineteen-year-old David Koker in 1940 and published to celebrate the beginning of the year 5702 in September 1941. "Within these walls, where joy all haste is spurning, / where in their sunlike, unassuming shine / white, slender Sabbath candles now are burning, / life's smallest things can seem both whole and fine." In the German-occupied Soviet Union, far away from Koker's Amsterdam home, the massacres of Jews had begun; outside the Koker family apartment, Jewish life was now severely constricted. But inside, the Kokers continued the observance of the Shabbat, as if the outside world did not matter. "Glimmering light-spots dancing on the ceiling / the table of a never-ending white, / with dishes motionless and softly gleaming, / the wine, the pure white bread. Oh how this sight // expressed such solemn presence, nonetheless, / seemed so aloof. We find ourselves constrained / for just one instant by bright giddiness / yet to what's innermost have been ordained, / and like the things around us self-contained // have we become as we observe each other, / re-find ourselves in space so bountiful. / Each in his solitude and yet together— / such was our Sabbath, and so wonderful." A non-Jewish friend, who often joined the Kokers on Friday evening, recalled after the war the deep-rooted love for the Shabbat that David and his father, Jesaja, expressed after the meal in song. Coming from a Communist household, the friend did not fully understand how to read such a sanctuary in time. "Things do not change that day," Abraham Joshua Heschel explained in 1951, ten years after the Shabbat celebrated in the poem and six years after the murder of David and Jesaja in a German concentration camp. "There is only a difference in the dimension of time, in the relation of the universe to God. The Sabbath preceded creation and the Sabbath completed creation; it is all of the spirit that the world can bear."

HOLD NO MAN INSIGNIFICANT, AND NO THING IMPROBABLE

In the late spring and summer months, Jews will study on Shabbat the *Pirkei Avot* (Chapters of the Fathers), published in English as *Ethics of the Fathers*. It is the only tractate of the Mishnah that is devoted solely to problems of ethics. Show kindness to others, it teaches; respect other people's condition. "Rabbi Shimon ben Elazar said: Do not try to appease your friend during his hour of anger; Nor comfort him at the hour while his dead still lies before him; Nor question him at the hour of his vow; Nor strive to see him in the hour of his disgrace." It instills the ethics that go with teaching and learning: "Rabbi Elazar ben Shammua said: Let the honor of your student be as dear to you as your own, and the honor of your colleague as the reverence for your teacher, and the reverence for your teacher as the reverence of heaven." And it counsels each person to stand up for him- or herself, always in an awareness of the larger community. "If I am not for myself, who will be for me?" Hillel asks. "And being for myself, what am 'I'? And if not now, when?" *Pirkei Avot* for many centuries provided both Jews and, more recently, also non-Jews guidance in their daily affairs, large and small, important and urgent. The book helps to establish the right proportion between people and people, people and thing, and thing and things: "[Shimon Ben Azzai] used to say: do not despise any man, and do not discriminate against anything, for there is no man that has not his hour, and there is no thing that has not its place." And, finally, it offers two pieces of advice from Rabbi Tarfon: "The day is short, and the work is plentiful, and the laborers are indolent, and the reward is great, and the master of the house is insistent." So get to work—that is, after the Shabbat has ended—and if one has some hesitation, given the magnitude of the task ahead, he added: "It is not your duty to finish the work, but neither are you at liberty to neglect it; If you have studied much Torah, you shall be given much reward. Faithful is your employer to pay you the reward of your labor; And know that the grant of reward unto the righteous is in the age to come."

Dąbrowa on My Mind (2016)

EXTEND THE BOUNDARIES OF THE HOME

The rules for what can be done on the Shabbat are strict, and one of them stipulates that nothing can be carried outside the house. "This is what the Lord says: Be careful not to carry a load on the Sabbath day or bring it through the gates of Jerusalem. Do not bring a load out of your houses or do any work on the Sabbath, but keep the Sabbath day holy, as I commanded your ancestors." As Talmudic scholars were a practical people, they found a way to make it possible to carry a few necessities from the home to the synagogue by conceptually enlarging the home, at the beginning of the Shabbat, to encompass the whole town—which was possible because the town was walled. The boundary that transforms the public domain into the private realm of the house is known as *eruv* (mixture), which refers to the mixing of food: all the households need to bring some food item to a common place in order to become a single household. An eruv was possible only if the town, which typically consisted of a majority of non-Jews, officially agreed to its establishment in a contract that stipulates that the Jewish community pays a rent for the right to do so. "For an eruv is not effective with the presence of an idolater," the Talmud states. "And they have no solution except for them to rent his domain, such that the idolater become as if he is a guest with them. And likewise if many idolaters were renting out their domains and the Israelites made an eruv, they would be permitted. And one Israelite who rents from an idolater may make an eruv with the other Israelites, and it thereby becomes permitted to all of them. And there is no need for each one to rent the domain of the idolater." Typically, the rental contract between the Jews and the non-Jews is not precise, but the boundary is. After the pulling down of the ghetto walls, Talmudic scholars determined that other means could be found to establish an eruv, such as canals, railways, and a wire stretched from pole to pole. It is important to note that the eruv helps to extend the boundaries of the home, but the boundaries of the public domain can never be extended into the home. The Jewish home remains inviolable.

TILL IT CRACKLES AND IS QUENCHED

The Shabbat is a three-part drama. It begins Friday evening with the festive arrival of the Shabbat like a bride, an arrival that is much anticipated and a cause for rejoicing. The second part, which unfolds on Saturday morning and afternoon, has little solemnity; it has a domestic scale and as a result carries a profoundly inward dimension. At its close, when the sun sets, the Shabbat reaches its climax. "The Third Sabbath Meal has the deep elements of true classical drama—the moment of parting," Yiddish poet Ephraim Auerbach observed. "The Sabbath Bride is seen out with no special rites. Even the meal is poor and humble, sometimes a piece of fish left over from the rich feast, sometimes only a bit of herring. But spiritually it rises to be pitch of high tragedy. The scenery is supplied by nature itself—the twilight that gradually deepens, till the departure is shrouded in shadows." A short, private ceremony known as *havdalah* (separation) pronounces the hope that something of the sweetness and holiness of the Shabbat will remain during the week. One person lights a braided candle, and every member of the family drinks a sip of wine, smells the fragrance of spices stored in a special box, sings blessings, and thus transitions back into the ordinary world. Executed in wood or silver, many spice boxes used in the havdalah ceremony are given architectural form as a tower—an architecture that suggests a measure of protection in the confused world beyond the Shabbat. Certainly from the tenth century onward, Jews lived an increasingly endangered life in Europe. And hence Heinrich Heine defined the end of Shabbat as an evil hour, when the prince "shudders, fearful of the canine / Metamorphosis that waits him." And so he smells the spices and accepts from the princess the cup of parting. "And he drinks in haste, till only / Drops a few are in the goblet. // These he sprinkles on the table, / Then he takes a little wax-light, / And he dips it in the moisture / Till it crackles and is quenched."

Havdalah Spice Boxes and Candle (2005)

Prague Ghetto (1980)

CLAUSTROPHILIA

Heinrich Heine's comparison of Jewish life with that of a dog in a world of humans was apt: for 2,000 years, the majority of the Jewish people had been subject to sustained prejudice, debilitating social and economic constraints, and episodes of more or less intense persecutions, ranging from riots and pogroms to expulsions and massacres. In such an uncertain world, the relative safety of the home and the Jewish neighborhood, as an extension of the home, might offer a fragile haven at best. Social isolation, the actual conditions of spatial confinement, and the possibility of sudden anti-Jewish violence, which remains a threat even today, cultivate a mindset of suspicion of outsiders. The perennial threat of hostility fostered a mental situation so acute that most Jews, even after the beginning of the emancipation initiated in the late eighteenth century, remained mentally locked up in a ghetto besieged by the majority society. This has resulted in a suspicion of the world, a condition in which every event is judged on the basis of one question only: "Yes, but is it good for the Jews?" Yet, at the same time, the conditions of Jewish life provided a unique if stern laboratory of the human condition, with the non-Jewish environment providing the still, and the ghetto the condenser in a centuries' long process of distillation. Because the Jews had taken with them such a rich tradition into their confinement, they had a unique opportunity as a nation to accomplish what hermits and contemplatives attempt to do as individuals: to achieve a state of purity. "Distilling is beautiful [...] because it involves a metamorphosis from liquid to vapor (invisible), and from this once again to liquid," chemist and Auschwitz survivor Primo Levi observed in his masterwork *Il sistema periodico* (The Periodic Table). "In this double journey, up and down, purity is attained, an ambiguous and fascinating condition." Ambiguous and fascinating: this applies to the ghetto, which Arthur Koestler described as both prison and nest, "where generations of Jews, huddled together in the warm twilight of the Shabbath-candles, developed that peculiar feature of Jewish communities which one might be tempted to name 'claustrophilia'"

THE SHATTERING OF THE VESSELS

Throughout the period that followed the destruction of the Temple, the covenant between God and the Jews remained valid—or at least that is what the rabbis taught. So, why did God allow the sufferings of his people? Philosophers have pondered the contradiction created by the presence of evil in a world created by an all-powerful, all-knowing, and righteous God. Because the just suffer injustice, God is either not all-powerful or not all-knowing, or he isn't righteous. In Judaism a mystical tradition developed in response to the great suffering of the people, a tradition that attempts to ask the age-old question: Where was God when ... ? The answer was that God was in exile himself, that the whole of creation is God in a state of contraction. On the basis of an older Jewish esoteric tradition known as Kabbalah, the sixteenth-century mystic Isaac Luria articulated a threefold understanding of the world centered on Contraction, the Shattering of the Vessels, and Repair. God began creation through a contraction of his own essence, light, creating an empty space in which a figure appeared with a human form that was without substance: Adam Kadmon (Primordial Adam). Subsequently arose ten vessels, one after the other, in which God's light streamed, as a waterfall. The first nine vessels were not strong enough to contain the impact of the light, and the vessels shattered one by one until the light reached the last vessel, named Kingdom. This became the world created at the beginning of Genesis. The third step, Repair, is the task of humanity to gather the sparks of divine light and the shards of the shattered vessels, raise them up, reestablish Adam Kadmon, and end God's exile—when he, seeing himself in the mirror of his creation, is able to say: *ehyeh asher ehyeh.* "I am who I am."

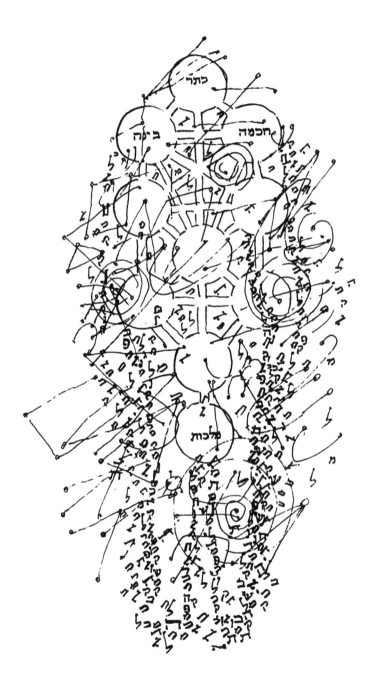

Combining Letters (1982)

Expulsion 1492 (2013)

WE ARE NOT ADVENTURERS

During the Middle Ages, the Muslim-ruled state of Andalus on the Iberian Peninsula was a haven for Jews. The Spanish conquered the last remaining part of Andalus in 1492 and then decided to give both Jews and Muslims a choice: conversion or expulsion. Many decided to leave. Muslims could cross into the Maghreb, where they had deep ties. The Jews had no obvious safe haven anywhere, and with fewer options, the catastrophe seemed greater and subsequently was compared to the Roman destruction of the Temple in 70 CE. Many lives were ruined, but collectively the expulsion also triggered a massive renewal within European Judaism. "Emigration represents a break and an impact fortunately realized by but a few," German Jewish physician Martin Gumpert observed in 1941, five years after his departure from Nazi Germany. He compared what had been a de facto expulsion with bankruptcy and the need to begin again from scratch. "To adventurers this offers a tremendous fascination, the chance of their lifetime. But we are not adventurers; we are doctors and businessmen with readily checked inventories. Yet it would be ungrateful to deny the tremendous stimulus brought on by emigration. Many of us over there were what many of you are over here [the United States]—dead men who walked, lives lived in a vacuum, adding machines, robots for whom there was virtually no salvation from the dreary inferno of life. We did not feel at ease in our skins—we began to ail and crumble. We all plainly suffered from a neurosis of civilization that consigned adult men to premature old age at the very prime of their life. When one is ruthlessly put out into the street at such a stage, the elements of youth are revitalized; one has to learn all over again, has to exert effort, skip a generation and find one's way in a modern life in which heretofore one had played but the role of pensioner." Did Gumpert touch on one of the secrets of the eternal youth of an old people?

The result of expulsions and flight from persecution was a diaspora that became increasingly global. In most countries, Jews could not participate in the trades or own land but were forced to make a living in either long-distance trade or banking, which both generated a cosmopolitan perspective. As it was difficult to enforce contracts from afar, it helped to possess an informal network of cousins and cousins of cousins who lived in many different places. Two common languages (Yiddish in western, central, and eastern Europe; Ladino around the Mediterranean) also allowed for the smooth functioning of bills of exchange and securities that could be traded internationally. In the early modern period, Jewish financiers provided their services primarily to rulers, but from the late eighteenth century onward, they struck out on their own. The House of Rothschild became a symbol of a global connectivity, not only because it had branches in many capitals but also, and more importantly, because it was the main source of the credit that paid for the railways, canals, and harbors bringing the world together in a single market, in which everything was in state of uninterrupted movement, competition, and agitation. "All fixed, fast-frozen relations, with their train of ancient and venerable prejudices and opinions, are swept away, all new-formed ones become antiquated before they can ossify," the German Jewish political philosopher Karl Marx observed about this new age. "All that is solid melts into air, all that is holy is profaned, and man is at last compelled to face with sober senses his real conditions of life, and his relations with his kind." While many who could not find their bearings in the new, cosmopolitan and uncertain world blamed the Jews for this state of affairs, Marx pointed the finger at the bourgeoisie and, in the tradition of the biblical prophets, issued the very first call for global political action that was to bring redemption to all: "The proletarians have nothing to lose but their chains. They have a world to win. Working Men of All Countries, Unite!"

The Torah Is the Map of the World (1994)

Torah Pointers and French Flag (2020)

IN PRAISE OF IMPURITY

At the end of the eighteenth century, the prospects for European Jews improved. Reason dictated that all humans—which meant, of course, in practice European men—were created equal and all deserved therefore an equal opportunity of self-realization within a unified nation-state. The Enlightenment project, which informed the ideals of the American and French Revolutions, initiated the political emancipation of the Jews as citizens—a process that took around fifty years in western and central Europe. The steps of emancipation included citizenship, the opportunity to participate in the body politic, freedom of movement, and entrance into every field of economic activity. Yet these gains came with an important loss: in premodern Europe, Jewish individuals had faced many restrictions, but Jewish communities had enjoyed a measure of autonomy and, as a result of that, authority over the Jewish population. If before emancipation the majority society supported the claims of the Jewish community over its members, now each Jewish individual was increasingly alone with the myriad of choices that came with the destruction of the ghetto walls and the opening up of civil society. Was one, for example, a "Frenchman of the Israelite faith" or a "Jewish Frenchman" or a "French Jew" or simply a "Jew who happens to live in France"? Each self-definition generated its own space of possibilities and also its own boundaries. The well-defined space of the ghetto had been cramped and crowded, but it also had supplied a certain clarity. That intelligibility was lost, and with it the spiritual purity—or at least the appearance of it—that had defined life in the ghetto. A different experiment began, which focused on the vitality generated by impurity. Considering the way pure zinc resists the attack of sulfuric acid, while zinc with tiny impurities will react with the acid and produce zinc sulfate, Primo Levi compared the "praise of purity, which protects from evil like a coat of mail," with "the praise of impurity, which gives rise to changes, in other words, to life." Both as chemist and a humanist, Levi found the second option more congenial.

LIKE EVERYONE ELSE, ONLY MORE SO

"Jews are like everyone else," German Jewish poet Heinrich Heine is supposed to have said in the early nineteenth century, adding, however, the all-important qualifier, "only more so." Before emancipation it would have been difficult to defend this seemingly simple assertion, but the whole point of both Christian and Jewish support of emancipation was to not only end the exceptional position of the Jews but also to transform them into "normal" people. However, eighteen centuries of persecution could not be undone at short notice. "And if the Jew, by not living the life of the nations, but living in a Biblical dream-world of his own, escaped the feudal point of view with its dispiriting consequences on the fortunes of the lower classes, this peculiar aloofness prevented the dreamier section from ever facing the realities of life," Israel Zangwill observed. "A class of beggar-students and rabbis and nondescript Bohemians was evolved, who still haunt the Ghettos of the world from New York to Jerusalem. '*Luftmenschen*' [Max] Nordau has ingeniously styled these airy tribes who look to miracles for their daily food, and scan the horizon for provision-bearing ravens. No people in the world possesses so many fantastic ne'er-do-wells as this nation mythically synonymous with success. Nor does any people possess so many individuals indifferent to moneymaking." Many of these *Luftmenschen* (German), or *luftmentshen* (Yiddish), were rooted in the traditions of Talmudic study but applied their critical skills to secular society around them, becoming at best ironic observers and at worst sarcastic judges of the follies of everyday existence. They became, among the social classes that valued stability, propriety, and decorum, the vital impurities that, as Primo Levi noted, allow the wheel of life to turn. "Dissension, diversity, the grain of salt and mustard are needed," Levi had learned in the late 1930s while observing the reactions of both pure and impure zinc in the lab. But he also had learned something else: "Fascism does not want them, forbids them, and that's why you are not a Fascist; it wants everyone to be the same, and you are not."

Tyrants Sought to Destroy Us (2011)

A SPECIAL PROBLEM

Many Christians were irritated by the increasingly obvious and noisy presence of Jews within civil society and also doubted the ability of Jews to function within the nation-state. "A powerful, hostilely disposed nation is infiltrating almost every country in Europe," German philosopher Johann Gottlieb Fichte observed in 1793 when the French Republic granted Jews civic rights. Fichte predicted that Jews would refuse to assimilate within the European nations, which were increasingly defined as communities of people with a shared character and appearance, a shared history of both triumphs and defeats, shared hopes, shared achievements, and shared grief—peoples that lived in well-defined territories that allowed for an easy distinction between "us" and "them": the French in France, the Germans in Germany, and so on. Of course, the concept of nation in the multiethnic Russian and Austro-Hungarian Empires was more complex, but everywhere, in the streamlined nation-state such as France, the more complex political construction of Germany, or the many nation-empires, the Jews always presented a special problem: they not only were a minority with a peculiar history that did not really fit that of the majority population but also were assumed to have deep ties to Jews in other countries. "Does this not recall to you the notion of a state within a state?" Fichte asked. "Does the obvious idea not occur to you, that Jews alone are citizens of a state which is more secure and powerful than any of yours? If you also give them civic rights in your states, will not your citizens be completely trod under foot?" This was, in a nutshell, the "Jewish Question" (so-called) that seemed to cry out for a "Solution." Fichte's verdict was straightforward: "I absolutely see no way of giving them civic rights; except perhaps, if one night we chop off all their heads and replace them with new ones, in which there would not be one single Jewish idea. And then, I see no other way to protect ourselves from the Jews, except if we conquer their promised land for them and send all of them there."

HOUSE OF LIFE

While Jews coped with the pressures, and philosophers debated the "Jewish Question" in sophisticated language, those who believed the conspiracy theories that had become part and parcel of nineteenth-century popular literature read with excitement about secret goings-on in the Jewish cemetery in Prague. "Beth-Chajim—the House of Life! is what the cemetery is called," the antisemite Hermann Goedsche wrote in his novel *Biarritz* (1868). "To be sure, this resting place of the dead is truly a House of Life! For it is from here that the mysterious, powerful impulse originates which makes the outcasts into the lords of the earth, the despised into the tyrants of nations, and which is supposed to fulfill for the children of the Golden Calf the promises once made to God's people in the fiery thorn bush." Toxic sentences, they set the tone for this first fiction of a nefarious cabal of Jewish elders who met once every century in the Prague cemetery to coordinate Jewish efforts to undermine Christendom. "Gradually our people is rising up and its power increases day by day," their chief pronounces in the meeting that will address their efforts in the nineteenth century. "Ours is that God of today whom Aaron raised up for us in the desert, that Golden Calf, that universal deity of the age. The day when we shall have made ourselves the sole possessors of all the gold in the world, the real power will be in our hands, and then the promises which were made to Abraham will be fulfilled." The speech continues, describing a Jewish financial network that controls the banks and stock exchanges, and makes a secret push for land reform measures to destroy the landed estates and, thus, the aristocracy, and so laying the ground for a direct attack on Christianity. Control of the editorial rooms of the newspapers would allow Jews to articulate a new set of values, control the masses, and ultimately make them a tool of rebellion and revolution—catastrophes that the elder describes as key steps to bring the cabal to their single aim: "World domination as was promised to our father Abraham."

Where Time Stands Still (1997)

PROTOCOLS

When *Biarritz* appeared in 1868, few of its readers would have believed a meeting in the Prague cemetery of Jewish elders who are planning world domination to be anything but fiction. But in the 1870s, two works began to circulate in Russia that claimed to uncover a real conspiracy centered on the Kahal, the local body that in Russia had run Jewish communities until 1844. Both *Evreiskie bratstva mestnye i vsemirnye* (Jewish Brotherhoods, Local and International) and *Kniga Kagala Vsemirnyi evreiskii vopros* (The Book of the Kahal) were written by Jacob Brafman, a Jewish-born man who had converted to the Russian Orthodox church. Given access to the archive of the Kahal of Minsk, Brafman published genuine documents to support his thesis about the Kahals' control over Russian Jewish life. Having achieved some authority on the basis of genuine archival research, Brafman now made a wild allegation that the Kahals had been part of a secret and well-coordinated network that had been established immediately after the destruction of King Herod's Temple and that continued to exist after 1844 as a deep state, seeking universal power in alliance with Jewish organizations elsewhere. The most important of these was the Paris-based Alliance Israélite Universelle (Universal Israelite Alliance), created by the Jewish Freemason Adolphe Crémieux to improve the conditions of Jews everywhere. Brafman's imagination now saw a universal conspiracy, in which the secret Kahal, using Freemasonry as its tool, aimed at universal dominance. In the 1890s, Matvei Golovinsky, a member of the Russian secret police in Paris, took the notion of a Judeo-Masonic plot, combined it with Goedsche's narrative, and grafted all of that onto the First Zionist Congress, held in Basel in 1897. Golovinsky's fabrication purported to be a series of "protocols," or minutes of secret deliberations held by a cabal of Jewish leaders gathered in Basel. If the public proceedings spoke of the desire to create a Jewish homeland, the document alleged that in secret proceedings, so-called elders had reported on a conspiracy to destroy Christendom and obtain universal power.

THE ARCHETYPE OF ALL INTERNMENT

An expanding literature "unmasking" secretive cabals of Jews meeting in cemeteries, Freemason lodges, and backrooms to engineer a social and moral degeneration by means of laissez-faire capitalism, urbanization, industrialization, secularization, democratization, social mobility, and cultural modernism began to charge the antisemitic imagination with a sense of urgency absent from the anti-Jewish theories of Church Fathers like Saint Augustine. Europe, for them, was too small to allow for a coexistence of non-Jews and Jews. This notion was also supported by a newly evolving theory that the world was divided into various incompatible races, that the Jews were of a different—"Semitic"—race from the "Aryan" Europeans, and that race mixing not only reinforced the social and moral degeneration kindled by modernity but also caused physical degeneration. By the late nineteenth century, antisemites believed that a forceful reversal of Jewish emancipation—that is, a return to the ghetto—was only a first step of a policy of expulsion. Some believed that the Americas might take the European Jews. The German orientalist and nationalist Paul de Lagarde proposed the African island of Madagascar as a Jewish homeland and assumed that once there, all Jews would slowly rot to death. But such a banishment was only the outward sign of an isolation that antisemitic racism had already achieved. Captured by the Germans and held between 1940 and 1945, but separated from other French prisoners of war in a special section for Jews, Emmanuel Levinas noted that he and his Jewish comrades were no longer part of the world. "Our comings and goings, our sorrow and laughter, illnesses and distractions, the work of our hands and the anguish of our eyes, the letters we received from France and those accepted for our families—all that passed in parenthesis. We were beings entrapped in their species; despite all their vocabulary, beings without language. Racism is not a biological concept; antisemitism is the archetype of all internment. How can we deliver a message about humanity which, from behind the bars of quotation marks, will come across as anything other than monkey talk?"

The Master Race (2016)

Four Children (2011)

A CONFUSING LABYRINTH

The sequence of emancipation and the new antisemitism transformed what had once been for European Jews a difficult but intelligible world into a confusing labyrinth. In response, they developed four options. The first one was to join mainstream society, without any buts or ifs, and attempt a full assimilation, which might even include conversion to the majority religion. Of course, after their assimilation or conversion, many discovered that they had exchanged their status as pariah for that of parvenu, remaining socially excluded. A second option was to persist in a life of semi-seclusion within the Jewish traditions, though adapted to the evolving conditions of the non-Jewish society around them. This was the path members of the various Jewish orthodoxies and ultra-orthodoxies chose. The key spaces for them remained the space of the Torah, the space of the Talmud, the space of the synagogue, and the space of the home—and in western and central Europe, also shared places of study and work: schools, universities, offices, factories, hospitals, warehouses, and so on (but not the restaurants, cafés, bars, and clubs of the Gentiles). Obviously, in the czarist Pale of Settlement such options to participate as Jews in the world of the Gentiles were fewer, if they existed at all. As a third option, many chose political engagement as Jews but in alliance with non-Jews, aiming for a social-democratic or even communist reform of society that, so they believed, would destroy the preconditions for antisemitism through the creation of economic equality and justice. And, finally, there were those who sought to begin a new life elsewhere, far away from Europe. The most obvious opportunities were in the Americas, and that is where most of the European Jews who decided on emigration ended up. However, a minority decided to take the exhortation made at the end of the seder meal both literally and seriously, and to make a new life in Ottoman-ruled Palestine.

SING OF ZION AS OF A BELOVED MISTRESS

"For eighteen centuries no Jew would pass under the Arch in Rome which Titus erected to celebrate his triumph, with its bas-reliefs of the spoils of the Temple: the seven-branched candlestick, the golden table and the sacred trumpets," Israel Zangwill observed in a short reflection on the continuing impact of the memory of the Temple of Jerusalem on the Jewish imagination. The conflict with Rome in particular had fueled the disastrous Bar Kokhba uprising, which had led to the removal of the last Jews from Jerusalem. "But even then the hope was not quenched, though the notion of conquest gradually gave place to that of a supernatural redemption, to be simultaneous with that 'one far-off divine event to which the whole creation moves.' The flickering flame was tended throughout all the Diaspora by the shadowy forms of the ancient prophets whose rhapsodies had become part of the liturgy; by the writers who added prayers for the Return to every sacred office; by the pious millions who in every century fasted on the ninth of Ab to commemorate the fall of Jerusalem; by the long chain of zealots whose tears have fallen every Friday on the ruined wall of the Temple; by the mediaeval Spanish poets who sang of Zion as of a beloved mistress; by the old men who in every generation went to die there and by the myriads who paid tribute to keep its students alive." In the nineteenth century, international politics made the reestablishment of a Jewish homeland in Palestine an issue of interest in first London and then Berlin. Russia had a foothold in the region because it was recognized by the Ottoman government as protector in Palestine of Orthodox Christians, and France was responsible for the Roman Catholics. Both the British and German governments believed that the presence of Jews in Jerusalem under their respective protectorates would give them influence in an increasingly important region.

Western Wall (1978)

The Attic (2008)

AN ALL-TOO-EASY SOLUTION

While they lived in the ghetto, Jews knew that, apart from God, they could not count on much protection. Their nominal protectors, the local king, duke, or count, proved to be fickle in their loyalty to their Jewish subjects. One famous rabbi, Judah Loew ben Bezalel, also known as the Maharal of Prague, decided his community needed extra protection. The result was the golem, a man formed from clay that could be animated to fend off danger. By 1897 the golem had been dormant for three centuries in the attic of the Altneuschul. That year the First Zionist Congress, convened by Theodor Herzl, resolved that Jews could emancipate themselves by establishing a Jewish state in Palestine and working the soil as settlers and farmers. Herzl knew that he needed support and approached Kaiser Wilhelm II with the proposal that this Jewish state, to be carved out of the Ottoman Empire, become a protectorate of the German Reich. The Kaiser and Herzl agreed to iron out the details in Jerusalem in the fall of 1898— it was to be a first visit to the city for both. On his way to Jerusalem, the Kaiser made a stop in Constantinople, where he tried to convince his ally Sultan Abdul Hamid II of the merits of this idea. The sultan responded with an emphatic *no*. When Wilhelm met Herzl in Jerusalem, he buried the plan in silence. Herzl was very disappointed, not only by the collapse of an all-too-easy solution to establish a Jewish state. "The musty deposits of two thousand years of inhumanity, intolerance, and uncleanliness lie in the foul-smelling alleys," he wrote in his diary on the eve of his meeting with the Kaiser. "If we ever get Jerusalem and if I am still able to do anything actively at that time, I would begin by cleaning it up." As for Wilhelm, having skipped a historical opportunity to help turn the history of the Jews around, he turned his back to their fate. Exactly twenty years later, faced with the defeat of Germany after four years of war, he fled to the Netherlands, renounced his imperial and royal titles, and spent the next twenty-three years in a state of rage, blaming an international conspiracy of Jews for his disgrace.

TEST OF PATRIOTISM

During the Great War, the British government decided that it would serve its interest, after the defeat of the German Reich and its allies, among them the Ottoman Empire, to sponsor a Jewish state in Palestine. By this time, the need for a Jewish state had become increasingly obvious. The war had been catastrophic for the Jewish masses in eastern Europe as the core of the Cherta Postoyannoy Yevreyskoy Osedlosti (Pale of Settlement), between Lodz and Lemberg (today's Lviv, Ukraine), became an extended battlefield. Suspecting that the Yiddish-speaking Jews favored the Germans—after all, Yiddish was closely related to German—the czarist government not only took Jews hostage to ensure the loyalty of the rest but also initiated regular pogroms, deported hundreds of thousands from their homes, and gave free reign to soldiers to engage in looting of Jewish property. If Russian Jews did not wish for a German victory in 1914, they certainly did so by the end of 1915. For Jews of the German Reich, considered to be the best place to live in the diaspora, defending the country became a test in patriotism Jews were supposed to fail. Antisemites claimed Jewish soldiers were not to be seen in the trenches. In the fall of 1916, the Reich's Ministry of War conducted a statistical investigation of the number of Jews in military service and the number at the front. The undertaking alone suggested to the public that something must be amiss. In the end, the "Jew count," as it was called, clearly demonstrated that German Jews were pulling their weight at the front, but the authorities refused to publish these results. Non-Jewish Germans rigidly refused to accord Jews respect. "If you became an officer, you had elbowed your way up," a German Jewish veteran observed after the war. "Even if you were in an engineering battalion and wounded at night in the first trench, you did not participate in the great German experience of the front. If you organized the economy—which would have collapsed after three months if not for the Jews—you were a shirker." And when, in November 1918, the German armed forces faced defeat, it did not take antisemites long to place blame for this on Jewish treason. *Judas Redivivus*.

And You Pummeled Me with Dung (2017)

HOLOCAUST BEFORE THE HOLOCAUST

After the Bolshevik Revolution, a vicious civil war broke out in Russia. Occupied by the German army in early 1918, the Pale of Settlement was initially spared the fighting. But when the armistice of November 1918 stipulated the end of the German occupation of Russian territory, the Pale became a battleground between the Reds, who tried to impose Bolshevik rule; the Whites, who tried to restore the czarist regime; and Ukrainian nationalists. The Whites considered Bolshevism a movement inspired by the writings of one Jew (Karl Marx) and dominated by other Jews (such as Leon Trotsky and Grigory Zinovyev); presses in White-held territory printed cheap editions of Golovinsky's *Protocols of the Elders of Zion* with a lurid addendum that blamed the Bolshevik Revolution on a worldwide Jewish conspiracy, linking it to the reign of the Antichrist. White forces focused their rage on the Jews in the areas under their control. Ukrainian peasant bands also robbed and slaughtered Jews, purportedly to prepare the ground for a Ukrainian nation-state. "The Jewish population was generally left stark naked, being deprived even of their shoes and underwear," the head of the Ukrainian Jewish community reported. "Ears, noses, and fingers would be cut off from individuals who were fully alive." Isaac Babel reported on the scenes his Red Army unit witnessed when it entered the shtetls: "Our soldiers, who have seen a thing or two in their time and have been known to chop off quite a few heads, staggered in horror at what they saw." We'll spare the reader the details. At least 120,000 Jews became victims of systematic massacres. It took the Red Army two years to defeat the White Army and the Ukrainian nationalists. White officers and civilians, who included many Germans who had belonged to the Russian professional elite, fled to Germany, taking their antisemitism with them. Having suffered the destruction of their world, with its hierarchy and comfort, they became obsessed with warning the Germans about the danger posed by a worldwide Jewish conspiracy, as articulated in the *Protocols*.

UNIVERSAL REFUGE

Yet, even as things worsened for Jews there was a horizon of promise. With the Balfour Declaration pledging the Jews a homeland in Palestine, and the British mandate for that territory, a solution to the problem of persecution seemed at hand. The Zionist project to create a universal refuge for all Jews now really got underway. It was clear, however, that it could not be an immediate solution for the hundreds of thousands of Jews suffering in postwar central Europe. Palestine was an underdeveloped country with little infrastructure and few resources. A proposal to transport 600,000 Jews from Ukraine to Palestine was rejected because it likely would have led to the death of at least half of them after arrival. The Zionist leadership and the British agreed that immigration of Jews should occur on the basis of the absorption capacity of the country and should follow sound demographic principles: the combination of the right skills and the right ideological motivation, not the fact of persecution, was to determine who was to be allowed to settle. It was expected to take many decades before the country would be able to offer hope to the majority of European Jews. Until then, those who were admitted and absorbed had to create the framework for a Jewish nation-state and, most importantly, to create a common language: in the 1920s, Jews arriving in Palestine spoke Yiddish, Ladino, Polish, German, and many other languages. Hebrew, which had ceased to develop as a spoken language since the late second century, serving only the purpose of prayer, was to become a modern tongue. Proposals to adopt the Latin alphabet came to naught. Arthur Koestler identified this decision as symbolic: "Though rationalized by arguments about technical difficulties, its real source is a deeply ingrained, instinctive resistance against the final breakdown of the cultural barriers between Jew and Gentile." Thus the new state was to arise in the shadow of the ghetto, "whose walls not only segregated from, but also offered protection against, a hostile environment."

Synagogue Menorah Surmounted with Polish Eagle (2021)

MINORITY SCORNED AND FEARED

The Great War transformed the map of Europe. The most dramatic change was the fragmentation of the multiethnic Austro-Hungarian Empire into a number of nation-states. Poles in Galicia joined their compatriots in Russian-ruled Congress Poland and the German province of Posen to resurrect an independent Poland, which quickly annexed a significant part of Ukraine. Of the 30 million Polish citizens, 10 million belonged to national minorities, of which the two largest groups comprised 3 million Ukrainians and 3 million Jews. Before 1918, Polish nationalists had dreamt of a nation-state of one people with a shared Polish language, culture, and history, and a shared Roman Catholic religion. They did not really know what to do with the minorities—especially the mostly Yiddish-speaking Jews, who unlike the Ukrainians were not concentrated in one geographical region. From the very outset, antisemitism was rife in Poland. Pogroms were common as the new state consolidated itself. While conditions for Jews improved in the 1920s, they worsened again during the Great Depression of the 1930s. Concerned about overpopulation in the countryside, which had led to crushing rural poverty, Warsaw advocated moving 1 million peasants to the cities. In order to house them, the government considered the deportation of 1 million poor Jews to a colony to be obtained through the good services of the League of Nations. However, no colony was to be had. Now, organized pogroms, random acts of street violence, the institution of special restrictions for Jewish students at the universities, boycotts of Jewish businesses, and the decision by a number of professional associations to bar Jews from membership were meant to make life as unpleasant as possible for an unwelcome minority. Yet, at the same time, Jewish communities, families, and individuals made the best of a difficult situation and, grasping whatever opportunities were available to them, became an important part of a new middle class that fully participated in the cultural life of the Polish nation.

SHOOTING STARS

German Jews did well in the Weimar Republic, the democratic state that arose from the 1918 defeat: Jews held government ministerial positions, joined the diplomatic and civil services, and advanced to professorships in the universities. Novelist Joseph Roth, composer Arnold Schönberg, playwright Ernst Toller, critic Walter Benjamin, journalist Kurt Tucholsky, theater director Max Reinhardt, and scholar Ernst Cassirer assumed pioneer roles in the experimental, innovative culture of the day. Salman Schocken modernized the retail economy radically through the establishment of large, modern department stores to mass-market the best of contemporary design. His architect, Erich Mendelsohn, was one of the leaders of expressionist architecture that arose from the experience of the trenches and the revolutionary upheavals of the immediate postwar period. His most famous building was the Einsteinturm (Einstein Tower) in Potsdam—an astrophysical observatory specially constructed to make observations and conduct experiments to validate Albert Einstein's relativity theory. In the Weimar Republic, Einstein quickly became a symbol of a new Germany associated not with militarism but with bold intellectual concepts and the most advanced science. Einstein did not close his eyes to the folly of those Jews who attempted to craft an identity as "German citizens of the Jewish faith." "I cannot suppress a pained smile," he wrote in 1920. "What lies behind this highfalutin' description? What is Jewish *faith* after all? Is there a kind of non-faith by virtue of which one ceases being a Jew?" He realized that in the eyes of antisemites he would be a Jew even were he to become a Christian, and so he became a Zionist, as he believed the establishment of a Jewish state in Palestine to be a crucial part of an emerging global Jewish consciousness and mutual solidarity.

Einstein Tower Inkwell (2021)

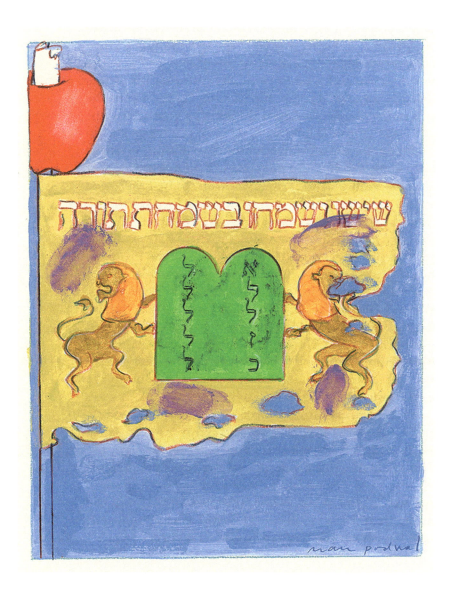

Be Strong, Be Strong (2013)

BRAVE LITTLE NATION

In 1925, Lion Feuchtwanger published his gripping historical novel describing the fate of eighteenth-century Jewish financier Joseph Süss Oppenheimer, who, after the sudden death of his client the Duke of Württemberg, was convicted of unspecified crimes and hanged. Despite Süss's tragic end, Feuchtwanger chose to take a long view on the Jewish ability to survive catastrophe. Canaan provided the key to understanding: a small country located at the three-way crossroads of the ancient world, it was exposed to radically different pressures from the Mediterranean, Egypt, and Mesopotamia. From the west came a desire for deeds, from the south a refusal to submit to death, and from the east a capacity of renunciation. In response, Canaan forged a small but attentive nation. "It must keep a sharp-look-out if it is not to be crushed unawares or swallowed up by giants. And it does not want to be swallowed up, it wants to exist, it is a clever and brave little nation, and it has no intention of being crushed. The three waves keep on coming with constant uniformity. But the little nation stands fast. It is not stupid, it does not stand up against the impossible: it bends its head when a wave comes that is too high for it, and quietly lets itself be submerged over the very crown. But then it emerges erect, and shakes itself, and is there again. It is stubborn, but not foolishly obstinate. It surrenders itself to all the waves, but not completely to any one of them. It takes to itself from the three currents what seems convenient and adapts it. Its standing danger compels the little nation to ignore no movement of its gigantic neighbours, to be always prudent, to feel, to guess, to sift, to recognize. To sift, classify, and recognize the world becomes second nature to it. A great love grows up within it for the means of such knowledge, the Word." Thus Feuchtwanger articulated the Jewish genius for survival. It was to be tested in the two decades that followed the publication of *Jud Süss*, when the three-millennia-old coping mechanism faced a threat radically more dangerous than any the Jewish people had encountered before.

Antisemites, increasingly concentrated in the so-called National Socialist movement, hated the Weimar Republic, with its rapid modernization of German *Kultur*. They believed that both the defeat of Germany in the Great War and the rapid changes in society were the result of a Jewish conspiracy foretold in the novel *Biarritz* and articulated in greater detail in its sequel, *The Protocols of the Elders of Zion*. A major propagandist was the Baltic German Alfred Rosenberg, who had lived in Russia until the revolution, when he fled to Germany, with a copy of the *Protocols* in his luggage. Rosenberg added a new and what proved to be a very dangerous trope to the antisemites' vocabulary: *Der Jude* (The Jew). "When a nation or a group of nations enters an age of drought for the soul, or a decline in creative spirituality, of rootless, sham, unnatural ambition, then one also sees the ascent of The Jew, symbol of decline, to a leading position. Because we have become disloyal to ourselves, The Jew is able to gain power; because we do not honor what is holiest to us, he can grab it. The Jew appears in our history as our metaphysical opposite. Never before have we really understood this. Today it appears that, finally, we perceive and hate the eternally alien and hostile because it has risen to such a great power. For the first time in history, instinct and insight unite in a clear understanding. As a result The Jew, standing on the highest pinnacle of power, which he so greedily ascended, faces a fall into the abyss. The last fall. After that fall there will be no place anymore for The Jew in Europe and America." National Socialism, conceived by Adolf Hitler but given much of its content by Rosenberg, proved a pressure cooker in which all older prejudices against Jews were transformed into a single obsession with an ogre-like specter: The Jew. In The Jew, any differences between particular Jewish dominations and even between individual Jews dissolved. This was utter nonsense, without any evidence to support it. But for those who believe in conspiracies, the very lack of evidence is, in fact, a proof of the power and efficacy of the conspirators. An infernal epistemology to be sure.

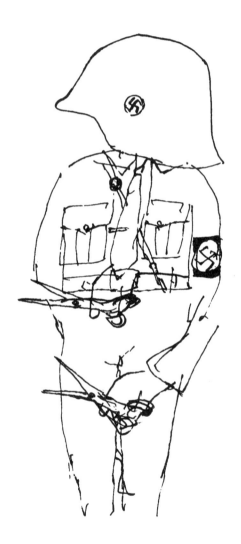

Cutting Jewish Beards (1980s)

The Enemy (2019)

PACK OF HUNTING DOGS

In the midst of the Great Depression, the National Socialists, led by Adolf Hitler, grabbed power. They claimed that a thousand-year descent of Germany, from its heights in the years of the Saxon emperors to the low of the Weimar Republic, had come to a halt, and a new millennium of German glory had begun. An essential tool employed to turn the German ship of state and society was to convince the German population that the Jew was the cause of all of Germany's ills. Reeducation began with a boycott of Jewish businesses. "Apart from the terror, the unsettling and depressing aspect of this first murderous declaration of intent was that it triggered a flood of arguments and discussions all over Germany, not about anti-Semitism but about the 'Jewish question,'" German journalist Raimund Pretzel (who was to become famous two years later when he published a best seller under the name Sebastian Haffner) recalled in British exile in 1938. "Suddenly everyone felt justified, and indeed required, to have an opinion about the Jews, and to state it publicly. Distinctions were made between 'decent' Jews and the others. If some pointed to the achievements of Jewish scientists, artists, and doctors to justify the Jews (justify? what for? against what?), others would counter that they were detrimental 'foreign influence' in these spheres. Indeed, it soon became customary to count it against the Jews if they had a respectable or intellectually valuable profession. This was treated as a crime or, at the very least, a lack of tact." Writing five years into Hitler's reign, Pretzel had no illusion as to what was unfolding in Germany: "It is something new in the history of the world: an attempt to deny humans the solidarity of every species that enables it to survive; to turn human predatory instincts, that are normally directed against other animals, against members of their own species, and to make a whole nation into a pack of hunting dogs."

WHERE ONE BURNS BOOKS ...

On May 10, 1933, students at the University of Berlin threw 25,000 books on a large pyre. Many were by Jewish authors such as Sigmund Freud and Albert Einstein, but they were in the company of books written by non-Jews, such as Bertolt Brecht and Thomas Mann, that showed the "Jewish spirit." An article in the Nazi Party daily hammered home the key message: "The flames are still crackling while stacks upon stacks of the collected Jewish subversive writings are thrown into them. With this demonstration, the continuing fight against the un-German mind has been started." In the days that followed, gleeful students mounted book burnings at all the major universities, apocalyptic spectacles that went back to the medieval Christian tradition of burning copies of the Talmud. The world sensed that some kind of terrible civilizational rupture was taking place in Germany, the country of *Dichter und Denker* (poets and philosophers). Not a few journalists remembered the poet Heinrich Heine's prediction a century earlier: "Where one burns books, one soon will burn people." In response, Salman Schocken, who had modernized the retail industry in the 1920s, determined to publish a library of books encompassing Judaism as a civilization that spans 3,000 years, the texts of which include the Bible, rabbinical writings, Kabbalah, philosophy, poetry, folklore, stories, novels, letters, and memoirs, as well as studies of Jewish history and even historical sources. The series was to educate the German Jews, who were increasingly thrown back on themselves, about the beauty and richness of their legacy—and also to provide consolation. At the same time Thomas Mann, who by the time of the book burnings had left Germany, wrote the third volume of his four-part novel cycle *Joseph und seine Brüder* (Joseph and His Brothers)—an epic attempt to tell his fellow Germans not only how the tales in the Torah touch on life in all its romantic, tragic, grotesque, and comedic dimensions but also why the world owes the Jews a debt of gratitude.

According to Heine (2020)

Great Synagogue of Munich Wrapped in a Prayer Shawl (2017)

TO HAVE NO NEIGHBOR

Antisemitic legislation, expropriation, and systematic violence pushed German Jews out of civil society. Jews tried to understand what was happening to them, and often tried to compare their situation to that of their ancestors before emancipation. "The fact that we are living in a ghetto is beginning to penetrate our awareness," Rabbi Joachim Prinz wrote in 1935. "On the basis of our experiences and the exigencies of our life we designate as a 'ghetto' the fact that *we are living in a country, we Jews of Germany, where they tell us without any prettification or adornment, on many occasions, that our lives are a burden on the German people.*" The new ghetto was radically different from the premodern one. "The medieval ghetto was sealed at night. The gate was shut strictly and aggressively. The bolt was thrown deliberately: one left the 'world' and entered the ghetto. Today the situation is just the opposite. When the door of our house closes behind us, we leave the ghetto and enter our homes. This is the basic difference. The ghetto is no longer a defined geographical area, at least not in the sense of the Middle Ages. The ghetto is the 'world.' It is outside that the ghetto exists for us. In the market, in the streets, in the hotels—the ghetto exists in every place. It has a sign. That sign is: no neighbors. *The Jewish destiny is to have no neighbor.*" As Jewish children were kicked out of schools and sport clubs, Jewish communities improvised to create Jewish schools and Jewish sports clubs, financed by rapidly impoverishing parents. Forbidden to participate in the public sphere, synagogues provided Jews some kind of refuge, acquiring in addition to their traditional purpose the function of community center, counseling office for those willing and able to emigrate, and concert hall, where Jews were allowed to enjoy the music composed by Jewish composers. The Great Synagogue in Munich fulfilled all these functions until June 1938, when Hitler visited the city to help it prepare for the annual Tag der deutschen Kunst (Day of German Art), which was to take place on July 8. Aspiring to make the whole of Germany into a *Gesamtkunstwerk* (total work of art), the German artist-in-chief, Hitler, ordered the immediate destruction of one of the finest and largest Jewish religious buildings in the Reich.

With Germany transforming into a ghetto, many German Jews tried to find a new life abroad. Emigration was difficult: immigration was not popular in countries with high unemployment as a result of the lingering Depression. Zionism, which had been an ideology supported by a small minority of German Jews before 1933, suddenly seemed to provide an answer. The odd, daggerlike shape of Mandatory Palestine that had entered atlases in the 1920s now became a sign of rescue. Yet, due to a strict immigration policy agreed upon by the British government, which was the Mandatory power in Palestine, and the Jewish Agency for Palestine, the number of immigration certificates issued each year was to be based on the economic and demographic absorption capacity of the country. And this was very limited. Nevertheless, thanks to German immigration in 1933, 1934, and 1935, which brought both know-how and some needed capital, the prospects of a viable, independent Jewish state in Palestine became real—and triggered an uprising of the Arab population. Subsequently, the Palestine Royal Commission recommended a partition of the territory, with a Jewish state in most of the coastal strip and Galilee, and an Arab state in the ancient heartland of Judah and Israel. Jerusalem was to remain under British rule. The British government, however, decided to stop Jewish immigration. Ten years, and in terms of Jewish history an epoch later, the United Nations assumed the mandate and proposed a second partition plan, which transferred the blade of the dagger to the Jewish state. More than seventy years after the establishment of the State of Israel, its eastern boundary with a still nascent Arab Palestine remains a moving target.

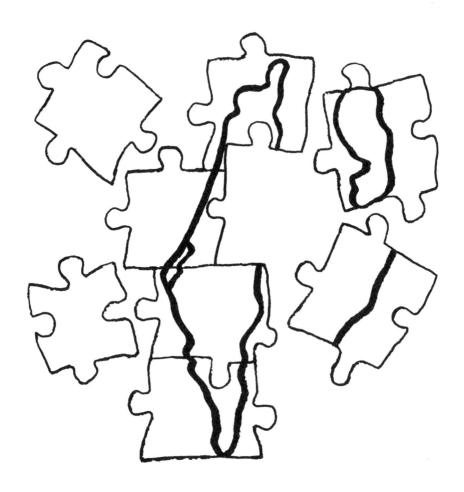

Israel (2001)

Kristallnacht (1988)

ANYWHERE BUT EUROPE

Until 1936, many German Jews were able to leave Germany, but for the Nazis their egress went too slowly—by early 1938, most borders were closed, and the British had effectively closed the borders of Mandatory Palestine. In order to "motivate" Jews who had nowhere to go to leave nevertheless, the German government engineered a nationwide pogrom in November 1938, in which almost all the synagogues went up in flames, and 30,000 Jewish men were imprisoned in concentration camps. With businesses expropriated, all opportunities to earn a living removed, and the last Jewish communal organizations closed, flight remained the only option. "They pleaded at the consulates and almost always in vain, for which country wanted newcomers who had been plundered to the skin, beggars?" Austrian Jewish writer Stefan Zweig wrote two years later in British exile. Many Jews who were lucky enough to make it to France, Belgium, the Netherlands, or Britain had only temporary visas and soon needed to move on. "I will never forget the sight which once met me in a London travel bureau," Zweig wrote. "It was filled with refugees, almost all Jews, every one of them wanting to go—anywhere. Merely to another country, anywhere, into the polar ice or the scorching sands of Sahara, only away, only on, because their transit visa having expired, they had to go on, with wife and child to new stars, to a new-language world, to folk whom they did not know and who did not want to receive them. [...] There they crowded, erstwhile university professors, bankers, merchants, landed proprietors, musicians; each ready to drag the miserable ruins of his existence over earth and oceans anywhere, to do and suffer anything, only away, away from Europe, only away! [...] It was a gigantic mass which, murderously roused and fleeing in panic before the Hitlerite forest fire, besieged the railway stations at every European frontier and filled the jails; the expulsion of a whole people which was denied nationhood but was yet a people which, for two thousand years, sought nothing so much as to stop wandering and rest their feet on quiet, peaceful earth."

THE CROAKING HOLE

The German leadership was very ambitious: it not only aimed to get rid of its Jewish population but also desired to restore territories lost in the 1919 Treaty of Versailles. This implied the liquidation of Poland. Yet Poland was inhabited by more than 3 million Jews. Thus, when Germany, in conjunction with the Soviet Union, invaded and subsequently partitioned Poland in 1939, it appeared that its partly successful policy, initiated in 1933, to expel the German Jews had come to naught. By 1940 the German government had revived an older plan to make Madagascar into a Jewish reservation. Yet deportations to that island had to wait until a peace had neutralized the British fleet and transferred Madagascar to German sovereignty. As an interim measure, the Germans set up closed ghettos in Polish cities. "People from all categories slept, breathed, and vegetated next to each other, strangers to each other despite the common suffering and same prospects for the future," the Austrian Jewish writer Oskar Rosenfeld observed after his deportation to the Lodz ghetto, where he was forced to live in overcrowded dormitories, separated from family and friends, suffering cold in the winter and hunger and humiliation at all times. "Yes, slowly it dawned on all of us, the merciless truth of the words with which the brown shirts had described the ghetto of Lodz: the *Krepierwinkel* (croaking hole) of Europe." Yet at the same time, individuals, groups, and communities did their best to hold on to their dignity, their responsibility to others, and their traditions. In the Warsaw ghetto, for three years, Rabbi Kalonymus Kalmish Shapira ran a secret synagogue, leading services, delivering homilies, conducting marriages, and maintaining a mikvah. He also kept a detailed record of his struggle to keep the faith in the ancient covenant when God seemed so far away. Shapira was willing to accept all that he saw and suffered because, taking the long view, he understood the German persecution as just another episode in the history of the Jews. "In every generation there are those who rise against us."

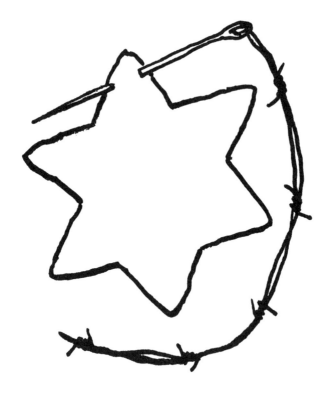

Jew (2005)

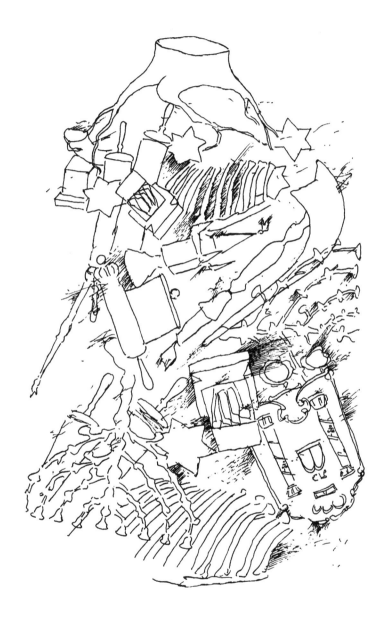

Babyn Yar (1980s)

DAYS OF AWE, DAYS OF TERROR

In June 1941, having conquered most of Europe, Hitler turned his gaze farther east. Driven by his hatred for communism and his promise to the German people of more living space, he broke the 1939 Molotov-Ribbentrop Pact by launching an attack on the Soviet Union. Nazi propaganda presented this war as an ideological crusade against "Judeo-Bolshevism"—one of the tools, so the Nazis believed, *Der Jude* wielded to control the world. If capitalism allowed the New York aspect of *Der Jude* to keep the West in a state of servitude, communism allowed the Moscow aspect of *Der Jude* to neutralize the power of the Russian, Ukrainian, Kazakh, and other Soviet peoples by reducing them to the state of *Untermensch* (subhuman). "We clearly recognize our mission to save European culture from the advancing Asiatic barbarism," German general Hermann Hoth told his troops. "This battle can only end with the destruction of one or the other." The war against the Soviet Union was an ideological and racial crusade: destruction of communism implied, in the view of the Germans, the genocide of all Soviet Jews. Within a month of the beginning of the invasion, special units of the SS (Schutzstaffel) and the German police known as Einsatzgruppen began massacring Jewish civilians in the occupied Soviet territories. The largest massacre in what has become known as the "Holocaust by bullets" happened on September 29 and 30, 1941, at the Babyn Yar ravine, just outside of Kyiv, Ukraine. An early forensic record of what transpired states: "The Germans ordered everyone, without exception—girls, women, children, and old men—to strip naked; their clothes were gathered up and placed in neat piles. Rings were torn from the fingers of the naked people, both men and women. Then the executioners placed the doomed people in rows along the edge of the deep ravine and shot them at pointblank range. The bodies fell over the cliff. Small children were pushed into the ravine alive." Thus Germans murdered 33,771 Jews in two days, a slaughter that, in the Jewish calendar, occurred in the Days of Awe of the year 5702. By the time Yom Kippur began, the shooting at the ravine had stopped, but searches for those who had gone in hiding in Kyiv continued, and those found were shot on the spot or out in the streets.

FINAL SOLUTION

Throughout 1940 and 1941, the Germans had not dared to massacre large groups of Jews in Poland because, locked up in ghettos, they were useful as hostages to ensure that the United States would not enter the war on the side of Great Britain and, from June 1941 onward, the Soviet Union. Berlin believed that *Der Jude* controlled Washington as he controlled New York and London and Moscow, and that *Der Jude* would not want to risk the future of the population base of the Jewish people in German-occupied Poland. This theory began to show signs of wear in August 1941, when the United States and Great Britain agreed on the Atlantic Charter, which included the expectation of "the final destruction of the Nazi tyranny," leading to the conditions of "a peace which will afford to all nations the means of dwelling in safety within their own boundaries." In the wake of this declaration, circumstances of Jews in western and central Europe worsened. On December 7, 1941, Japan attacked the American fleet in Pearl Harbor, Hawaii. The United States declared war on Japan. In support of its ally, Germany declared war on the United States. The European war had become a world war. Hitler responded immediately in a speech to the Nazi leadership; in 1939 he had prophesied that a new world war would mean the annihilation of the Jews—now he was determined to make his prophecy come true: all Jews of German-occupied Europe were to be murdered. The justification was, of course, that *Der Jude* had it coming: this ogre of the antisemitic imagination, rooted in centuries of anti-Talmud rhetoric, had been the sinister force behind the modernization that had uprooted German *Kultur*, had held the dagger that was thrust into the back of the German soldier in 1918, had caused the great inflation that had bankrupted so many in 1923, and had triggered the Great Depression of 1930. *Der Jude* was to be defeated once and for all by the murder of every last Jewish man, Jewish woman, and Jewish child. For Jews, all of Europe was now a single big trap.

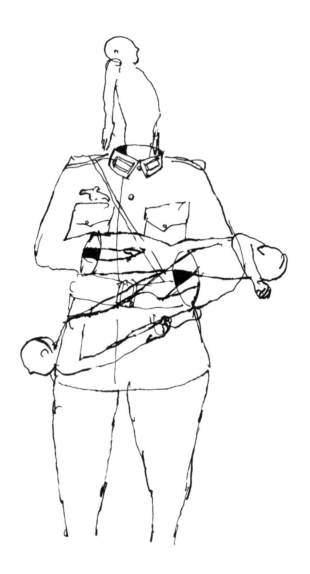

Final Solution (1988)

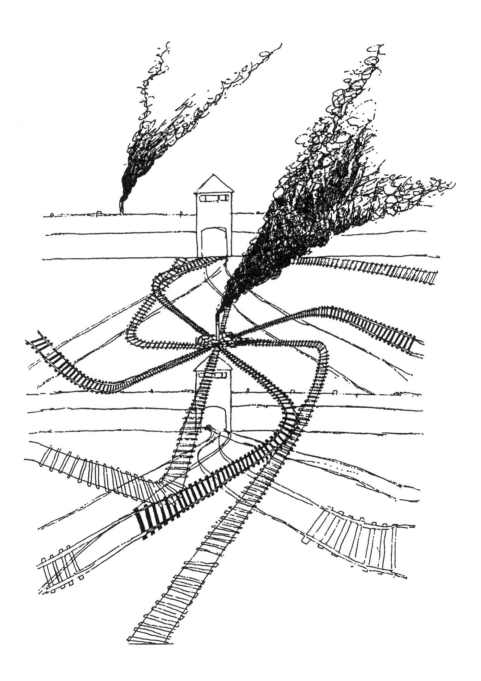

Roads to Extinction (1985)

UNPRECEDENTED AND UNPARALLELED

All over German-occupied Europe, Jews had been limited to a highly restricted life at home, whatever "home" meant in 1942. Robbed of all their possessions, denied access to libraries, museums, schools, and clubs, they had seen their lives reduced to a nervous waiting: for the knock on the door, for an Allied victory—which seemed always so near and remained so far—or for the Messiah. For most, the knock on the door came first. Rounded up while their neighbors watched, Jews from western and central Europe were brought to railway sidings, loaded in freight wagons, and transported to places with names that have haunted the conscience of humanity ever since: Kulmhof (Chelmno), Belzec, Sobibor, Treblinka, Auschwitz. Only a small minority was able to find protection, often from strangers who refused to look away when the roundups happened. For these few, the world shrank to the size of a room or a closet, and they were forced to live lives of total dependence on the goodwill of others, lives of despair about the fate of family, lives in the fear of betrayal, of hopelessness that this would never end, of rage against the world in which the Nazis thrived—and God was silent. There were Jews of faith who still tried to console themselves with thoughts that their experience was not unlike that of their ancestors, and that Jews and Judaism had survived, and so would they. But in Warsaw, Rabbi Shapira changed his mind in July 1942, when the Germans initiated the liquidation of the ghetto on the ninth of Av. The preceding Shabbat, Shapira had given a sermon in which he had implored God to really look at the suffering of his people, to really listen to their screams. In November of that year, Shapira added a note to the transcript of his sermon. "Only such torment as was endured until the middle of 1942 has ever transpired previously in history. The bizarre tortures and the freakish, brutal murders that have been invented for us by the depraved, perverted murderers, solely for the suffering of Israel. Since the middle of 1942, are, according to knowledge of the words of our sages of blessed memory, and the chronicles of the Jewish people in general, *unprecedented and unparalleled*. May God have mercy upon us, and save us from their hands, in the blink of an eye."

THE WORDS ARE BINDING

In December 1942, the Allies declared that the Germans had already murdered 2 million Jews, and that they were committed to continue with the slaughter. Most people who heard this chose not to believe, declaring it to be the usual atrocity propaganda. And those who believed didn't know what to do. Having finished, in Californian exile, the last page of the fourth volume of his Joseph cycle in early January 1943, Thomas Mann immediately began to write a novella about what appeared to him, in view of the news from Europe, to be the most important event in the history of humankind: Moses's pronouncement of the Ten Commandments. The result, both playful and stern, was a meditation on the power of education as the new God and the possibility for the savage human race to emancipate itself from a slavery to its instincts and passions by means of a conscience. The long sojourn in the desert was intentional: Moses needed time. "It meant that somewhere out there in the open he would have for himself all this mass of bewildered flesh wavering among various traditions, these procreating men, lactating women, impulsive youths, snotty-nosed children, the blood kin of his father; that he would inculcate them with the holy-invisible God, the pure, the spiritual one; that he could set up this God as their collective, formative center and shape them in his image." Moses was realistic about the prospects of success: "I know well and God knows beforehand that His commandments will not be kept and that there will be transgressions against His words always and everywhere. But if any man breaks one of them, his heart shall turn ice-cold, because they are written into his flesh and blood, and he knows well that the words are binding. But accursed be the man who stands up and says: 'They are no longer binding.' Accursed be he who teaches you, 'Rise up and free yourselves of them! Lie, murder, and steal, whore, defile, and deliver your father and mother over to the knife, for that is human, and you should praise my name, because I proclaimed freedom to you.'"

Birkenau (1980s)

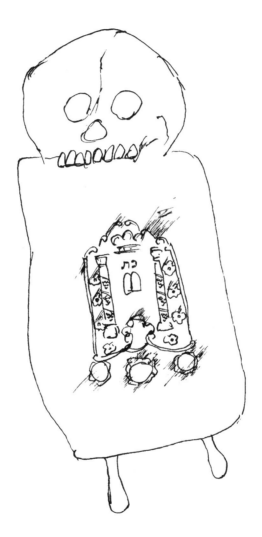

The Jews Are All Gone, Never to Return (1980s)

A PEOPLE HAS BEEN MURDERED

After the Wehrmacht's defeat in Stalingrad, the Red Army regained territory formerly occupied by the Germans. The Soviet soldiers found empty cities, towns, and shtetls everywhere. "Stillness. Silence," Vasily Grossman reported in late 1943. "A people has been murdered. Murdered are elderly artisans, well-known masters of trades: tailors, hatmakers, shoemakers, tinsmiths, jewelers, housepainters, furriers, bookbinders; murdered are workers: porters, mechanics, electricians, carpenters, furnace workers, locksmiths; murdered are wagon drivers, tractor drivers, chauffeurs, cabinet makers; murdered are millers, bakers, pastry chefs, cooks; murdered are doctors, therapists, dentists, surgeons, gynecologists; murdered are experts in bacteriology and biochemistry, directors of university clinics, teachers of history, algebra, trigonometry; murdered are lecturers, department assistants, candidates and doctors of science; murdered are engineers, metallurgists, bridge builders, architects, ship builders; murdered are pavers, agronomists, field-crop growers, land surveyors; murdered are accountants, bookkeepers, store merchants, suppliers, managers, secretaries, night guards; murdered are teachers, dressmakers; murdered are grandmothers who could mend stockings and bake delicious bread, who could cook chicken soup and make strudel with walnuts and apples; and murdered are grandmothers who didn't know how to do anything except love their children and grandchildren; murdered are women who were faithful to their husbands, and murdered are frivolous women; murdered are beautiful young women, serious students and happy schoolgirls; murdered are girls who were unattractive and foolish; murdered are hunchbacks; murdered are singers; murdered are blind people; murdered are deaf and mute people; murdered are violinists and pianists; murdered are three-year-old and two-year-old children; murdered are eighty-year-old elders who had cataracts in their dimmed eyes, cold transparent fingers and quiet, rustling voices like parchment; murdered are crying newborns who were greedily sucking at their mothers' breasts until their final moments. All are murdered, many hundreds of thousands, millions of people."

KILL OFF THE SPIRIT

The Nazis targeted for murder all Jewish men, women, and children, but they also targeted other groups: Roma and Sinti, Slavs, German male homosexuals, and so on. What made the Holocaust different from the genocide of the Roma and Sinti, the mass murders of Poles and Russians, and the persecution of others is that removing the Jews from the space of Europe was only one part of the Holocaust; the second was the extirpation of any manifestation of the "Jewish spirit" from the world. To the Nazis, Jews were not simply an ethnic "other" nor an inferior "other" to be enslaved, expelled, or murdered. And they were not simply the people who had given the world the Ten Commandments, teachers, as Nietzsche had claimed, of a slave morality. They were, above all, part of a global physical and spiritual reality that the Nazis identified as *Der Jude*, a spiritual principle, both inferior and superior at the same time. It was inferior because it polluted humanity with ideas that negated the natural—in the Nazi world picture—hierarchy of humankind. Christianity, liberal democracy, capitalism, internationalism, pacifism, and communism were all Jewish inventions to neutralize the natural instincts and undermine the hierarchical distinctions between the races, which the Nazis arranged in a pyramid with the Nordic Germans at the apex. But *Der Jude* was also superior because these offerings were so enticing, so tempting, to not only the masses but also the middle classes—that is, the majority of humankind, which did not know where its self-interest was located. Therefore it was necessary not only to remove Jews from the space of the world but also to destroy Jewish spiritual space, represented in books, libraries, music, the visual arts, architecture, and so on. Thus the Holocaust was an attempt to burn up a people and also everything that this people had contributed to humanity.

Białystok Synagogue Memorial and Cathedral (2016)

NO ONE COULD SAY, "I WAS THERE"

When in early 1945, Auschwitz survivors arrived in the Buchenwald concentration camp after a death march, they told those whom they could trust, in whispers, about the murder, year after year, of countless Jews in gas chambers. Buchenwald inmate Jorge Semprún immediately realized that the gas chambers had introduced something new in history. Throughout history, Semprún observed, there were direct witnesses to massacres: survivors and perpetrators. But not of the death in the gas chambers. "We have the proofs, but not the testimonies. In Humanity's collective memory, legendary or historical, fable or document, there will always be this ontological vacuum: […] no one could ever tell us that he has been there." Nevertheless, many have tried to imagine the scenes within that room, hear the echoes of last words spoken. "When the layers of gas had covered everything, there was silence in the dark sky of the room for perhaps a minute, broken only by shrill, racking coughs and the gasps of those too far gone in their agonies to offer a devotion." Thus, in the 1950s, the French Jewish novelist André Schwarz-Bart, whose parents were murdered in Auschwitz, imagined this most important threshold in both Jewish and human history. "And first a stream, then a cascade, an irrepressible, majestic torrent, the poem which, through the smoke of fires and above the funeral pyres of history, the Jews—who for two thousand years never bore arms and never had either missionary empires or coloured slaves—the old love poem which the Jews had traced in letters of blood on the earth's hard crust—the old love poem unfurled in the gas chamber, surrounded it, dominated its dark, abysmal sneer: 'SHEMA ISRAEL ADONAI ELOHENU ADONAI EH'OTH. […] Hear O Israel, the Eternal our God, the Eternal is One. O Lord, by your grace you nourish the living, and by your great pity you resurrect the dead; and you uphold the weak, cure the sick, break the chains of slaves; and faithfully keep your promises to those who sleep in the dust. Who is like unto you, O merciful Father, and who could be like unto you?'"

A PERFECTLY NORMAL MEASURE

In May 1945, a young German Jewish refugee, Peter Weiss, treated himself to a movie in Stockholm. The newsreels that preceded the feature film reported on the liberation of the concentration camps in Germany. "On the dazzlingly bright screen I saw the places for which I had been destined, the figures to whom I should have belonged." He saw an inconceivable and incomprehensible world. "A sobbing could be heard and a voice called out: Never forget this! It was a miserable senseless cry, for there were no longer any words, there was nothing more to be said, there were no declarations, no more admonitions, all values had been destroyed." Weiss observed the mountains of corpses and, between them, "shapes of utter humiliation in their striped rags. Their movements were interminably slow, they reeled around, bundles of bones, blind to one another in a world of shadows." Weiss racked his brain for a parallel, for some kind of conceptual framework that would help him understand what he saw. He turned to the traditional iconography of the underworld as told in great works of literature and depicted in great visions of art. Yet he couldn't make the connection. "Everything was reduced to dust and we could never think again of looking for new comparisons, for points of departure in the face of these ultimate pictures." Watching the same images in New York, German Jewish refugee Hannah Arendt was struck by an "atmosphere of insanity and unreality" and noticed that "to the unprejudiced observer they are just about as convincing as the pictures of mysterious substances taken at spiritualist séances." The apparent unreality of the camps arose from the fact that within the camps, "the human masses sealed off in them are treated as if they no longer existed, as if what happened to them were no longer of any interest to anybody." Arendt realized with a shock that this very fiction, imposed by the jailers on the prisoners, not only produced that surreal aura of the camps but also convinced those who ran the camps that the extermination of the inmates was "a perfectly normal measure."

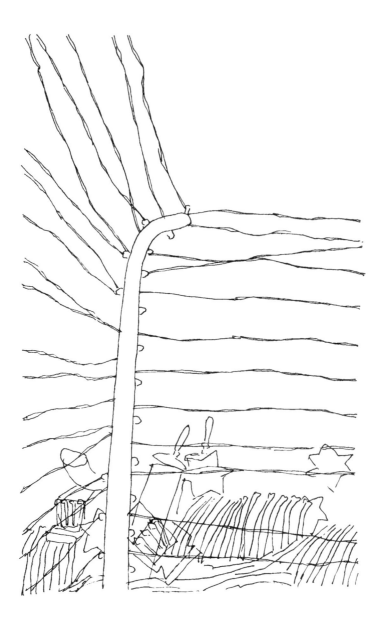

An Incomprehensible World (1980s)

The Seven Species of Israel (2014)

AN INTERROGATION MARK

In 1922, the League of Nations had given Great Britain a mandate over Palestine, with the aim that it would create conditions for a Jewish homeland. Confronted with increasing civil unrest between the Jewish and Arab populations, London had become increasingly frustrated with its responsibilities in Palestine, and in 1947 it announced that in 1948 it would return the mandate to the league's successor organization, the United Nations. A vote of the UN General Assembly decided on a partition of the territory into a Jewish state and an Arab state, which resulted in the proclamation of the State of Israel on May 14, 1948. The Israeli government adopted as its symbol the menorah of King Herod's Temple, sculpted in a relief on the Arch of Titus in Rome, which celebrates the destruction of that temple—a somewhat paradoxical choice to be sure. The creation of the first independent Jewish state since 70 CE was greeted with jubilation among Jews, but conditions on the ground were harsh. "Life in Israel is lacking in tradition and style, form and color, humor and grace," Arthur Koestler reported in 1949. He acknowledged that it was unfair to judge Israeli society "by the standards of mellower civilizations." But one had to face that Zionist propaganda and millennial dreams about the return to the Promised Land had created expectations about a land of milk and honey that could not be met by the new state. "It is a hard pioneer country and a bitter refugee country, disillusioned by experience, stubbornly fighting for life, with an aching void in its past and an interrogation mark for its future. The muses and the social graces are still under embargo; most of the things which make life attractive and worth living are for tomorrow."

THEY REMAIN STRANGERS

In 1935, Rabbi Joachim Prinz had told the German Jews, who by then were being reduced to Jews who (still) happened to be living in Germany, that their destiny was to live without neighbors. After the Holocaust, this did not dramatically change. The State of Israel, legitimate under international law as the result of a vote in the UN General Assembly, and a fact on the map of the Middle East as the result of remarkable feats of arms, was for the first thirty years of its existence a country without a single neighbor. And while a 1979 treaty with Egypt and a 1994 treaty with Jordan brought some improvement in the neighborhood, and the establishment of diplomatic relations with Bahrain, the United Arab Emirates, Sudan, and Morocco marked some progress, truly amiable relations remain to be achieved. In Europe, survivors who returned to the places from which they had been deported had difficulty regaining their homes from new occupants. As to the treasures given in trust to neighbors: countless are the tales of returnees confronted with outright denial of such transactions. Those who could not swallow their rage about such betrayal left, for Palestine or the New World. Those who could, or who were too tired to make a new beginning elsewhere, tried to make a new living in the midst of a society that had not really welcomed them back. "My neighbor greets me in a friendly fashion, *Bonjour, Monsieur*," Hanns Chaim Mayer (also known as Jean Améry) noted a quarter of a century after his return from Auschwitz. "I doff my hat, *Bonjour, Madame*. But Madame and Monsieur are separated by interstellar distances; for yesterday a Madame looked away when they led off a Monsieur, and through the barred windows of the departing car a Monsieur viewed a Madame as if she were a stone angel from a bright and stern heaven, which is forever closed for the Jew. [...] As a Jew I go through life like a sick man with one of those ailments that cause no great hardships but are certain to end fatally. [...] *Bonjour, Madame, Bonjour, Monsieur*. They greet each other. But she cannot and will not relieve her sick neighbor of his mortal illness at the cost of suffering to death from it herself. And so they remain strangers to one another."

Former Jewish Owned Property (2021)

PREPARED FOR THE FUTURE

Not all looked the other way, of course. There were Christians who risked their lives to save Jews, sometimes driven by charity, sometimes by the opportunity to make ends meet, sometimes because of hatred for the Germans, but most often by a mixture of motives. A Jewish native of Zbarazh (then Poland, now Ukraine), Ida Landau was blond and blue-eyed, and survived the Holocaust with false papers. After the war she married Bruno Fink, and in the 1950s began to write short stories based on her wartime experiences. In one of them, set after the war, the narrator meets on a train a Jewish couple that is returning from a visit to the peasants who had hidden them in their hut, equipped with a bricked-in area in the cellar where they spent time when a visitor came or Germans arrived in the village. Money had changed hands, and now the peasants had constructed a house that they were eager to show. "We began in the kitchen, then we went into the living room, the bedroom, and another room for the son who had returned from the army," the woman told their new acquaintance. "We thought they had shown us everything, but then they said, 'And we kept you in mind, too. Here, take a look!' The husband pushed aside a wardrobe and I looked—a white, blank wall. But when he went down and touched the floor, I grabbed Olek's hand. I didn't see anything yet, but that gesture was familiar. He lifted a red, waxed board and told us to look closely. 'There, now, just in case something happens, you won't have to roost like chickens, a shelter as pretty as a picture, with all the comforts!' I leaned over and saw stairs leading down into a small dark room, without any windows or doors. It had two beds, two chairs, and a table. [...] 'What are we supposed to make of that?' asked the man. 'Sentenced to a hiding-place, sentenced to death once again? And by whom? By good people who wish us well. It's appalling. To build a hiding-place out of the goodness of one's heart! That's what's so horrible. There, in that house, it was as if I were kneeling above my own grave.'" As the train pulls into the station, the narrator continues: "'Horrible,' I repeated. I said something else about how the war twisted people, and I felt ashamed; it was so banal, so polite. But they didn't hear me. They were hurrying towards the exit, and their quick, nervous steps gave the impression of flight."

THE INTIMACY OF THE HOME

Born in the Pale of Settlement, Emmanuel Levinas studied philosophy in France and Germany in the 1920s. As a naturalized Frenchman, he served in the French army in 1940, was captured by the Nazis, and survived as a prisoner of war while his wife and daughter were hidden in a French convent. In the wake of the Holocaust, Levinas articulated an understanding of human existence that was rooted in his understanding of Judaism, which, in turn, reflected the experience of the persecuted who had survived because they had true neighbors. "If Judaism is attached to the here below, it is not because it does not have the imagination to conceive of a supernatural order, or because matter represents some absolute for it; but because the first light of conscience is lit for it on the path that leads from man to his neighbor." Thus Judaism became the basis of a philosophy of dwelling and property that centers on the dialectic of recollection and hospitality, the way we become ourselves in our homes, and the way that very sense of being *at home* allows us to open our homes to, and share our possessions with, strangers who present themselves on our doorstep—who we receive inside our home, so that they can share a meal at our table and, in undoubtedly rarer instances, a night in our beds. The intimacy of the home, Levinas proposed, creates a condition in which we are freed from the constant interaction with a world in which we are not at home, creating a clearing in which we can pay attention to ourselves, assess our place in the world, and consider our options. Yet this separation and recollection in the interiority of the home, which is filled with our possessions, is only a first step. The security of the home is meaningless if it does not initiate the second step, which is the extension of the boundary of the home in such a way that it also embraces the unfamiliar, the stranger—an act that is possible because, in the final analysis, the person who is at home is, at least since Abram left Ur of the Chaldeans, also an exile in the world. "In order that I be able to free myself from the very possession that the welcome of the Home establishes, in order that I be able to see things in themselves, that is, represent them to myself, refuse both enjoyment and possession, I must know to *give* what I possess."

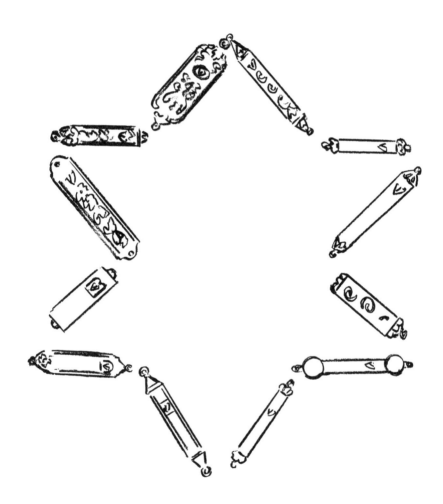

Mezuzahs (2021)

Broken Jewish Tombstones (2016)

WRITE AND RECORD!

"This is what we are fighting against," Hitler announced to a small gathering of Nazis in early 1933 and, as we have already seen, he went on to list not only "the masochistic spirit of self-torment" but also "the curse of so-called morals" as shackles that bound the German nation. Yet Hitler's struggle against conscience, which he assumed to be a Jewish invention of universal impact, was difficult: even the SS, charged with the key role in the so-called Final Solution, was not immune. "Most of you here must know what it means to see a hundred corpses lie side to side, or five hundred, or a thousand," SS chief Heinrich Himmler, who was in charge of the Final Solution, told his subalterns in 1943. "To have stuck this out and—excepting cases of human weakness—to have kept our integrity, that is what made us hard. In our history, this is an unwritten and never-to-be-written page of glory." If German decency demanded that the Final Solution be buried in silence, Jewish decency, and a deep sense of justice toward the perpetrators, victims, and the world as a whole, demanded that every single aspect of the Holocaust be committed to the annals of history. "Write and record!" Throughout the twelve years of the assault, people wrote down what happened to the Jews, and in the decades that followed, their best minds submitted it to profound analysis. Witnessing the trial of an important Nazi perpetrator, Hannah Arendt noted that the Nazis had transformed the commandment "Thou shalt not kill" into "Thou shall kill." "Evil in the Third Reich had lost the quality by which most people recognize it—the quality of temptation," she observed. She assumed that many Germans must have been tempted not to kill, not to become direct or indirect accomplices in the deportation of their neighbors and the destruction of a people. "But, God knows, they had learned how to resist temptation." But Arendt considered not only the guilt of the perpetrators. She also considered with a relentless intellectual honesty the compliance of the Jewish leadership with German orders. "To a Jew this role of the Jewish leaders in the destruction of their own people is undoubtedly the darkest chapter of the whole dark story," Arendt observed.

WHEN PEACE AND A LITTLE REPOSE FINALLY COME

When the Jews returned from Babylonian exile, they did not immediately reconstruct the Temple of Jerusalem. In the Israeli-Arab war that followed the proclamation of the State of Israel, the Israelis proved able to hang on to the newly constructed suburbs of Jerusalem but not the Old City, with the Temple Mount. When in 1967, a third Israeli-Arab war restored the Old City, and also the territories that had been the heartland of the Hebrew tribes under Israeli control, the moment seemed almost messianic. In the words of army chief of staff Yitzhak Rabin, "There was one moment in the Six-Day War which symbolized the great victory: that was the moment in which the first paratroopers—under Gur's command—reached the stones of the Western Wall, feeling the emotion of the place; there never was, and never will be, another moment like it." However, these territorial gains turned out to be another example of the weary wisdom that one should be careful of what one wishes, because one might get it. The rose offered by history proved to have many sharp thorns. The Promised Land of old now became a cauldron of Jewish messianism, which ranged from those who simply desired to annex the conquered territories to those who even considered destroying the Dome of the Rock so the Temple could be constructed, and a Palestinian nationalism that had at the time an equal zero-sum approach to the land and that saw that very same Dome of the Rock, located a stone's throw from the Western Wall, as the symbol of its national identity. Trying to understand the pressures of expectations, desires, and resentments, Israeli writer Amos Oz traveled the whole of the land between the Jordan and the Mediterranean in the fall of 1982. Of all the places he saw, he liked Ashdod best, an unpretentious port town without a contested past that had been established in the late 1950s. "All those who secretly long for the charms of Paris and Vienna, for the Jewish shtetl, or for heavenly Jerusalem: do not cut loose from those longings—for what are we without longings?—but let's remember that Ashdod is what is there. […] And from her we shall see what will flower when peace and a little repose finally come."

Jerusalem: The Impossible Partition (2003)

Torah Shield Engraved with Chodorów Synagogue (2020)

PIECING THE FRAGMENTS TOGETHER

The most important sites of Jewish martyrdom in Nazi-ruled Europe have become destinations of annual pilgrimages of young people, who walk the last mile or two that the victims were forced to walk to the mass graves or the gas chambers. These tours are optimistically named: March of the Living, March of Remembrance and Hope, and so on. But few go to the thousands upon thousands of shtetls where so little remains to remind either the current inhabitants or the occasional visitor of past Jewish life. A whole architectural tradition was wiped out by fire: of the hundreds of often exquisitely decorated wooden synagogues that dotted the eastern reach of today's Poland, of Belarus and Ukraine, a couple stand as empty husks, but none remains intact. Volunteers have re-created the painted ceiling of the Chodorów (Khodoriv, Ukraine) synagogue, but it is a museum installation about a lost civilization. Most of the brick and stone synagogues were destroyed also, and many of the few dozen that remain are now used as warehouses or garages. A small number have been restored with foreign funds but lack a Jewish community to bring them to life. As to the graveyards, the onetime pride of each of those now Jew-free towns and villages? The Nazis and their allies not only murdered the living and destroyed their houses of worship but also broke up the tombstones, using the fragments for the pavement of roads. But the children and children's children of the few survivors remember and have begun to return to these places of life, places of dead, and places of destruction—and with the help of the current non-Jewish inhabitants have begun to piece the fragments together, into a story and a presence.

SONG OF ASCENT

"I heard there was a secret chord / That David played and it pleased the Lord," thus begins Leonard Cohen's "Hallelujah." The next line suggests: "But you don't really care for music, do you?" Indeed, we have lost touch with music as a key that opens an infinity of auditory, existential, and historical spaces, the way the rhythms, chords, and melodies of the prayers, blessings, readings in synagogues or the songs that celebrate the Shabbat in the Jewish home break the confinement of the here and now. So Cohen provides a small lesson to the present generation on the perfect, diminished, and augmented intervals that connect music to the soul: "It goes like this, the fourth, the fifth, / the minor falls, the major lifts, / the baffled king composing Hallelujah." Cohen's David was first and foremost not the famously loving, famously intrepid, nor famously artistic king, but a continuously bewildered man, and in this he touched on the hidden core of the secret chord, not only of the man David but also of his people. David's Psalm 133 is one of the oldest lyrics. Historically chanted by pilgrims approaching Jerusalem from the Judaean valleys or the coastal plain over ascending roads, it has been heard ever since in synagogues, in Jewish homes, Jewish youth camps, and in the planes that carried the Israeli Defense Force commandos during their audacious rescue mission of the Entebbe hostages in 1976. *Hine ma tov u'ma-nayim, shevet ach-im gam ya-chad*. "How good and pleasant it is when God's people live together in unity." Psalm 133 is reimagined and reinvented every time it is sung. Sung as a round, it makes every person listen to the other, then grouping to grouping, creating an upward spiral of expanding space in which individuals become connected in a community, and the community with the world at large.

That Old Song – Do You Still Know It? (2017)

Shofars (2017)

LIKE A SUMMONS, SOUNDING INTO EVERY CORNER

While song may be the secret chord of Jewish history, the foundation and aspiration of that history transcends the power of the human voice. On Rosh Hashanah, the Jewish new year, and at the end of Yom Kippur, the Day of Atonement, a series of primal but at the same time precisely calibrated blasts of a ram's horn—the shofar—are meant to shatter the separation between the earth and the heavens. The shofar is an instrument that evokes the *Akedah*, the binding of Isaac. The boy survives God's peculiar test of Abraham's faith when a ram sent by God takes his place, just in time. The shofar is a difficult instrument that is blown only sporadically in religious services and never for entertainment in social settings. Thus the person who is given the honor to produce the prescribed blasts has little opportunity to gain full control over it—making it, unlike the fiddle, even when played on a roof in pogrom-prone czarist Russia, a perfect symbol of human life itself. "The shofar blares out; everyone is awakened." Thus Bella Chagall née Rosenfeld remembered in 1939 the blowing of the shofar in her native Vitebsk thirty years earlier. "They are all very still. They wait. The shofar gives another blast. The sound is chopped off, as though the horn were out of breath. People exchange glances. The shofar trumpets hoarsely. A murmur ripples through the shul. What manner of shofar blowing is that? He lacks strength. Perhaps another man should be called up. And then suddenly, as though the trumpet blower had pushed out the evil spirit that was clogging the instrument, there comes a pure, long sound. Like a summons it runs through the whole shul, sounding into every corner. The congregation is relieved: one gives a sigh, another nods his head. The sound rises upward. The walls are touched by it, it reaches me and my handrail. It throbs up to the ceiling, pushes the thick air, fills every empty space. It booms into my ears, my mouth, I even feel an ache in my stomach. When will the shofar finish trumpeting? What does the New Year want of us?" And thus a people of history faces judgment, and the future.

Coda—and a New Beginning

On September 21, 1941, began the Rosh Hashanah that inaugurated the year 5702. In Kyiv, German troops had entered the city two days earlier, after a bitter, four-week-long battle that had brought much destruction to the city. Of the 230,000 Jews who had lived there three months earlier, both Soviet citizens and Polish refugees, only 60,000 to 70,000 remained—many of them elderly people, women, and children. Most of the men had been drafted into the Red Army, and tens of thousands had been evacuated to the East. Did the Jews who remained gather to hear the Shofar that Rosh Hashanah? It is unlikely: German soldiers had terrorized Jews from the first day of the occupation. Persecution quickly turned into massacre: nine days after the beginning of the German occupation, posters appeared everywhere in the city instructing Jews to appear at eight a.m. on Monday, September 29, 1941, at a particular location near the Jewish cemetery. The stick: refusal to appear carried an automatic death sentence; the carrot: the rumor was that the Jews would be sent to Palestine, aka Eretz Israel, aka the Promised Land. They were to bring documents, money and other valuables, warm clothing, and bed linens. According to a German tally, 33,771 Jews assembled at the designated place. They were marched under guard of Einsatzkommando 4a (Task Force 4a), one of the special German units created with the singular task to murder Jews, toward the Babyn Yar ravine. There they were murdered within the next eighteen hours.

It is almost impossible to imagine what went on at Babyn Yar, or at any of the other sites in the German-occupied Soviet Union where the mobile murder squads sought to wipe out a people and a civilization in a minimum of time and with a minimum of fuss. Eyewitness testimonies are few, and most of them were recorded decades after the event. The first such witness statement, taken on November 10, 1945, was given by Hermann Friedrich Gräbe, a German construction manager who had been dispatched to the Ukrainian city of Dubno to build grain-storage facilities at the airport. Unlike the great majority of his countrymen, Gräbe arrived in the occupied territories with both a moral compass and an ethical rudder, and he not only tried to record the crimes that were committed but also took great risks to save Jews by providing false papers, giving shelter, and organizing several daring escapes. On October 5, 1942, he could do no more than bear witness. That morning his foreman, Hubert Moennikes, told him that a massacre of Jews was under way near the construction office, and they decided to observe the events.

"Moennikes and I went directly to the pits. Nobody bothered us. Now I heard rifle shots in quick succession from behind one of the earth mounds. The people who had got off the trucks—men, women and children of all ages—had to undress upon the order of an SS man who carried a riding or dog whip. They had to put down their clothes in fixed places, sorted according to shoes, top clothing and undergarments. I saw heaps of shoes of about 800 to 1000 pairs, great piles of under-linen and clothing. Without screaming or weeping these people undressed, stood around in family groups, kissed each other, said farewells, and waited for a sign from another SS man, who stood near the pit, also with a whip in his hand. During the fifteen minutes I stood near, I heard no complaint or plea for mercy. I watched a family of about eight persons, a man and a woman both of about fifty, with their children of about twenty to twenty-four, and two grown-up daughters about twenty-eight or twenty-nine. An old woman with snow white hair was holding a one-year-old child in her arms and singing to it and tickling it. The child was cooing with delight. The parents were looking on with tears in their eyes. [...] At that moment the SS man at the pit started shouting something to his comrade. The latter counted off about twenty persons and instructed them to go behind the earth mound. Among them was the family I have just mentioned. I well remember a girl, slim with black hair, who, as she passed me, pointed to herself and said, 'twenty-three years old.' I walked around the mound and found myself confronted by a tremendous grave. People were closely wedged together and lying on top of each other so that only their heads were visible. Nearly all had blood running over their shoulders from their heads. Some of the people shot were still moving. Some were lifting their arms and turning their heads to show that they were still alive. The pit was nearly two-thirds full. I estimated that it already contained about a thousand people. I looked for the man who did the shooting. He was an SS man, who sat at the edge of the narrow end of the pit, his feet dangling into the pit. He had a tommy-gun on his knees and was smoking a cigarette. The people, completely naked, went down some steps which were cut in the clay wall of the pit and clambered over the heads of the people lying there to the place to which the SS man directed them. They lay down in front of the dead or wounded people; some caressed those who were still alive and spoke to them in a low voice. Then I heard a series of shots. I looked into the pit and saw that the bodies were twitching or the heads lying already motionless on top of the bodies that lay beneath them. Blood was running from their necks.

The next batch was approaching already. They went down into the pit, lined themselves up against the previous victims and were shot."

This is what happened in Dubno in October 1942, and what happened in so many other places. And this is what happened in September 1941 in Babyn Yar, the place that has come to represent in our collective memory all those different places—a symbol, because of the size of the massacre, because it happened adjacent to the largest city in the German-occupied Soviet Union, and because of its date: the murder went on for eighteen hours, to end at Erev Yom Kippur, the eve of the holiest of Jewish holy days.

When in November 1943 the Red Army pushed the Germans out of Kyiv, the troops found a city that was empty of Jews, and Kyiv was no different from the other cities, towns, and villages. "In gullies and deep ravines, in anti-tank ditches of sand and clay, under heavy black soil, and in swamps and pits, there lie hastily flung bodies of professors and workers, doctors and students, old people and children," war reporter Vasily Grossman observed. He mourned those murdered, as individuals and as a people, but in his reflection on the emptiness that he encountered, he did not remark on the systematic destruction of Jewish cultural legacy, embodied above all in the masonry synagogues that stood in the cities and larger towns and the wooden houses of prayer in smaller towns and villages. Some of the masonry structures survived as ruins, but all the wooden synagogues had been burned to the ground. Soviet officials did not care. The synagogue was not a legacy that was meaningful to the functionaries of a state that characterized religion as "the opium of the people." In the words of Vladimir Ilyich Lenin, all religions were "instruments of bourgeois reaction that serve to defend exploitation and to befuddle the working class."

Eighty years later, the destruction of the hundreds of wooden synagogues that were constructed in the seventeenth and eighteenth centuries in the territory of the Polish-Lithuanian Commonwealth—an area that covers most of today's Poland, all of Lithuania, Belarus, and the western and central part of Ukraine, including Kyiv—is seen by many as an enormous loss to world heritage. These buildings dating from the seventeenth and early eighteenth centuries embodied a vital and highly original architectural tradition that occupies a unique position in the artistic and cultural history of the Jewish people. While the spatial organization of these buildings reflected Jewish principles, their structure was typically realized by non-Jewish builders, as Jews were excluded from the building trade. Many of these craftsmen were employed by the aristocrats who owned the towns where these buildings were erected. Sophisticated and ambitious in their taste, these landowners tried to revive the rural economy in the wake of a series of disastrous wars that had laid waste to the Polish-Lithuanian Commonwealth. They realized that a beautiful synagogue in a shtetl occasioned the arrival of Jewish tailors, shoemakers, furriers, and perhaps also a physician or two. And with a bit of luck, the Jewish community might grow to such a size that it might also provide enough work for a glazier, a painter, a bookbinder, a goldsmith, and of course a moneylender, five trades that were particularly useful in maintaining the comfort and beauty of a magnate's castle, the quality of his library, the happiness of his wife, and the cash flow of the estate. All in all, it was an early example of an approach to development articulated by the mysterious voice that speaks in the movie *Field of Dreams* to Iowa corn farmer Ray Kinsella: "If you build it, he will come."

The need to attract Jews explains, for example, the remarkable synagogue constructed in Wołpa (aka Volpe or Voupa), Belarus. Sponsored by the princely Sapieha family, which owned the town, the sanctuary had a spectacular wooden ceiling that leapt upward in three recessed and curved steps, culminating in a fourth and final vault, from which descended four slender wooden pillars that framed the polygonal bimah. The forced perspective made an already soaring space appear much higher than it was, while the central bimah, framed by the four posts, generated the characteristic centrifugal space embodied in so many central and eastern European synagogues. Typically, Jewish artists executed the polychrome painted interiors of these wooden houses of prayer and sculpted the richly carved ark and bimah. Sixty years ago, Stephen Kayser, the pioneering scholar of Jewish ceremonial art, reflected on the unique position of these wooden synagogues in Jewish history. "If there ever was a truly close relationship between a house of worship and its populace, it lay in the affection which the inhabitants of an Eastern European Jewish country community felt for their synagogue, the home of their souls." Born of a collaboration of Jewish and non-Jewish neighbors, the synagogues represented "a truly original and organic manifestation of artistic expression—the only real Jewish folk art in history."

Wooden marvels like the Wołpa synagogue were testimonies of the onetime relative affluence and, as important, the interconnectedness of these shtetls. However, by the nineteenth century, the prosperity of the rural areas in what was by then the Russian Pale of Settlement declined as the result of urbanization and increasingly antisemitic policies, and by the end of that century, many of these buildings were in a bad state of repair. Industrialization allowed some of those small towns to expand, but that almost always led to the demolition of the wooden synagogue and the construction of a larger masonry one. No one protested: these wooden synagogues were beyond the horizon of the emerging discipline of architectural history, which at that time had little interest in vernacular traditions. While some did attract the attention of folklorists and ethnographers, these scholars were not equipped to understand and document the structures' architectural significance.

The year 1891 marked a turning point in the appreciation of these buildings when the twenty-three-year-old non-Jewish Polish painter Karol Zyndram Maszkowski began a documentation of the Gwoździec synagogue. Shortly thereafter, the Warsaw-based entrepreneur, banker, and amateur historian Mathias Bersohn initiated a project to document wooden synagogues by commissioning local photographers. Between 1910 and 1913, a non-Jewish architecture student at the Vienna University of Technology, Alois Breier, undertook the first systematic survey of many synagogues, but it was another twenty years before a bare-bones summary of his work to be published.

Only in 1915, when a twenty-five-year-old architecture graduate, typographer, and illustrator of Yiddish children's books, Lazar Markovich Lissitzky, arrived at the wooden Mahilyow (aka Mogilev or, in Yiddish, Molev) synagogue, did this building type find its match in an artistic, and also a Jewish, sensibility that was able to fully appreciate its marvels. Lissitzky had traveled widely, absorbing firsthand the canonical works of European architecture. Yet, when he entered the Mogilev shul, he was stunned. "No, this was something different from that first surprise I received when I visited the Roman basilicas, the Gothic cathedrals, the Baroque churches of Germany, France, and Italy. Maybe, when a child awakens in a crib that is covered with a veil upon which flies and butterflies are sitting and the entire thing is drenched by the sun, maybe the child sees something like that. The walls—wooden, oaken beams that resound when you hit them. Above the walls, a ceiling like a vault made of boards. The seams all visible. Although the work of the carpenter is without artfulness, without imagination, the whole interior of the shul is so perfectly conceived by the painter with only a few uncomplicated colors that an entire grand world lives there and blooms and overflows this small space."

Upon closer inspection, Lissitzky changed his mind about the architectural composition, which he now recognized as remarkably sophisticated, but the major delight of the building was to be found in the decorative scheme, which offered both an infinite plenitude of forms and ideas and a commanding vision that aligned every detail with both the building and, even more important, the world outside. "The treasury of forms used by the painter is inexhaustible. One sees how it all flowed from him, as from a cornucopia, and how the hand of the virtuoso never grew tired and never allowed itself to be outpaced by the speed of thought. On the back of the holy ark I discovered the first sketches in pencil of the outline of the entire painting, which served as the foundation of the later work in paint. This outline was sketched on the wall by a master with intense confidence, for whom the pencil is perfectly under the control of his will." Much of the magic resulted from the interplay between the work and the ever-changing light, made possible by the windows that breached each of the four walls. "As the sun completes its circle, every hour each wall—and especially the sloping parts of the ceiling—is lit in a different way. This gives the entire thing an unending play." Immersing himself in the tradition of the wooden synagogues gave Lissitzky a profound sense of Jewish identity; yet, within two years he shifted his concern from identity and lineage to the future: El Lissitzky, as he was to be known, became the cofounder of two radical movements in twentieth-century art and architecture: Suprematism and Constructivism.

While the Russian Revolution and the utopian project of a perfectly equitable society diverted El Lissitzky from further engagement with wooden synagogues, the Russian architect George Lukomski (also spelled Loukomski), a minor aristocrat who escaped the mixed blessing of the Bolshevik Revolution in 1920 to eke out an émigré's existence initially in

Berlin and then in Paris, turned to drawing Polish synagogues in 1933; that year he visited and sketched no fewer than 144 of them. In 1934, he began to exhibit his work, first in London. This led to an invitation to publish an article on wooden synagogues in the *Burlington Magazine for Connoisseurs*. Thus, Lukomski introduced the building type, which was unknown in western Europe, to a lofty sphere of mostly wealthy aesthetes, few of whom would have any understanding of Jewish or, certainly, eastern European traditions. Lukomski had an urgent message: all those synagogues faced destruction because wood typically lasts only 400 years. "Thus, the synagogues of the sixteenth and seventeenth centuries will soon be in a ruinous condition, impossible of restoration. It is, therefore, all the more necessary to compile an iconography of these unique buildings and make them known to the world." In 1935, Lukomski's drawings were exhibited in Paris, and in early 1936 they could be seen first in Lisbon and then in Casa de Velázquez in Madrid—where they were all destroyed when, in November of that year, General Franco's airplanes bombed the city.

A sense of urgency to record what was seen as an imperiled legacy also shaped surveys undertaken in Poland in the 1920s and 1930s. The independence of Poland—which resulted in 1918 from the collapse of the three empires that had dismembered the Polish-Lithuanian Commonwealth in the three partitions of 1772, 1793, and 1795—created a surge in Polish nationalism that, in turn, generated within the new state an interest in the history and forms of Polish national architecture. At the Politechnika Warszawska (Warsaw Polytechnic), Professor Oskar Sosnowski established the Zakład Architektury Polskiej (Institute of Polish Architecture) and—remarkably, in terms of our understanding of the meaning of the adjective *Polish* in that name—immediately initiated a comprehensive project to document the wooden synagogues that were within the borders of the new state (those located in the Soviet Union were, of course, out of reach). One of the important collaborators in the project was Jewish art historian and photographer Szymon Zajczyk, who knew both Yiddish and Hebrew and was able to read the many liturgical texts on the synagogues' walls. Many architecture students were involved in producing survey drawings. Those by Mieczysław Kuźma stood out for their skill and beauty. The project was still underway when Germany invaded Poland in 1939. The Germans executed Sosnowski shortly after their occupation of Warsaw in

October 1939; Zajczyk was murdered in 1942—and by that time the Germans had systematically destroyed wooden synagogues wherever they found them.

While much of the material created and collected by Sosnowski, Zajczyk, and others was lost, enough survived World War II to allow two of Sosnowski's former students, Maria Piechotka (née Huber) and her husband, Kazimierz Piechotka, to pull this research together into the first monumental study of the wooden synagogues. Published in 1957 under the title *Bóznice Drewniane* (Wooden Synagogues), the book documents sixty-nine wooden synagogues in great detail and remains a landmark in the historiography of the wooden synagogue. Two years later appeared a splendidly produced English-language edition. "This book commemorates martyred buildings," Stephen Kayser noted in a special introduction. "To be sure, only a few of those interested in art and architecture knew of these charming wooden structures even at the time when most of them could still be seen. Now that practically all of them have fallen to the destructive madness of the Nazi horde, they deserve to be remembered like the six million human beings who perished with them in unspeakable agony—and who to a considerable extent were part of them."

The Piechotkas' pioneering work had appeared just at the time when Polish officials instructed Polish architectural historians not to include buildings that stood east of the Polish-Soviet border established in 1945 as part of the Polish national patrimony—these were now to be considered as paradigms of Belarusian or Ukrainian architecture. This meant that many of the most splendid examples of wooden synagogue architecture, such as those in Wołpa, Mogilev, and Gwoździec, were now out of bounds. In addition, increasing antisemitism, masking as anti-Zionism, made the study of Jewish history difficult. But thanks to the Piechotkas, architect Robert Boyle had enough material at hand to construct, in 1970, a wooden synagogue for the film set of *Fiddler on the Roof*. By 1985, the singular importance of the wooden synagogues of eastern Europe was well understood. That year, American architectural historian Carol Herselle Krinsky published her monumental *Synagogues of Europe: Architecture, History, Meaning*. She stressed the key importance of the wooden synagogue as a building type and, significantly, chose to illustrate the book's dust jacket with Mieczysław Kuźma's perspective cross section of the Wołpa synagogue. By the time Krinsky's book appeared, two decades of political repression in Poland were coming to an end, and the Piechotkas were able to pick up their research on wooden synagogues. This ultimately led to the revised and much expanded second edition of their book, published in 2015 under the title *Bramy Nieba: Bóznice drewniane na ziemiach dawnej Rzeczypospolitej* and two years later in an English edition as *Heaven's Gates: Wooden Synagogues in the Territories of the Former Polish-Lithuanian Commonwealth*.

Both books were published by the Polin Museum of the History of Polish Jews, in Warsaw. The largest artifact in the collection is the reconstructed ceiling and roof structure of the small synagogue that stood from the late seventh century to the 1940s in the small town known under Polish rule as Gwoździec and today, located in Ukraine, as Hvizdets. This synagogue was very well documented, thanks to Maszkowski and Breier, and the subject of a substantial monograph written by American architectural historian Thomas C. Hubka. This book inspired Rick and Laura Brown of Handshouse Studio, in Massachusetts (US), to seek ways to reconstruct either the whole or part of the Gwoździec synagogue. They approached the Polin Museum's chief curator, Barbara Kirshenblatt-Gimblett, who was charged with developing the museum's core exhibition, with this idea and found that she welcomed them. Thus, the painted ceiling and the trusses of the roof above it, and the equally splendid painted bimah—each one at 85 percent of the original size—were reconstructed and are an important part of the museum's presentation of early modern Jewish history in the Polish-Lithuanian Commonwealth. A hugely impressive artifact, it fails, however, to generate that magical experience described by Lissitzky: the ceiling is suspended too low in the exhibition space, the painted walls that belonged to the original composition are absent, and the natural light that charged the paintings with life is lacking.

Much of the construction of the ceiling and trusses of the Gwoździec synagogue was undertaken on the grounds of the Museum of Folk Architecture in Sanok, where many wooden buildings from different parts of rural Poland had been brought and reassembled and where, as a result, traditional wood-construction crafts were maintained. The Sanok collection of buildings did not contain an original synagogue—after 1945 none were left—but the work done for the Polin

Museum led the Sanok museum to decide to create a replica of the wooden synagogue in Polaniec, destroyed in 1943, as part of a small-town market square to be constructed on the museum site.

At the same time, property developer Tadeusz Kuźmiński heeded the message "If you build it, he will come" and initiated an undertaking to create a replica of the Wołpa synagogue in the small town of Biłgoraj, over 400 kilometers south of its original location. The maternal family of Isaac Bashevis Singer, the only Yiddish writer to be a Nobel laureate and, in a different ranking, one of just six Polish-born recipients of this most prestigious award in literature, came from Biłgoraj. As an adolescent and young adult, Singer had spent the years 1917–23 in the house of his maternal grandmother, Chana Zylberman, widow of the well-known Rabbi Jacob Mordechaj Zylberman. Through the Biłgoraj XXI Foundation, which summarizes its purpose as, "Civic entrepreneurship for the benefit of integration, economic development, culture, tourism, and sport and preserving traditions of borderland regions," Kuźmiński began to develop the town's brand with the establishment of the Isaac Bashevis Singer Museum in a reconstruction of the Zylberman house. "We want to give the climate of prewar times by moving those who are interested to a place that is unquestionably unique, that is to the Singer's House," the website of the foundation announces. "Just like at the beginning of the last century, the house of Isaac Singer's grandfather Rabbi Zylberman was steeped in […] the smell of old books, sacred books and the local wood burned in the local furnace, and also now above the threshold of today's Singer's House, we will feel the smell of a pine board from the forests of Biłgoraj, we would warm up in the heat beating from the faithfully reconstructed clay hearth, we can relax holing up in the volume of our favourite reading which will take us into the previous Singer's age."

It is, of course, a bit of absurd theater: the museum is to present a nostalgic view of pre-Holocaust Jewish life in Poland that stands in a dramatic opposition to the evocation of that culture in Singer's work. By the time he left Poland for America, in the mid-1930s, Singer had become convinced that in Poland the pious, observant Jews who followed the traditions of earlier time, the assimilated Jews, and all the Jews in between had failed to find a synthesis between Judaism and the modern world, and that the two could not be meaningfully integrated. As a consequence, he believed that whatever remained of Jewish culture was both spiritually corrupt and morally exhausted, an obsolete world marked by perversion and decay, and that even without the Holocaust, it would not have survived the twentieth century.

Kuźmiński does not appear to have understood Singer's work but chose to memorialize the writer with a museum solely because he was a famous man associated with the town. The museum was to be one of the anchors of a gated community that looked like a traditional shtetl. Because a shtetl centered on a synagogue, Kuźmiński needed one and, guided by the scholarship of the Piechotkas and undoubtedly inspired by Kuźma's drawing, picked the one that had stood in Wołpa. It was to be an embellished version of the original: while the triple-vaulted ceiling of the original Wołpa synagogue consisted of bare boards, that of the replica was to be decorated with an expanded and enriched version of the Gwoździec ceiling. Today, in 2021, the exterior shell of the building has been completed, but the interior has not, and with Kuźmiński's passing in 2020, it is not clear whether it will ever happen. Certainly, without the support of a well-established institution, as is the case in Sanok, or without the presence of a Jewish community, the prospects are not bright—especially in a time when the issue of cultural appropriation has become increasingly fraught with controversy.

"What would Singer have thought or written about Kuźmiński's renascent Biłgoraj?" Israeli writer Zack Rothbart asked in a blog post published by the National Library of Israel, whose readers presumably knew of Singer's dark view of traditional Jewish life. "Would he have seen humor in the idea of a replica shtetl with no Jews? Or the notion of a once-iconic synagogue transported through space and time, plopped down in tiny Biłgoraj, steps away from a modest museum in his honor (despite the fact that he himself only lived there for a brief period)?" Rothbart turned for an answer to the short speech Singer gave at the Nobel Prize banquet on December 10, 1978. In a few witty remarks, he addressed the question of why he wrote in Yiddish, a dying language. "Firstly, I like to write ghost stories and nothing fits a ghost better than a dying language. The deader the language the more alive is the ghost. Ghosts love Yiddish and as far as I know, they all speak it." And immediately thereafter he turned to the question of why he had begun, after having established himself as the foremost living writer in an (almost) dead language, he had turned to writing children's stories, publishing eighteen books of them in the final eighteen years of his life. He provided ten answers, but they all came down to the fact that children know how to read for the pleasure of it, unself-consciously and ready to accept the magic that each book reveals the moment one opens its covers. In summary, Rothbart's view of Singer's view of Kuźmiński's project to reconstruct the Wołpa synagogue in Biłgoraj was: he would have enjoyed it because he liked to write children's books.

Wooden synagogues constructed to be viewed in a museum setting or as a magnet for financial investment are tokens of a nostalgia for a world that is gone, irrevocably. While there is a modest revival of some measure of Jewish life in the larger cities of Poland, Lithuania, Belarus, and Ukraine, it is unlikely that the smaller towns and villages of eastern Europe, the places where the wooden synagogues belonged to the local vernacular, will ever see the establishment of viable Jewish communities that might be able to support a new generation of wooden synagogues that reinterpret those created in the seventeenth and eighteenth centuries. But we are fortunate that a large literature exists that allows us to understand the many dimensions of that lost world, with Isaac Bashevis Singer revealing its contradictions and perversions; poet, storyteller, dramatist, and satirist Isaac Leib Peretz articulating its inhabitants' hopes and aspirations; and popular author Sholem Aleichem creating a vivid image of its comic aspects.

In her 1939 memoir of life in pre-1914 Vitebsk, Bella Chagall (née Rosenfeld) provided a moving portrait of the absolute unity between space, liturgy, and congregation during the final hour of Yom Kippur, in which the architecture and space of the synagogue, as perceived from the women's gallery, and the movement of the gathered community fused into a single experience of holiness. "The heavy curtain of the holy ark is drawn aside. Now there is silence, the air has become motionless. Only the rustle of prayer shawls can be heard. The men hurry toward the holy ark. The shining scrolls of the Torah, like princesses awakened from sleep, are carried out from the ark. On their white and dark red velvet mantles great stars gleam—shields of David embroidered in silver and gold. The handles are mounted with silver, encrusted with mother-of-pearl, and crowns and little bells hang from them." Held high above the crowd, the Torah scrolls are carried through the synagogue. Every male worshipper, fully covered by his white *talis* (prayer shawl), attempts to touch the scrolls, and Bella and the other women in the gallery must be satisfied with just a glance. Then they are returned to the ark, and the curtain is drawn. "As though to drown the sadness, the men begin at once to pray aloud," Bella recalled. "I remain standing by the window. I am attracted by the men's section, its clamorous air, filled with white talesim, like upraised wings surging through the shul, covering every dark spot. Only here and there a nose or an eye peeps out. The talis stripes sway like stairs above the covered heads. One talis billows up, emits a groan, and smothers the sound within itself. The shul grows dark. I am seized by fear. The talesim bend, shake, move upward, turn to all sides. Talesim sigh, pray, moan. Suddenly my legs give away. Talesim quiver, drop to the ground like heavy sacks. Here and there a white woollen sock sticks out. Voices erupt as from underground. Talesim begin to roll, as on a ship that is sinking and going down amid the heaving waves. I do not hear the cantor at all. Hoarse voices outshout one another. They pray, they implore, asking that the ceiling open for them. Hands stretched upward. The cries set the lamps shaking. At any moment now the walls will crumble and let Elijah the Prophet fly in. Grown up men are crying like children. I cannot stand it any longer. I myself am crying more and more. I recover only when I perceive at last a living, weeping eye behind a crouching talis, when I hear trembling voices saying to one another: 'Gut yom-tov! Gut yom-tov!'" And thus, the drama of the Day of Atonement reaches its conclusion.

Some thirty-five years later, during the Yom Kippur of the year 5702, things were very different, of course, in Vitebsk and all the other cities, towns, and shtetls of the German-occupied territory of the Soviet Union. As to Kyiv …

A few weeks after Yom Kippur 5781, the Babyn Yar Holocaust Memorial Center commissioned Manuel Herz to design a synagogue at Babyn Yar. He did not come unprepared. Over two decades earlier, when the Jewish community of the German city of Mainz ran a competition for a new synagogue and community center, Herz proposed a particularly felicitous combination of a building that, in the arrangement of its sanctuary, was quite traditional but as a whole, as a protagonist in the urban space, was radical. The *parti pris* was grounded in the Hebrew noun *davar*, which means both "word" and "thing"—a direct reflection of the fact that in the biblical account of Creation, God speaks the world into being. Thus, Herz conceived the massing of the building as the noun *Kedushah* (holiness). With the Babyn Yar Synagogue, Manuel pushed, for a second time in his career, the conceptual envelope of synagogue design—and it is to his credit that he managed to avoid, in the beautiful words of William Shakespeare's Sonnet 59, which considers the age-old question of whether innovation is possible, "The second burthen of a former child."

Three original ideas shaped the Babyn Yar project. The first one was Herz's ambition to repair the interrupted tradition of the eastern European wooden synagogues in a manner that boldly transcends the antiquarian efforts at Polin, Sanok, and Biłgoraj. In the choice of both its material and its decoration, and in its purpose as a place of prayer and perhaps even study and debate, Herz's synagogue was to communicate to the world a resolve to continue despite the odds, a faith expressed in 1943 by Hirsh Glick, a young Jewish inmate of the Vilna ghetto, in the song that became a source of strength to European Jews fighting for their lives. *Zog nit keyn mol, az du geyst dem letstn veg, / Khotsh himlen blayene farshteln bloye teg. / Kumen vet nokh undzer oysgebenkte sho, / S'vet a poyk ton undzer trot: mir zaynen do!* (Never say that you're going your last way / Although the skies filled with lead cover blue days / Our promised hour will soon come / Our marching steps ring out: We are here!).

The second was Herz's conception of the Babyn Yar Synagogue as an oversize *siddur* (prayer book) that is closed when not in use and will be opened in a collective effort by the members of the minyan before the service commences, and that can be closed afterward—taking into account, of course, Halakhic rules as to what work can be done when.

Finally, the synagogue project was also informed by a third idea, closely linked to the second: when the oversize wooden siddur shul opened, it was to unfold its parts in the manner of a children's pop-up book—which has movable parts made out of specially cut and folded paper that, by means of paper gears, pull tabs, or little strings, arise from a flat position into a complex three-dimensional scene with the unfolding of a spread of pages. Rooted in the paper mechanics used to illustrate astronomical ideas about the rotation of the heavens or anatomical notions about the workings of the human body, the pop-up became a storytelling device in children's books in the nineteenth century. At a time that began to understand the special place of early childhood in the development of each individual, a new genre of children's literature emerged that spurned a didactic purpose and instead aimed to stimulate the imagination. One way to do so was to allow readers to participate in the telling of the story by triggering the pop-up mechanism through the simple movement of a page from right to left, producing in the transformation from surface to sculpture an always surprising result.

Thus, we have a resurrection of one of the most authentically Jewish forms of architecture, unique to the conditions that existed in the Polish-Lithuanian Commonwealth in the seventeenth and eighteenth centuries; a siddur, which stands for the discipline, composure, and integrity of religious devotion; and a children's pop-up book, which has no roots in the Jewish tradition and represents, instead, the innovation, fun, and games that come with secularization. This tripartite origin of the Babyn Yar Synagogue certainly would have delighted Singer, who more than any other Jewish writer of the past two centuries, had a broad appreciation for the impossible choices that accompany any attempt to create a meaningful Jewish existence within the conditions of modernity, and who believed that only in the full embrace of life in all its possibilities can the triangular opposition of history, piety, and delight be fused into a paradox worthy of an artistic form.

As a wooden synagogue, the Babyn Yar shul invokes the sense of community that Bella Chagall evoked and that is the bedrock of Jewish history and of the Jewish understanding of the sacred. "Our share in holiness we acquire by living in the Jewish community," Rabbi Abraham Joshua Heschel observed in 1950. "What we do as individuals is a trivial episode, what we attain as Israel causes us to grow into the infinite." This "Israel" is both a community in the here and now, embracing Jews everywhere, and a community in time, which reaches back to Abraham and forward to generations yet unborn.

As a siddur, the Babyn Yar shul refers to the sense of self-discipline and stubborn persistence generated by the lengthy set of prescribed prayers that religiously observant Jewish men conduct three times a day and women once a day. Unlike prayer in Christianity, which easily becomes a free-flowing conversation with God as a person of faith articulates sentences that express his or her feelings at that very moment, prayer in the Jewish tradition is a precisely defined recitation in which every word is prescribed. Because of the very immutability of the words spoken, the guidance of a text is essential, and this can be found in the siddur. It provides the firmness of thrice-daily custom, and the structure for all the other Jewish observances, including that on the Shabbat. "In the morning I arise and match again / my plans against my cash. / I wonder now if the long morning-prayers / were an utter waste of an hour / weighing, as they do, hopes and anguish, / and sending the believer out into the street / with the sweet taste of the prayers on his lips. / […] / How good to stop / and look out upon eternity a while; / and daily—at *Shahris*, *Minha*, *Maariv*, / in the morning, afternoon, and evening— / be at ease in Zion." Thus, American Jewish poet Charles Reznikoff summarized the solace provided by the thrice-daily prayer.

As a pop-up book, the Babyn Yar shul offers the experience of surprise and evokes a sense of wonder. The unexpected, often defined as a miracle, is, of course, a major theme in Jewish history. The most important miracle is the survival of the Jewish people and the impact of that very small nation on the history of the world. "If the statistics are right, the Jews constitute but one percent of the human race. It suggests a nebulous dim puff of stardust lost in the blaze of the Milky Way. Properly the Jew ought hardly to be heard of, but he is heard of, has always been heard of." Thus, American writer Samuel Langhorne Clemens, aka Mark Twain, reflected in 1899 on the surprising history of the Jews, noting their prominence in finance and commerce, in the sciences and in the arts. "He has made a marvellous fight in this world, in all the ages; and has done it with his hands tied behind him." All the great empires that once had ruled the world of the Jews—Egyptian, Babylonian, Persian, Greek, and Roman—had passed away.

> "The Jew saw them all, beat them all, and is now what he always was, exhibiting no decadence, no infirmities of age, no weakening of his parts, no slowing of his energies, no dulling of his alert and aggressive mind. All things are mortal but the Jew; all other forces pass, but he remains."

Twain did not reflect on the reason for the miraculous survival of the Jews, but in the wake of a history of catastrophes, which include massacres, expulsions, centuries of exile, and of course the Holocaust, the question must be raised: Why? Leaving aside faith-based arguments about a special protection God might have given to the People of the Covenant over the past 3,000 years, a more empirical approach to this question might begin with God's remark in a conversation with Moses after the latter, having descended from Mount Sinai, encounters the Hebrews worshipping the Golden Calf and angrily smashes the tablets on which he had inscribed the Ten Commandments. "'I have seen these people,' the Lord said to Moses, 'and they are a stiff-necked people.'" Certainly, in this context, "stiff-necked" was intended pejoratively, meaning both impudent and stubborn. And this is how Christians who seek to convert Jews see them when they face a 2,000-year-old refusal of the majority of the Jewish nation to accept the Gospel.

> However, as Jews, for most of the past 2,000 years a small, persecuted minority within Christendom, successfully resisted the demand of conversion imposed upon them by the Christian majority, they did not consider the designation "stiff-necked" to be a negative tag, and they learned to take pride in their obstinacy to remain who they are—a sentiment that certainly ought to earn some respect. The late rabbi Jonathan Sacks reflected on this in a sermon on the twenty-first *parashah* (weekly Torah portion in the annual cycle of Torah reading), which covers Exodus 30:11 to 34:35 and includes the episode of the Golden Calf. In the wake of this troubling episode, God ordered Moses to carve a pair of new tablets. "And Moses hurried and knelt to the ground and bowed," Sacks observed, "and he said, 'If I have found favour in your eyes, my Lord, may my Lord go among us, because it is a stiff-necked people, and forgive our wickedness and our sin, and take us as your inheritance.' The difficulty in the verse is self-evident. Moses cites as a reason for God remaining with the Israelites the very attribute that God had previously given for wishing to abandon them. [...] How can Moses invoke the people's obstinacy as a reason for God to maintain his presence among

them?" After a quick review of a few older explanations of this apparent contradiction, Sacks invoked a line of interpretation that, during the Holocaust, found a powerful expression in the words of Rabbi Yitzhak Nissenbaum, who died in the Warsaw ghetto. As the Jews faced the greatest crisis in their history, Nissenbaum argued that when Moses faced God after the debacle of the Golden Calf, he told God that the very obstinacy that was their greatest vice would turn out to be the core of a great loyalty. "Nations will call on them to assimilate, but they will refuse. Mightier religions will urge them to convert, but they will resist. They will suffer humiliation, persecution, even torture and death because of the name they bear and the faith they profess, but they will stay true to the covenant their ancestors made with You."

The annals of Jewish martyrdom show that this loyalty was put to the test again and again. The Kabbalist Abraham ben Eliezer Halevi, who experienced the expulsion from Spain and many difficult years thereafter, wrote a lengthy consideration on the way Jews might prepare themselves for both persecution and the temptation to escape such a fate through conversion—an option that, incidentally, the Nazis did not provide. And thus, if the inquisitioner were to interrupt the torture for a moment and offer the salvation of the Cross, there was only one way forward. "This shall be your answer: 'What do you want of me? Yes, I am a Jew. As a Jew will I live, and as a Jew will I die—as a Jew, a Jew, a Jew!' And then he shall resolve what his lips have shaped and his mouth has spoken, and he shall be steadfast and of firm purpose to sanctify his Creator, and not to desecrate the name of God."

The triple *parti pris* of Herz's Babyn Yar Synagogue merges into a single, unified organizing idea when it is seen against the background of 3,000 years of Hebrew-Israelite-Judahite-Jewish history, seemingly organized on a Möbius-strip-like continuum in which the miracle of persistence morphs into the persistence of miracle, which creates and sustains a community that, in turn, supports the miracle of persistence, and so on. It does not turn its back to the events that happened there in the first days of 5702, September 1941 of the common era. It rests on cursed ground and does so as gingerly as is possible, given the laws of nature. And when the siddur shul opens, and the bimah and the seats and the women's gallery unfold, also a canopy rises into place. Like the ceiling of the Wołpa, it suggests the heavens, but at Babyn Yar it shows the constellations as they appeared in the sky at Erev Yom Kippur 5702, set within a decorative scheme that recalls the painted interiors of the Mogilev, Gwoździec, and countless other wooden synagogues.

The Babyn Yar canopy is both terrifying in its specific reference to the massacre that ended at Erev Yom Kippur 5702 and also beautiful in both its execution and its reference to the universe of wooden synagogues that, like the universe of Jewish humanity, was destroyed in the Holocaust. In this unity, it refers, in general, to the paradox of the holy, which emerges from a merger of the *mysterium tremendum*, the mystery that makes one tremble, and the *mysterium fascinans*, the mystery that attracts—a unity of opposites that is not only the precondition of all thought, as Hegel observed, but also of all Creation, as suggested by Rabbi Isaac Luria's articulation of the Jewish esoteric discipline known as Kabbalah (tradition). Lurianic Kabbalah arose in the wake of the expulsion from Spain, which was experienced by its contemporaries as the single greatest catastrophe to befall the Jewish people since the destruction of the Temple. It shattered the belief that a peaceful existence in exile was possible and led to an overwhelming sense of the fragmentariness of Jewish life, one filled with contradiction and paradoxes. And this sense Luria and his disciples projected back into the universe and its creation, in a remarkable reversal of traditional Jewish esoteric thought, which had held that Creation resulted from God projecting his own self into space, that Creation was God's emanation, a one-way trajectory from center to periphery. Luria claimed the opposite: Creation was the result of God's retreat.

The late Gershom Scholem, without doubt the most important scholar of the history of Jewish mysticism to date, has provided the classic description of this process. "Luria begins by putting a question which gives the appearance of being naturalistic and, if you like, somewhat crude. How can there be a world if God is everywhere? If God is 'all in all,' how can there be things which are not God? How can God create the world out of nothing if there is no nothing?" The answer was straightforward: God had to make place for the world by abandoning a region within Himself. "Instead of emanation we have the opposite, contraction. The God who revealed himself in firm contours was superseded by one who descended deeper into the recess of His own Being, who concentrated Himself into Himself, and had done so from the very beginning of creation." The result was that Creation was God's retreat into exile, "of banishing Himself from His totality into profound seclusion." Only after God has contracted can he fill the space that he abandoned with light and thus begin the process of Creation. And this applies to every emanation and manifestation of God: it must be preceded by contraction and retraction. "The cosmic process becomes two-fold. Every stage involves a double strain, i.e., the light which streams back into God and that which flows out from Him, and but for this perpetual tension, this ever repeated effort with which God holds Himself back, nothing in the world would exist."

In his testimony about the murder of 5,000 Jews in Dubno, Hermann Friedrich Gräbe spoke with great empathy about the victims. One pair stands out: "The father was holding the hand of a boy about ten years old and speaking to him softly; the boy was fighting his tears. The father pointed to the sky, stroked his head and seemed to explain something to him." It is here, in the self-possession of the two whose lives are about to be extinguished, that Gräbe's account touches, if only for a moment, on the question of meaning, if not for the witness, then for two of the 5,000 Jewish victims that October day: a father and his son. Many of the Jews who were led to the edge of existing ravines or freshly dug mass graves must have looked at the sky and said the final sentences of the Viddui, the confessional prayer to be said at the moment of death: *Adonai melech; Adonai malach; Adonai yimloch l'olam va'ed* (God reigns; God has reigned; God will reign forever and ever). *Baruch shem k'vod malchuto l'olam va'ed* (Blessed be God's name whose glorious dominion is forever). *Shema Yisrael Adonai eloheinu Adonai echad* (Hear, O Israel: Adonai is our God, Adonai is One). But, undoubtedly, many will have also asked the question that provides another rhythm of Jewish history: "Where is God ..?" Perhaps a few of the victims might have been sufficiently initiated into the paradoxes of Lurianic Kabbalism and considered the unification of opposites that structures the Kabbalist understanding of the world. Yet, it would not have been of much solace at such a moment, and thus it is likely that even those who did have an explanation, like the father, would have simply swallowed it to tell himself and whomever was with him to just say the hallowed words: *Shema Yisrael Adonai eloheinu Adonai echad.*

Yet, eighty years later, the representation of that sky that stretched over Babyn Yar at Erev Yom Kippur 5702 in the beautiful ceiling of the Babyn Yar Synagogue might provide a trigger for us, the second, third, and even fourth generation to consider the answer to the problem of evil given by Isaac Luria in the wake of the catastrophe of 1492. It would be an exploration of the paradoxical relationship between negation and creation, between the shattering of the nine vessels, that is the destruction of nine worlds, and the making of the tenth world, our world—one that is a finite universe of plenitude and variety, filled with beauty and ugliness, with fragments of the divine light and the shards of the destroyed worlds. And it would be a meditation on the concept of *Tikkun* (restitution), the universal task of all human beings in restoring the original unity, and the particular role of the Jews, the only people who in the view of Lurianic Kabbalists, share an essential condition with God: that of *Galuth* (exile). In defining God's exile as the beginning of everything, the exile of the Jews was the end of everything—an end, in the sense of a turning point, that allows the world to be reunited with God. As Scholem observed, this was a concept that spoke to the Jewish imagination, at the depth of catastrophe. "For *Galuth* acquires here a new meaning. Formerly it had been regarded either as a punishment for Israel's sins or as a test of Israel's faith. Now it is still this, but intrinsically it is a mission: its purpose is to uplift the fallen sparks from all their various locations." As I consider the ceiling of the Babyn Yar Synagogue, I not only see a universe represented by a beautiful but indifferent sky, a world of exile, but I also perceive in the constellations the flowers of the fields—or are they the fragments of the painted decoration of the wooden synagogues that were destroyed?—the ascent of fallen sparks, the so-much-anticipated conversion toward the point of origin, that first step to the redemption of the world, and God.

The Babyn Yar Synagogue is an ingenious, witty, profound, and profoundly moving reinterpretation of Jewish tradition, and it comes at a crucial moment in Jewish history. It is designed, constructed, and dedicated at a time marked by the passing of the last Holocaust survivors, of those who belonged to the crucial generation that, in the wake of the Holocaust, had to salvage Judaism. "We are either the last, the dying, Jews, or else we are those who will give new life to our tradition," Abraham Joshua Heschel noted with a measure of anxiety one decade after the liberation of Auschwitz. "Rarely in our history has so much depended upon one generation. We will either forfeit or enrich the legacy of the ages.

[…] Our existence is either superfluous or indispensable to the world; it is either tragic or holy to be a Jew. It is a matter of immense responsibility that we are here and Jewish teachers everywhere have undertaken to instil in our youth the will to be Jews today, tomorrow and for ever and ever. Unless being a Jew is of absolute significance how can we justify the ultimate price which our people was often forced to pay throughout history?"

> Sixty-five years after Heschel raised the question of the future of the Jewish people in the wake of the Holocaust, it has become clear that the generation of Holocaust survivors was destined not to be the last, and everywhere in the world are markers created by them and their children, and now also grandchildren, that new life is being given to old traditions.
> The synagogue at Babyn Yar is just the latest one in that chain that almost snapped, eighty years ago, but nevertheless held and continues to hold, from generation to generation:
>
> *Mir zaynen do!*

Bibliography & References

BIBLIOGRAPHY

I conceived and wrote this book during a lockdown, on the basis of an understanding of the issues at stake formed over a forty-year period. In my apartment, I had only a small collection of books at hand, as the bulk of my scholarly library was out of reach in my university office, and both academic and public libraries were closed. The list below provides the most important sources either directly available to me during the lockdown or accessed by means of notes taken many years ago. In addition, I had the backup provided by the JSTOR digital library of academic journals and the very important collection of Jewish writings, including the Babylonian Talmud, made available by means of the online Sefaria Library, conceived a decade ago by Joshua Foer and Brett Lockspeiser and accessible at Sefaria.org. But, writing in a very short time, I did not conduct significant research to expand on what I thought I knew about the matters at hand, and this might be both the strength and weakness of the current book. Any reader who wishes to follow up on issues will be able to navigate his, her, or their way through the internet to articles that provide in-depth information on stories told and issues raised in the narrative of this book.

The English translation of the Bible used in this book is the New International Version (NIV). This edition of the Bible has earned a stellar reputation for its precision, clarity, and elegance of language. In an early draft I used for quotations from the Tanakh text published by the Jewish Publication Society (JPS). At certain points the JPS translation of key passages appears to reflect a Jewish understanding of the original more precisely. Most importantly, this occurs in the translation of Deuteronomy 6:4, which the JPS translates as, "Hear, O Israel! The Lord is our God, the Lord alone," and NIV as "Hear, O Israel: the Lord our God, the Lord is one." But in general, the English in the NIV translation is superior to that in the JPS version, and this proved decisive.

Abraham ben Elezier ha-Levi. "The Death of the Martyrs." In *In Time and Eternity: A Jewish Reader*, ed. Nahum N. Glatzer, 201–4. New York: Schocken Books, 1946.

Aleichem, Sholem. "The Town of the Little People." In *The Old Country*, trans. Julius and Frances Butwin, 15–20. London: Andre Deutsch, 1918.

Améry, Jean. *At the Mind's Limits: Contemplations by a Survivor on Auschwitz and Its Realities*. Trans. Sidney and Stella P. Rosenfeld. Bloomington: Indiana University Press, 1980.

Arendt, Hannah. "The Concentration Camps." *Partisan Review* 15, no. 7 (July 1948): 743–63.

—. *Eichmann in Jerusalem: A Report on the Banality of Evil*. New York: Viking, 1963.

Auerbach, Ephraim. "The Song of Sabbath." In *The Way We Think: A Collection of Essays from the Yiddish*, 2 vols., ed. Joseph Leftwich, 1:210–17. South Brunswick, NJ: Thomas Yoseloff, 1969.

Avodah Zarah. *The William Davidson Talmud*. Sefaria edition. https://www.sefaria.org/Avodah_Zarah?lang=bi.

Babel, Isaac. "Murderers Who Have Yet to Be Clubbed to Death." In *Complete Works of Isaac Babel*, ed. Nathalie Babel, trans. Peter Constantine, 371–73. New York and London: Norton, 2002.

Bartov, Omer. *Hitler's Army: Soldiers, Nazis and War in the Third Reich*. New York and Oxford: Oxford University Press, 1991.

"The Book of Enoch." In *The Apocrypha and Pseudepigrapha of the Old Testament*, 2 vols., ed. Robert H. Charles, 2:163–281. Oxford, UK: The Clarendon Press, 1913.

Brecht, Bertolt. *Life of Galileo*. Trans. John Willet. London: Methuen Drama, 1980.

Busink, Theodor A. *Der Tempel von Jerusalem*. 2 vols. Leiden, 1970–80.

Chagall, Bella. *Burning Lights*. Trans. Norbert Guterman. New York: Schocken, 1946.

Clifford, Richard J. *The Cosmic Mountain in Canaan and the Old Testament*. Cambridge, MA: Harvard University Press, 1972.

Cody, Aelred. *A History of Old Testament Priesthood*. Rome: Pontifical Biblical Institute, 1969.

Cross, Frank Moore. *Canaanite Myth and Hebrew Epic: Essays in the History of the Religion of Israel*. Cambridge, MA: Harvard University Press, 1973.

Dawidowicz, Lucy S., ed. *A Holocaust Reader*. New York: Behrman House, 1976.

Ehrenburg, Ilya, and Vasily Grossman, eds. *The Complete Black Book of Russian Jewry*. Trans. David Patterson. New Brunswick and London: Transaction, 2002.

Einstein, Albert. *Einstein on Politics*. Eds. David E. Rowe and Robert Schulman. Princeton: Princeton University Press, 2007.

"Enlil in the E-Kur (Enlil A)." The Electronic Text Corpus of Sumerian Literature. Faculty of Oriental Studies, University of Oxford. https://etcsl.orinst.ox.ac.uk/cgi-bin/etcsl.cgi?text=t.4.05.1#.

Eusebius of Caesarea. "Life of Constantine." In *A Select Library of Nicene and Post-Nicene Fathers of the Christian Church: Second Series*, 14 vols., eds. Philip Schaff and Henry Wallace, 1:481–560. New York: The Christian Literature Company, 1890–1895.

Feuchtwanger, Lion. *Power*. Trans. Willa and Edwin Muir. New York: Viking, 1926.

Fichte, Johann Gottlieb. "A State Within a State (1793)." In *The Jew in the Modern World: A Documentary History*, eds. Paul Mendes-Flohr and Jehuda Reinharz, 283–84. Oxford: Oxford University Press, 2011.

Fink, Ida. "Shelter." In *A Scrap of Time and Other Stories*, trans. Madeline Levine and Francine Prose, 127–34. Evanston, IL: Northwestern University Press, 1994.

Flavius Josephus. *Josephus*. 9 vols. Trans. Henry St. John Thackeray. Cambridge, MA: Harvard University Press, 1950–67.

Fournet, Caroline. *The Crime of Destruction and the Law of Genocide: Their Impact on Collective Memory*. Aldershot, UK: Ashgate, 2007.

Friedman, Richard Elliott. *Who Wrote the Bible?* New York: Summit, 1987.

Fussenegger, Gertrud. "Aus Reiseaufzeichnungen." *Das innere Reich* 10 (1943–44): 65–73.

Goedsche, Hermann (aka Sir John Retcliffe). *Biarritz*. Berlin: Carl Sigismund Liebrecht, 1868.

—. "The Rabbi's Speech." In *The Jew in the Modern World: A Documentary History*, eds. Paul Mendes-Flohr and Jehuda Reinharz, 336–39. Oxford: Oxford University Press, 2011.

Golomb, Abraham. "What Is Jewish Tradition?" In *The Way We Think: A Collection of Essays from the Yiddish*, 2 vols., ed. Joseph Leftwich, 1:172–81. South Brunswick, NJ: Thomas Yoseloff, 1969.

Grossman, Vassily. "Ukraine Without Jews." Trans. Polly Zavadivker. *Jewish Quarterly* 58, no. 1 (2011): 12–18.

Gumpert, Martin. *First Papers*. Trans. Heinz and Ruth Norden. New York: Duell, Sloan and Pearce, 1941.

Haffner, Sebastian. *Defying Hitler: A Memoir*. Trans. Oliver Pretzel. New York: Farrar, Straus and Giroux, 2002.

The Haggadah of Passover for Members of the Armed Forces. Eds. David and Tamar de Sola Pool. New York: Jewish Welfare Board, 5703/1943.

Halpern, Baruch. *The Constitution of the Monarchy in Israel*. Leiden: Brill, 1981.

—. "The Uneasy Compromise: Israel Between League and Monarchy." In *Traditions in Transformation: Turning Points in Biblical Faith*, eds. Baruch Halpern and Jon D. Levenson, 59–96. Winona Lake, IN: Eisenbrauns, 1981.

—. *The First Historians: The Hebrew Bible and History*. San Francisco: Harper & Row, 1988.

Heine, Heinrich. "Princess Sabbath." In *The Works of Heinrich Heine*, 12 vols., trans. Charles Godfrey Leland, 12:3–9. London: Heinemann, 1905.

Hermann, Georg. *Unvorhanden und Stumm, doch zu Menschen noch redden*. Ed. Laureen Nussbaum. Mannheim: Persona Verlag, 1991.

Herzl, Theodor. *The Complete Diaries of Theodor Herzl*. 3 vols. Ed. Raphael Patai, trans. Harry Zohn. New York and London: Herzl Press and Thomas Yoseloff, 1960.

Heschel, Abraham Joshua. *The Sabbath: Its Meaning for Modern Man*. New York: Farrar, Straus and Giroux, 1951.

—. *God in Search of Man: A Philosophy of Judaism*. London: John Calder, 1956.

—. *The Earth Is the Lord's: The Inner World of the Jew in Eastern Europe*. Woodstock, NY: Jewish Lights Publishing, 1995.

—. *In This Hour: Heschel's Writings in Nazi Germany and London Exile*. Ed. Helen Plotkin. Philadelphia: Jewish Publication Society, 2019.

Howe, Irving. *World of Our Fathers*. New York: Harcourt Brace Jovanovich, 1976.

Hubka, Thomas C. *Resplendent Synagogue: Architecture and Worship in an Eighteenth-Century Polish Community*. Hanover, NH: Brandeis University Press, 2003.

Kayser, Stephen S. Introduction. *Wooden Synagogues*, by Maria and Kazimierz Piechotka, 5–6. Trans. Rulka Langer. Warsaw: Arkady, 1959.

Kirshenblatt-Gimblett, Barbara, and Antony Polonsky, ed. *POLIN: 1000 Year History of Polish Jews*. Warsaw: Museum of the History of Polish Jews, 2014.

Koestler, Arthur. *Promise and Fulfilment: Palestine, 1917–1949*. New York: Macmillan, 1949.

Koker, David. *At the Edge of the Abyss: A Concentration Camp Diary, 1943–1944*. Ed. Robert Jan van Pelt, trans. Michiel Horn and John Irons. Evanston, IL: Northwestern University Press, 2012.

Kraus, Hans-Joachim. *Worship in Israel: A Cultic History of the Old Testament*. Trans. Geoffrey Buswell. Oxford, UK: Blackwell, 1966.

Krinsky, Carol Herselle. *Synagogues of Europe: Architecture, History, Meaning*. New York: Architectural History Foundation, 1985.

Lenin, Vladimir Ilyich. "The Attitude of the Workers' Party to Religion." In *Collected Works*, vol. 15, 402–13. Moscow: Progress Publishers, 1960–70.

Levi, Primo. *The Periodic Table*. Trans. Raymond Rosenthal. New York: Schocken, 1984.

Levinas, Emmanuel. *Totality and Infinity*. Trans. Alphonso Lingis. Pittsburgh: Duquesne University Press, 1969.

—. "The Name of a Dog, or Natural Rights." In *Difficult Freedom: Essays on Judaism*, trans. Seán Hand, 151–53. Baltimore: Johns Hopkins University Press, 1990.

—. "Place and Utopia." In *Difficult Freedom: Essays on Judaism*, trans. Seán Hand, 99–102. Baltimore: Johns Hopkins University Press, 1990.

Lissitzky, El. "On the Mogilev Shul: Recollections." Trans. Madeleine Cohen. *In Geveb: A Journal of Yiddish Studies*, July 2019.

Lukomski, George K. "The Wooden Synagogues of Eastern Europe." *Burlington Magazine for Connoisseurs* 66, no. 382 (January 1935), 14–21.

Mann, Thomas. *The Tables of the Law*. Trans. Marion Faber and Stephen Lehmann. Philadelphia: Paul Dry Books, 2010.

Marx, Karl, and Friedrich Engels. *The Communist Manifesto*. Ed. Gareth Stedman Jones. London: Penguin, 2002.

Mendenhall, George. *The Tenth Generation: The Origins of the Biblical Tradition*. Baltimore and London: Johns Hopkins University Press, 1979.

Mendes-Flohr, Paul, and Jehuda Reinharz, eds. *The Jew in the Modern World: A Documentary History*. Oxford: Oxford University Press, 2011.

Michman, Dan. *The Emergence of Jewish Ghettos During the Holocaust*. Trans. Lenn J. Schramm. Cambridge: Cambridge University Press, 2011.

Mishneh Torah, Eruvim. Trans. Francis Nataf. Sefaria edition. https://www.sefaria.org/Mishneh_Torah,_Eruvin?lang=bi.

Nietzsche, Friedrich. "Of the People of Israel." In *The Jew in the Modern World: A Documentary History*, eds. Paul Mendes-Flohr and Jehuda Reinharz, 325–26. Oxford: Oxford University Press, 2011.

Orwell, George. "In Front of Your Nose." In *The Collected Essays, Journalism, and Letters of George Orwell*, 4 vols., eds. Sonia Orwell and Ian Angus, 4:122–25. London: Secker & Warburg, 1968.

Oz, Amos. *In the Land of Israel*. Trans. Maurie Goldberg-Bartura. London: Chatto & Windus, 1983.

—. *How to Cure a Fanatic*. London: Vintage, 2012.

Parkinson, Richard Bruce, ed. *The Tale of Sinuhe and Other Ancient Egyptian Poems 1940–1640 BC*. Oxford: Oxford University Press, 1997.

Patai, Raphael. *Man and Temple in Ancient Jewish Myth and Ritual*. 2nd ed. New York: Ktav, 1967.

—. *The Jewish Mind*. New York: Charles Scribner's Sons, 1977.

Pepys, Samuel. *The Diary of Samuel Pepys*. Ed. Kate Loveman. New York: Knopf, 2018.

Piechotka, Maria, and Kazimierz Piechotka. *Wooden Synagogues*. Trans. Rulka Langer. Warsaw: Arkady, 1959.

—. *Heaven's Gates: Wooden Synagogues in the Territories of the Former Polish-Lithuanian Commonwealth*. Trans. Krzysztof Z. Cieszkowski. Warsaw: Polish Institute of World Art Series / POLIN Museum of the History of Polish Jews, 2015.

Philo of Alexandria. *Philo*. 10 vols. Trans. Francis Henry Colson. Cambridge, MA: Harvard University Press, 1929–62.

Pirkei Avot. Sefaria edition. https://www.sefaria.org/Pirkei_Avot?lang=bi.

Rauschning, Hermann. "Preface: A Conversation with Hitler." In *The Ten Commandments: Ten Short Novels of Hitler's War Against the Moral Code*, ed. Armin L. Robinson, ix–xiii. New York: Simon and Schuster, 1943.

Reeves, John C. "Sefer Zerubbabel: The Prophetic Vision of Zerubbabel ben Shealtiel." In *Old Testament Pseudoepigrapha: More Noncanonical Scriptures*, 2 vols., 1:448–66. Grand Rapids, MI: Eerdmans, 2013.

Reznikoff, Charles. "New York: 1951—Seven Poems," *Commentary* 12 (1951), 573–75.

Romik, Natalia, "Post-Shtetl: Spectral Transformations and Architectural Challenges in the Periphery's Bloodstream." In *Re-Centring the City: Global Mutations of Socialist Modernity*, ed. Jonathan Bach and Michał Murawski, 129–48. London: UCL Press, 2020.

Rosenberg, Alfred. "Die Protokolle der Weisen von Zion und die jüdische Weltpolitik." In *Schriften und Reden*, 2 vols., 2: 249–428. Munich: Hoheneichen-Verlag, 1943.

Rosenfeld, Oskar. *In the Beginning Was the Ghetto: Notebooks from Łódź*. Trans. Brigitte M. Goldstein. Evanston, IL: Northwestern University Press, 2002.

Rosenzweig, Franz, *The Star of Redemption*. Trans. William W. Hallo. New York: Holt, Rinehart and Winston, 1971.

Rothbart, Zack. "The Ghost Shtetl of Isaac Bashevis Singer's Youth," *The Librarians* (blog), National Library of Israel, January 1, 2021, https://blog.nli.org.il/en/lbh-bilgoraj-isaac-bashevis-singers/.

Sacks, Jonathan. "A Stiff-Necked People," February 18, 2019, Office of Rabbi Sacks, https://rabbisacks.org/a-stiff-necked-people-ki-tissa-5779/.

Schedel, Hartmann. *Nuremberg Chronicle*. Trans. Walter Schmauch. Madison: University of Wisconsin Digital Collections Center, 2010. https://search.library.wisc.edu/search/digital.

Schiffman, Lawrence H., ed. *Texts and Traditions: A Source Reader for the Study of Second Temple and Rabbinic Judaism*. Hoboken, NJ: Ktav, 1998.

Scholem, Gershom. *Major Trends in Jewish Mysticism*. London: Thames and Hudson, 1955.

Schulz, Bruno. "The Mythologizing of Reality." In *The Collected Works of Bruno Schulz*, ed. Jerzy Ficowski, 371–73. London: Picador, 1998.

Schwarz-Bart, André. *The Last of the Just*. Trans. Stephen Becker. London: Secker & Warburg, 1961.

Sextus Propertius. *The Love Elegies*. Trans. Anthony S. Kline. https://www.poetryintranslation.com/klineaspropertius.php.

Shakespeare, William. *The Complete Sonnets and Poems*. Ed. Colin Burrow. Oxford: Oxford University Press, 2002.

Shapira, Kalonymus Kalmish. "'Love God with all your heart': The Lesson of Rabbi Akiva." In *Writing in Witness: A Holocaust Reader*, ed. Eric J. Sundquist, 323–28. Albany: State University of New York Press, 2018.

Singer, Isaac Bashevis, "Banquet Speech." December 10, 1978. https://www.nobelprize.org/prizes/literature/1978/singer/speech/.

Smith, Jonathan Z. *To Take Place: Toward Theory in Ritual*. Chicago and London: University of Chicago Press, 1987.

Stein, Joseph. *Fiddler on the Roof*. Film script, dialogue transcription. http://www.script-o-rama.com/movie_scripts/f/fiddler-on-the-roof-script.html.

Sundquist, Eric J., ed. *Writing in Witness: A Holocaust Reader*. Albany: State University of New York Press, 2018.

Toman, Jindrich. "Making Sense of a Ruin." *Bohemia* 52, no. 1 (2012), 108–22.

Twain, Mark. "Concerning the Jews." *Harper's New Monthly Magazine* 99 (June–November 1899), 527–35.

United Hebrew Congregations of the British Commonwealth of Nations. *The Authorized Daily Prayer Book*. London: Eyre and Spottiswoode, 5722/1962.

United States, Office of the United States Chief of Counsel for Prosecution of Axis Criminality, *Nazi Conspiracy and Aggression*, 12 vols. Washington, DC: United States Government Printing Office, 1946.

Vilnay, Zev. *Legends of Jerusalem*. Philadelphia: The Jewish Publication Society of America, 1973.

Voegelin, Eric. *Order and History: Israel and Revelation*. Baton Rouge and London: Louisiana State University Press, 1956.

Weiss, Peter. *Exile*. Trans. E. B. Garside, Alastair Hamilton, and Christopher Levenson. New York: Delacorte Press, 1968.

—. "My Place." Trans. Roger Hillman. *Transit* 4, no. 1 (2008). https://transit.berkeley.edu/2008/hillman/.

Wensinck, Arent Jan. *The Ideas of the Western Semites Concerning the Navel of the Earth*. Amsterdam: Johannes Müller, 1916.

Wilken, Robert Louis. *The Land Called Holy: Palestine in Christian History and Thought*. New Haven and London: Yale University Press, 1992.

Zangwill, Israel. *The Voice of Jerusalem*. New York: Macmillan, 1921.

Zweig, Stefan. *The World of Yesterday*. London: Cassell, 1943.

REFERENCES

17
"How beautiful are your tents, Jacob" Numbers 24:5.
"But, Lord! to see the disorder" Pepys, *The Diary of Samuel Pepys*, 222–23.

18
"We are building our houses" Schulz, "The Mythologizing of Reality," 372.

19
"To say that Israel's was an historical religion" Halpern, "The Uneasy Compromise," 60.

20
"The cities I lived in" Weiss, "My Place."

21
"In this period our people attained" Heschel, *The Earth Is the Lord's*, 10.

27
"A fiddler on the roof. Sounds crazy, no?" Stein, Fiddler on the Roof.

31
"… orphaned, dreaming, bewitched" Aleichem, "The Town of the Little People," 15.
"… like loaf of bread" Ibid., 18.
"… the synagogues, the meeting houses" Ibid., 19.

34
"… and the poorhouse where the old men die" Ibid.

35
"I have no religion—after all, I am a Jew" Zangwill, *The Voice of Jerusalem*, 30.
"to see what is in front of one's nose" Orwell, "In Front of Your Nose," 125.

38
"Everywhere people die the same death" Aleichem, "The Town of the Little People," 19.

39
"I will establish my covenant" Genesis 17:7.

"Blessed art thou, O Lord our God" United Hebrew Congregations, *The Authorized Daily Prayer Book*, 71.
"… each producing the generation to come" Rosenzweig, *The Star of Redemption*, 298.

42
"We are fighting against the perversion" Rauschning, "Preface: A Conversation with Hitler," xii–xiii.

43
"I found myself displaced" Fussenegger, "Aus Reiseaufzeichnungen," 65–68.

46
"There's trouble in the world" Stein, *Fiddler on the Roof*.

47
"Adam made love to his wife again" Genesis 4:25.

51
"… the lofty bond between heaven and earth" "Enlil in the E-Kur (Enlil A)."
"Now the whole world had one language" Genesis 11:1–7.

54
"Go from your country" Genesis 12:1.
"Whatever God fated this flight" Parkinson, *The Tale of Sinuhe*, 34.

55
"Villagers in Israel would not fight" Judges 5:7.

58
"The Lord said to Moses" Numbers 11:16–17.

59
"Whenever the spirit from God came on Saul" 1 Samuel 16:23.
"Then the men of Judah came to Hebron" 2 Samuel 2:4.
"When all the elders of Israel" 2 Samuel 5:3.

62
"The king and his men marched to Jerusalem" 2 Samuel 5:6–11.

67
"Each of you will eat fruit from your own vine" Isaiah 36:16.
"… brief breathing-space in scenes of genial cheerfulness" Philo of Alexandria, "The Special Laws I," *Philo*, 7:139.

70
"In the beginning God" Genesis 1:1.

71
"In the desert the whole community grumbled" Exodus 16:2–5.

75
"… all the men in Israel" Numbers 1:45.
"The Lord had said to Moses" Numbers 1:48–50.
"… each of them under their standard" Numbers 2:2.
"How beautiful are your tents" Numbers 23:24.

78
"Put limits for the people around the mountain" Exodus 19:12–13.

79
"I am the Lord your God" Exodus 20:2–5.
"Everything in Judaism must remain fluid" Golomb, "What Is Jewish Tradition?" 174.
"Remember the Sabbath day" Exodus 20:8–11.

82
"In the beginning God created the heavens and the earth" Genesis 1:1.
"By the seventh day God had finished the work" Genesis 2:2–3.
"This is a radical departure" Heschel, *The Sabbath*, 8–9, 15.

83
"The king stood by the pillar" 2 Kings 23:3.

86
"If you fully obey the Lord your God" Deuteronomy 28:1.
"However, if you do not obey the Lord your God" Deuteronomy 28:15.
"Then the Lord will scatter you among all nations" Deuteronomy 28:64–67.

87

"He took the Asherah pole from the temple of the Lord" 2 Kings 23:6–7.

"Just as he had done at Beth-El" 2 Kings 23:19–20.

"The king gave this order to all the people" 2 Kings 23:21–23.

"… the mediums and spiritists, the household gods" 2 Kings 23:24.

"I will remove Judah also from my presence" 2 Kings 23:27.

90

"Go to the ant, you sluggard" Proverbs 6:6–11.

"When pride comes, then comes disgrace" Proverbs 11:2.

"Better to be a nobody and yet have a servant" Proverbs 12:9.

"The Lord tears down the house of the proud" Proverbs 15:25.

91

"He: 'I have come into my garden'" Song of Songs 5:1–8.

"For all of eternity in its entirety is not as worthy" Rabbi Akiva ben Yosef, as quoted in Schiffman, *Texts and Traditions*, 120.

94

"In the ninth year of Zedekiah's reign" 2 Kings 25:1.

"Nebuzaradan the commander of the guard" 2 Kings 25:11.

"By the rivers of Babylon we sat and wept" Psalm 137:1.

"If I forget you, Jerusalem" Psalm 137:5–6.

"This is what the Lord says" Jeremiah 30:18–22.

95

"It was during the troubled interval" Zangwill, *The Voice of Jerusalem*, 70.

98

"I saw a man whose appearance was like bronze" Ezekiel 40:3–4.

"He measured the east side with the measuring rod" Ezekiel 42:16–20.

99

"Passion is often greater in absent lovers" Sextus Propertius, *The Love Elegies*, book 2, chap. 33.

"Listen to me, you who pursue righteousness" Isaiah 51:1–3.

"The children of your oppressors will come" Isaiah 60:14–18.

102

"Is it a time for you yourselves to be living in your paneled houses" Haggai 1:4–9.

103

"All the people came together as one" Nehemiah 8:1–3.

"Then all the people went away to eat and drink" Nehemiah 8:12.

106

"But will God really dwell on earth?" 1 Kings 8:27.

114

"Among the other nations" Philo of Alexandria, "The Special Laws I," *Philo*, 7:155.

"But one may well be astonished at the hatred" Flavius Josephus, "Jewish Antiquities," *Josephus*, 4:403.

115

"Some hold that" Philo of Alexandria, "Moses II," *Philo*, 6:497–99.

118

"Moses saw that though the bush was on fire" Exodus 3:3–4.

"All this is a description" Philo of Alexandria, "Moses II," *Philo*, 6:313.

"Again fire, the element which works destruction" Ibid.

119

"While Jesus was having dinner at Matthew's house" Matthew 9:10–12.

"You have heard that it was said" Matthew 5:38–39.

122

"My own childhood in Jerusalem" Oz, *How to Cure a Fanatic*, 42.

123

"At that time Michael, the great prince" Daniel 12:1–3.

"This is the son of man who has righteousness" "The Book of Enoch," 214–15.

126

"In Yavne the foundation was laid for a pyramid" Heschel, *In This Hour*, 39–40.

127

"The Romans brought Rabbi Hanina ben Teradyon for judgment" Avodah Zarah, 1:17b, 18a.

"Unhappy the land that has no heroes" Brecht, *Life of Galileo*, 98.

130

"And by the merits of our ancestors" Vilnay, *Legends of Jerusalem*, 185.

"Before the Temple was built" As quoted in Patai, *Man and Temple in Ancient Jewish Myth and Ritual*, 121.

131

"The navel is the seat of natural and civil order" Wensinck, *The Ideas of the Western Semites*, 65.

134

"By the rivers of Babylon we sat and wept" Psalm 137:1–4.

135

"I will destroy this temple made with human hands" Mark 14:58.

138

"When everything had been arranged like this" Epistle to the Hebrews 9:6–8, 11–12, 24.

139

"Then I saw 'a new heaven and a new earth'" Revelation 21:1–3.

"I did not see a temple in the city" Revelation 21:22–23.

"Nothing impure will ever enter it" Revelation 21:27.

142

"Moses was faithful as a servant in all God's house" Epistle to the Hebrews 3:5–6.

"Behold, the days are coming, says the Lord" Jeremiah 31:31.

143

"On the very spot which witnessed the Saviour's sufferings" Eusebius of Caesarea, "Life of Constantine," 529.

"His blood is on us and on our children!" Matthew 27:25.

146
"Then the Lord will lower the celestial Temple" Reeves, "Sefer Zerubbabel," 464.

147
"Then Umar said to him" Quoted in Wilken, *The Land Called Holy*, 236–37.

155
"Hear, O Israel: the Lord our God, the Lord is one" Deuteronomy 6:4.
"You must act according to the decisions they give you" Deuteronomy 17:10.

162
"When the Jews residing in this city" Schedel, *Nuremberg Chronicle*, fol. 254.

163
"To every six hundred Germans there was one Jew" Feuchtwanger, *Power*, 163–64.
"In Europe […] they have gone through an eighteen-century schooling" Nietzsche, *Daybreak*, 325.

166
"What shall I do, then, with Jesus who is called the Messiah?" Matthew 27:22–25.
"Being a Jew was thus a dangerous occupation" Zangwill, *The Voice of Jerusalem*, 211–12.

167
"They had no state, holding them together" Feuchtwanger, *Power*, 165–66.

171
"Descendant and ancestor" Rosenzweig, *The Star of Redemption*, 346–47.

174
"One of the most striking features" Golomb, "What Is Jewish Tradition?" 179–80.

178
"Then God said" Genesis 1:26.
"… a plebian God, perhaps immanent but hardly transcendent" Howe, *World of Our Fathers*, 11.

179
"The Day of Atonement, which climaxes the ten-day period of redemption" Rosenzweig, *The Star of Redemption*, 323–24.

182
"The land must not be sold permanently" Leviticus 25:23–24.
"In a most profound sense possible" Rosenzweig, *The Star of Redemption*, 300.

186
"Hear, O Israel: the Lord our God, the Lord is one" Deuteronomy 6:4–9.

187
"So beginning with the fifteenth day of the seventh month" Leviticus 23:34–35.
"Live in temporary shelters for seven days" Leviticus 23:42–43.
"On that day there will be neither sunlight nor cold" Zechariah 14:6–9.
"Jerusalem will be raised up high" Zechariah 14:10–11.

190
"Behold the bread of affliction" *The Haggadah of Passover*, 21.
"How different is this night from all other nights?" Ibid. 23–25.

191
"In the beginning our ancestors were idolaters" Ibid., 31.
"This promise made to our fathers" Ibid., 35.
"May it bring to them together with sweet associations" Ibid., i.

195
"In every generation one must look upon oneself" Ibid., 61.
"Next year in Jerusalem" Ibid., 113.

195
"I stumble into the black chamber" Chagall, *Burning Lights*, 36–37.

"So God created mankind in his own image" Genesis 1:27–28.

198
"In Arabia's book of fable" Heine, "Princess Sabbath," 3–4.

199
"She quickly washes her face and hands" Chagall, *Burning Lights*, 48–49.
"The white table with the candles" Ibid., 51.

202
"We looked up at each other" Koker, *At the Edge of the Abyss*, 24–25.
"Things do not change that day" Heschel, *The Sabbath*, 21.

203
"Rabbi Shimon ben Elazar said" Pirkei Avot, 4:18.
"Rabbi Elazar ben Shammua said" Pirkei Avot, 4:12.
"If I am not for myself, who will be for me?" Pirkei Avot, 1:13.
"[Shimon Ben Azzai] used to say: do not despise any man" Pirkei Avot, 4:3.
"The day is short" Pirkei Avot, 2:15.
"It is not your duty to finish the work" Pirkei Avot, 2:16.

206
"This is what the Lord says" Jeremiah 17:21–22.
"For an eruv is not effective with the presence of an idolater" Mishneh Torah, Eruvim, 2:10.

207
"The Third Sabbath Meal" Auerbach, "The Song of Sabbath," 214.
"… shudders, fearful of the canine" Heine, "Princess Sabbath," 9.

210
"Distilling is beautiful" Levi, *The Periodic Table*, 57–58.
"… where generations of Jews" Koestler, *Promise and Fulfilment*, 315.

214
"Emigration represents a break" Gumpert, *First Papers*, 30–31.

215
"All fixed, fast-frozen relations" Marx and Engels, *The Communist Manifesto*, 223.
"The proletarians have nothing to lose" Ibid., 258.

218
"… praise of purity, which protects from evil" Levi, *The Periodic Table*, 34.

219
"Jews are like everyone else" This pithy statement cannot be found in Heine's published works.
"And if the Jew, by not living the life of the nations" Zangwill, *The Voice of Jerusalem*, 210.
"Dissension, diversity, the grain of salt" Levi, *The Periodic Table*, 34.

222
"A powerful, hostilely disposed nation" Fichte, "A State Within a State (1793)," 283.
"Does this not recall to you the notion of a state within a state?" Ibid., 284.

223
"Beth-Chajim—the House of Life!" Goedsche, *Biarritz*, 141, as quoted in Toman, "Making Sense of a Ruin," 115.
"Gradually our people is rising up" Goedsche, *Biarritz*, 166, as quoted in Goedsche, "The Rabbi's Speech," 336.

227
"Our comings and goings" Levinas, "The Name of a Dog, or Natural Rights," 153.

231
"For eighteen centuries" Zangwill, *The Voice of Jerusalem*, 221.

234
"The musty deposits of two thousand years of inhumanity" Herzl, *The Complete Diaries*, 2:745–46.

235
"If you became an officer" Hermann, *Unvorhanden und Stumm*, 233–34.

238
"The Jewish population was generally left stark naked" As quoted in Zangwill, *The Voice of Jerusalem*, 21.
"Our soldiers, who have seen a thing or two in their time" Babel, "Murderers Who Have Yet to Be Clubbed to Death," 372.

239
"Though rationalized by arguments" Koestler, *Promise and Fulfilment*, 315.

243
"I cannot suppress a pained smile" Einstein, "A Letter of Confession, 3 April 1920," in *Einstein on Politics*, 146–47.

246
"It must keep a sharp-look-out" Feuchtwanger, *Power*, 350.

247
"When a nation or a group of nations" Rosenberg, "Die Protokolle der Weisen von Zion," 428.

250
"Apart from the terror" Haffner, *Defying Hitler: A Memoir*, 142.

251
"The flames are still crackling" "Undeutsches Schrifttum auf dem Scheiterhaufen," *Völkischer Beobachter*, 12 May 1933.
"Where one burns books, one soon will burn people" The quote is from Heinrich Heine, Almansor. http://www.gutenberg.org/files/45600/45600-h/45600-h.htm.

154
"The fact that we are living in a ghetto" Joachim Prinz, as quoted in Michman, *The Emergence of Jewish Ghettos*, 39.
"The medieval ghetto was sealed at night" Ibid.

258
"They pleaded at the consulates" Zweig, *The World of Yesterday*, 319–20.

259
"People from all categories slept" Rosenfeld, *In the Beginning Was the Ghetto*, 37–38.
"In every generation there are those who rise against us" *The Haggadah of Passover*, 35.

262
"We clearly recognize our mission" As quoted in Bartov, *Hitler's Army*, 130.
"The Germans ordered everyone" Ehrenburg and Grossman, *The Complete Black Book of Russian Jewry*, 8.

263
"… the final destruction of the Nazi tyranny" Atlantic Charter, August 14, 1941. https://avalon.law.yale.edu/wwii/atlantic.asp.

266
"Only such torment as was endured" Shapira, "Love God with all your heart," 327.

267
"It meant that somewhere out there in the open" Mann, *The Tables of the Law*, 21–22.
"I know well and God knows beforehand" Ibid., 110–11.

270
"Stillness. Silence. A people has been murdered" Grossman, "Ukraine Without Jews," 13.

274
"We have the proofs, but not the testimonies" Jorge Semprún, as quoted in Fournet, *The Crime of Destruction and the Law of Genocide*, 32.
"When the layers of gas had covered everything" Schwarz-Bart, *The Last of the Just*, 407.

275
"On the dazzlingly bright screen I saw the places" Weiss, "Vanishing Point," in *Exile*, 194.
"… atmosphere of insanity and unreality" Arendt, "The Concentration Camps," 750–51.

278
"Life in Israel is lacking in tradition and style" Koestler, *Promise and Fulfilment*, 324.
"… by the standards of mellower civilizations" Ibid., 326.
"It is a hard pioneer country" Ibid., 327.

279
"My neighbor greets me in a friendly fashion" Améry, "On the Necessity and Impossibility of Being a Jew," in *At the Mind's Limits*, 95.

282
"We began in the kitchen" Fink, "Shelter," 133–34.

283
"If Judaism is attached to the here below" Levinas, "Place and Utopia," 100.
"In order that I be able to free myself" Levinas, *Totality and Infinity*, 170–71.

286
"This is what we are fighting against" Rauschning, "Preface: A Conversation with Hitler," xiii.
"Most of you know what it means to see a hundred corpses lie side by side" Heinrich Himmler, as quoted in Dawidowicz, *A Holocaust Reader*, 131–33.
"Evil in the Third Reich had lost the quality" Arendt, *Eichmann in Jerusalem*, 134.
"To a Jew this role of the Jewish leaders" Ibid., 104.

287
"There was one moment in the Six-Day War" Israel Ministry of Foreign Affairs, Press Room, 1995: Yitzhak Rabin's speech to the Knesset, May 29, 1995.
"All those who secretly long" Oz, *In the Land of Israel*, 241.

291
"How good and pleasant it is" Psalm 133:1.

294
"The shofar blares out; everyone is awakened" Chagall, *Burning Lights*, 76–77.

298
"Moennikes and I went directly to the pits" United States, "Document 2992-PS," *Nazi Conspiracy and Aggression* 5, 697–98.

299
"In gullies and deep ravines" Grossman, "Ukraine Without Jews," 18.
"instruments of bourgeois reaction" Lenin, "The Attitude of the Workers' Party to Religion," 403.

300
"If there ever was a truly close relationship between a house of worship and its populace" Kayser, "Introduction," 5.

301
"No, this was something different from that first surprise" Lissitzky, "On the Mogilev Shul."

302
"The treasury of forms used by the painter" Ibid.

303
"Thus, the synagogues of the sixteenth and seventeenth centuries" Lukomski, "The Wooden Synagogues of Eastern Europe," 18.

304
"This book commemorates martyred buildings" Kayser, "Introduction," 5.

306
"Civic entrepreneurship for the benefit of integration" Biłgoraj XXI, "Who are we?" http://www.bilgoraj21.pl/en/kim-jestesmy/.
"We want to give the climate of prewar times" Biłgoraj XXI, "In an attempt to draw on future," http://www.bilgoraj21.pl/en/dom-singera/.

307
"What would Singer have thought" Rothbart, "The Ghost Shtetl of Isaac Bashevis Singer's Youth."
"Firstly, I like to write ghost stories" Singer, "Banquet Speech."

308
"The heavy curtain of the holy ark is drawn aside" Chagall, *Burning Lights*, 91–94.

310
"The second burthen of a former child" Shakespeare, *The Complete Sonnets and Poems*, 499.
Zog nit keyn mol "Do Not Ever Say: The Partisans' Song," http://hebrewsongs.com/?song=zognitkeynmol.

311
"Our share in holiness" Heschel, *God in Search of Man*, 423.

312
"In the morning I arise and match again" Reznikoff, "New York: 1951—Seven Poems," 574.
"If the statistics are right" Twain, "Concerning the Jews," 535.

313
"'I have seen these people,' the Lord said to Moses" Exodus 32:9.
"And Moses hurried and knelt to the ground and bowed" Sacks, "A Stiff-Necked People."

314
"Nations will call on them" Ibid.
"This shall be your answer" Abraham ben Elezier ha-Levi, "The Death of the Martyrs," 202.

315
"Luria begins by putting a question" Scholem, *Major Trends in Jewish Mysticism*, 260–61.

316
"The father was holding the hand of a boy about ten years old" United States, "Document 2992-PS," *Nazi Conspiracy and Aggression* 5, 697.

317
"For *Galuth* acquires here a new meaning" Scholem, *Major Trends in Jewish Mysticism*, 284.
"We are either the last, the dying, Jews" Heschel, *God in Search of Man*, 421.

Acknowledgments

AUTHOR'S ACKNOWLEDGMENTS

Wer nicht von dreitausend Jahren / sich weiß Rechenschaft zu geben, / bleib im Dunkeln unerfahren, / mag von Tag zu Tage leben. "A person who does not know / the history of the last 3,000 years / wanders in the darkness of ignorance, / unable to make sense of the reality around him." Over half a century ago my grandparents Hans Bunge and Jenny Bunge-Hanf first presented me with Johann Wolfgang von Goethe's understanding of the temporal scale of any credible attempt to orient oneself in the world, and this lesson I have taken to heart. It has shaped my career as professor at the University of Waterloo School of Architecture, Canada, where my students over a thirty-five-year teaching career were willing to read old texts and consider old buildings to understand the issues of the present, confirming to me that Goethe's pronouncement remains relevant today—of course, as long as one is willing to critically assess questions of what history is taught, and whose history, issues that are increasingly the focus of invigorating debates. I thank all of them, as I want to express my gratitude to my colleagues at Waterloo, who have accepted with good humor certain idiosyncrasies in my research and teaching leading to a peculiar double-track career as a cultural historian and a Holocaust historian within the context of a professional school that, through its Co-op education program, is uniquely focused on educating architects who are ready for the real-world challenges of architectural practice.

My fellow members of the Architectural Advisory Board of the Babyn Yar Holocaust Memorial Center and my direct collaborators within the foundation—Nick Axel, Ilya Khrzhanovskiy, Anna Kamyshan, Marina Otero Verzier, Troy Conrad Therrien, Ines Weizman—accepted my argument that our discussion on the future of Babyn Yar should be informed also by an understanding of the formation and nature of Jewish understandings of space, both physical, intellectual, and emotional. Their response to my presentation, and the endorsement it received from Manuel Herz, who both as a scholar and as an architect understands more of the issues I have tried to address than anyone else I know, led to a couple of conversations between Nick, Manuel, and their publisher, Thomas Kramer, that laid the foundations for this book: without their votes of confidence, *An Atlas of Jewish Space* would not exist. *Gracias, Danke,* Дякую, Спасибо, Thank you!

In the preface I provided a quick sketch of the stimulating collaboration with Mark Podwal. My wife, Miriam Greenbaum, introduced me to his work, and my friend Alice Marxova, editor of the Czech Jewish monthly *Rosh Hodesh*, helped to make the contact. Miriam read all the drafts of the text—including the embarrassingly shitty first one—and returned each page with notes, questions, suggestions to tighten many arguments, and observations on how to expand some underdeveloped ones. Most importantly, she also identified some significant blind spots in the narrative. In this adventure she was my daily companion and counselor. Early on in the pandemic, poet, colleague, and friend Bob Wiljer and I had begun a weekly conversation on Third Reich historiography, with a particular focus on Hitler biographies—a topic that seemed of contemporary relevance in the last year of the Trump administration. When I had finally produced a Miriam-approved draft, I sent it to Bob with the request that he have a look at it. As he is a tough critic, I expected some rough weekly sessions that might leave me shaken, but he proved remarkably supportive of the effort—or at least, that's my takeaway, even as I continue to ponder Bob's somewhat ambiguous judgment as to the "Kafkaesque" character of the story as a whole. Finally, Amy K. Hughes, with whom I had a wonderful collaboration in perfecting the text of *Auschwitz. Not long ago. Not far away.*, the catalogue of the traveling exhibition of the same name organized by Musealia Exhibitions and Museums S.L., helped me to polish the text to a level worthy of the Park Books imprint. Miriam, Alice, Bob, and Amy: please accept my profound gratitude.

Coordination of the production was in the capable hands of Nick Axel, and Kai Udema provided a very effective design that allowed the creative friction between text and images to be explicit, while also offering in the typography of the Prologue and the Coda a sense of the uncertainty that accompanies all attempts to make sense of a world marked by words such as Auschwitz and Babyn Yar. All preparation leads to a point of no return, when (in alphabetical order) glue, grease, ink, paper, plate and thread are brought together to make the physical copy of the book you have in your hand. That final stretch in the making of *An Atlas of Jewish Space* was in the hands of the lithographers at Widmer & Fluri and the printers at Druckerei zu Altenburg. *Danke!*

This project was both conceived and executed during the Covid-19 pandemic. In an essential way, the need to maintain one's mental equilibrium in a state of lockdown shaped the narrative of the book: while the first and last parts, which deal with biblical history and Jewish history in the modern age, respectively, describe history as change, often dramatic, at times revolutionary, and occasionally catastrophic, the center of the text deals with a society that endured many centuries of lockdown in a hostile world. In such a condition the heroes of the story are not people who begin things or people who change things, but those who maintain things, who persist against all the odds in their stewardship of an impossible legacy. Anyone who takes Goethe's advice, and considers our current situation against a 3,000-year horizon, will of course marvel at the great developments and evolutions that are visible but even more so at the constancy of purpose, the loyalty to what has been handed down from generation to generation, and the decency of everyday people in everyday life—something that is easily overlooked amidst the noise of apparent change. Today, that constancy, loyalty, and decency are embodied in the many, many people who are now designated as "essential," and who allowed me to write this book in a heated and illuminated house, with a stocked pantry and access to information, located in a relatively well-run country with a universal, publicly funded health system that has been capable, until now, of absorbing the shock of the pandemic thanks to the dedication of the medical, nursing, and support staff, the constancy of policies promulgated by elected officials and a professional civil service on the best scientific advice, and the ability of the great majority of citizens to understand the gravity of the situation and the ethical demands it puts on each of us individually. As this book begins with Balaam's blessing of the well-ordered arrangement of a community living in a time of emergency, I like to think that Balaam would have spoken similar words seeing many such states and societies today.

Robert Jan van Pelt

ARTIST'S ACKNOWLEDGMENTS

Ecclesiastes 12:12 warns, "Of making many books there is no end, and much study wearies the body." While *Ecclesiastes* is among my favorite biblical books, a book I hope to illustrate one day, I've long neglected that advice. Making many books and study are my favorite preoccupations. With the making of my many books there is no end to the list of those who, for nearly fifty years, previously published images included in this work. My most recent publishers have been Marta Hallet of Glitterati, Patrick Alexander of Penn State University Press, Altie Karper of Schocken Books, and Jason Kalman of Hebrew Union College Press. Moreover, I would like to acknowledge my son Ariel, who was extremely helpful in digitally refining the art for reproduction. And of course, my gratitude to the Babyn Yar Holocaust Memorial Center for supporting this publication and to publisher Thomas Kramer and designer Kai Udema for producing such an elegant volume.

As this book includes numerous drawings and paintings created specially to illuminate Robert Jan van Pelt's text, other pictures previously published to accompany the words of Elie Wiesel, Harold Bloom, Heinrich Heine, Francine Klagsbrun, and Francine Prose, as well as my own, fit flawlessly.

Among sources for the images are my own books:
A Jewish Bestiary. University Park: Penn State University Press, 2021.
A Collage of Customs: Iconic Jewish Woodcuts Revised for the Twenty-First Century. Cincinnati: Hebrew Union College Press, 2021.
Kaddish for Dąbrowa Białostocka. Amherst, MA: Yiddish Book Center, 2018.
Reimagined: 45 Years of Jewish Art. New York: Glitterati Inc., 2016.
Built by Angels. New York: Houghton Mifflin Harcourt, 2009.
Jerusalem Sky. New York: Random House, 2005.
A Sweet Year. New York: Random House, 2003.
The Menorah Story. New York: Greenwillow Books, 1998.
The Book of Tens. New York: Greenwillow Books, 1994.

Books by others:
Wiesel, Elie. *The Tale of a Niggun*. New York: Schocken Books, 2020.
Heine, Heinrich. *Hebrew Melodies*. University Park: Penn State University Press, 2019.
Mishkan HaNefesh for Youth. New York: CCAR Press, 2017.
Mishkan T'filah for Youth. New York: CCAR Press, 2014.
Yoffie, Alan S. *Sharing the Journey: The Haggadah for the Contemporary Family*. New York: CCAR Press, 2012.
Bloom, Harold. *Fallen Angels*. New Haven: Yale University Press, 2007.
Wiesel, Elie. *King Solomon and His Magic Ring*. New York: Greenwillow Books, 1999.
Sobel, Ileene Smith. *Moses and the Angels*. Introduction by Elie Wiesel. New York: Delacorte Press, 1999.
Prose, Francine. *The Angel's Mistake: Stories of Chelm*. New York: Greenwillow Books, 1997.
Klagsbrun, Francine. *Jewish Days*. New York: Farrar, Straus and Giroux, 1996.
Wiesel, Elie. *A Passover Haggadah*. New York: Simon and Schuster, 1993.
The Elie Wiesel Collection. Paris: The Bibliophile Library, 1985–88.
Let My People Go: A Haggadah. Introduction by Theodore Bikel. Foreword by Abba Eban. New York: Macmillan, 1972.

Solo exhibition catalogues:
All this has come upon us … Terezín: Terezín Memorial, 2014.
Wiesel, Elie. *Mark Podwal: Jewish Dreams*. Prague: Jewish Museum, 1997.

Mark Podwal

Index

INDEX OF TEXTS

A Bond Is Sealed, 62
Accept the Yoke of His Kingdom, 179
A Confusing Labyrinth, 230
A Forbidden Place, 78
Alchemy of Memory, 172
An All-Too-Easy Solution, 234
A New Jerusalem, 139
An Interrogation Mark, 278
Anywhere but Europe, 258
A People Has Been Murdered, 270
A Perfectly Normal Measure, 275
A Plebian God, 178
Appointed Time for Deliverance, 146
Architecture of Promise, 98
Architecture of the Talmud, 159
A Single Obsession, 247
A Special Problem, 222
Aspiration versus Obligation, 107
A World Lost, 30
A World to Win, 215

Backbone of the Shtetl, 34
Blood of Christ, 138
Boundaries, 79
Boundless Redemption, 99
Brave Little Nation, 246
Catastrophic Destruction, 47
Center of the Earth, 131
Claustrophilia, 210
Come, Light the Menorah, 110
Concentration City, 67
Console, O Lord, the Mourners of Zion, 142
Contested Refuge, 255
Covenant, 39
Covenant of the Heart and Soul, 83

Dark Stammerings, 42
Days of Awe, Days of Terror, 262
Divinely Revealed, 50
Domain as Throne, 66

Embracing Tradition, 126
Endurance in Fearful Situations, 163
Everywhere and Nowhere, 71
Exiled but Not Abandoned, 94
Extend the Boundaries of the Home, 206

Final Solution, 263
Folie de Grandeur, 111
Foundation Stone, 134
Founding Fathers and Mothers, 55
From Oldest to Youngest, 171

God Does Not Repent of the Gifts He Makes, 151
Good News, 135

Head and Heart Alike Uplifted, 198
Hold No Man Insignificant, and No Thing Improbable, 203
Holocaust Before the Holocaust, 238
House of Assembly, 106
House of Life, 223

I Am Who I Am, 70
In Every Generation, 191
In Praise of Impurity, 218
In Scorn of Christ our Saviour, 162
In with the New, Out with the Old, 143
It's Just a Place, 46
It Takes Ten, 183

Kill Off the Spirit, 271

Light One Candle After Another, 199
Like a Summons, Sounding into Every Corner, 294
Like Everyone Else, Only More So, 219

Mah Tovu Ohalekha, Yaakov, 43
Man or Messiah?, 123
May It Give You Health, 195
Melting-Pot Kingdom, 119
Minority Scorned and Feared, 242

Neighbor or Pilgrim?, 175
Next Year in Jerusalem, 194
No One Could Say, "I Was There", 274

On the Doorframes of Your Houses, 186
On This Night, 190

Pack of Hunting Dogs, 250
Passover Cleansing, 87
Peripheral Sanctuary, 102
Piecing the Fragments Together, 290
Poppy-Seed Loaf, 31
Prepared for the Future, 282
Protocols, 226
Provide for the Redemption of the Land, 182

Rhythms and Truths, 90
Rock at the End of the Mosque, 147

Saul and David, 59
Sanctitude by Design, 74
Shine Out in Glory, 118
Shooting Stars, 243
Sing of Zion as of a Beloved Mistress, 231
Solomon's Temple, 63
Song of Ascent, 291
Space So Bountiful, 202
Stairway to Understanding, 115

Tabernacle as Declaration, 114
Temporary Shelters, 187
Test of Patriotism, 235
Text as Temple, 103
The Archetype of All Internment, 227
The Center Holds, 170
The Croaking Hole, 259
The Crucible of Captivity, 95
The Intimacy of the Home, 283
The Jerusalem Syndrome, 122
The Land I Will Show You, 54
The Lofty Dwelling, 51
The Lord Will Scatter You, 86
The People's Field, 38
The Seventh Day, 82
The Shattering of the Vessels, 211
The Talmud Says …, 158
The Tent of Meeting, 58
The Words Are Binding, 267
They Remain Strangers, 279
Thought Is Fluid, Ever-Continuing, 174
Till It Crackles and Is Quenched, 207
To Have No Neighbor, 254
Tradition on Edge, 27
Twelve Precious Stones, 75

Universal Refuge, 239
Unprecedented and Unparalleled, 266

Way of Walking, 35
We Are Not Adventurers, 214
We Were Taught, 155
What Remained Was the Word, 167
Where One Burns Books …, 251
Why Did the Stars Not Withdraw Their Brightness?, 154
Window of Heaven, 130
Wiping Out the Debtor, 166
When Peace and a Little Repose Finally Come, 287
Write and Record!, 286

Your Beloved Is Knocking, 91
Your Speeches Are Made in Vain, 150

INDEX OF ILLUSTRATIONS

Abraham Smashes the Idols (1994), 53
Accept the Prayers of Your People (2008), 181
According to Heine (2020), 252
A Dome Of Gold Shining Like A Second Sun (2004), 148
After the Pogrom (2020), 237
A History (1988), 40
Ancestors (2008), 37
And You Pummeled Me with Dung (2017), 236
An Incomprehensible World (1980s), 276
A Wondrous Star Announced the News of Jesus's Birth (2004), 136
A World That Is No More (2021), 45

Babyn Yar (1980s), 261
Becomes a Human Again (2017), 197
Be Strong, Be Strong (2013), 245
Began His Education with the Holy Book, the Torah (2017), 172
Białystok Synagogue Memorial and Cathedral (2016), 272
Birkenau (1980s), 268
Boskovice Synagogue and Castle (2017), 156
Broken Jewish Tombstones (2016), 285

Canaanite City in Ruins (2020), 56
Carrying the Deceased to the Cemetery (2019), 36
Combining Letters (1982), 212
Come and Read (1997), 49
Cutting Jewish Beards (1980s), 248

Dąbrowa Białostocka Synagogue in Shape of Tzedakah (Charity) Box (2016), 33
Dąbrowa on My Mind (2016), 205
Destruction of the Temple (1980), 141
Disputation (2021), 149

Earthly and Heavenly Jerusalem (2004), 140
Ecclesia and Synagoga (2013), 152
Einstein Tower Inkwell (2021), 244
Elijah Leading the Messiah at the Golden Gate (1990s), 124
Every Generation (2013), 192
Exile of the Tribes (1990s), 85
Expulsion 1492 (2013), 213

Ezekiel 41:1 And He Brought Me to the Temple (2013), 97

Fallen Angels (2006), 177
Fiddlers on Roofs (1995), 28
Film Strip (2021), 273
Final Solution (1988), 264
Flying Letters (2006), 128
Former Jewish Owned Property (2021), 280
Fortified City (1997), 61
Four Children (2011), 229
Fragment of Wooden Synagogue Interior (2021), 29

Ghetto Cemetery (2001), 44
Ghetto Wall (1997), 168
Giftschrank (2021), 41
Good and Evil (2020), 84
Great Synagogue of Munich Wrapped in a Prayer Shawl (2017), 253

Hanukkah Menorah (2011), 109
Havdalah Spice Boxes and Candle (2005), 208
Hebrew Zodiac (2001), 132
Heinrich Heine (2021), 220
High Priest (1997), 113
Holy Ark (1997), 116
Holy of Holies (2020), 64
Holy Opening (2004), 129

Israel (2001), 256

Jacob's Ladder over Jerusalem (2004), 133
Jerusalem Rose with Thorns (2012), 121
Jerusalem: The Impossible Partition (2003), 288
Jew (2005), 260
Jewish Time (2017), 81

Kahals (1996), 225
Kristallnacht (1988), 257

Manna (1998), 72
Matzoh Moon (2004), 88
Mezuzah (2021), 185
Mezuzahs (2021), 284
Mikvah Blueprint (2020), 196
Moses (1990s), 77
Murdered in Those Days (2020), 165

Nebuchadnezzar (1980s), 93
Ninth of Av (2012), 48
Now Crowned by a Great Church (2004), 144

Outside the Ghetto Wall Sat the Drummer (2020), 164

Pilpul ("Dialectical Exegesis") (1977), 160
Pirkei Avot (2018), 204
Praise (2013), 69
Prague Ghetto (1980), 209

Roads to Extinction (1985), 265

Samaritan Alphabet (2020), 120
Sea of Talmud (1992), 157
Seder (1991), 189
Seder Plate (2011), 193
Sefer (1980), 96
Shabbat (2002), 201
Shabbat Lamp (2017), 200
Shofars (2017), 293
Shtetl Synagogue (1993), 57
Sinai (2011), 80
Some Believe That Halfway Between Heaven and Earth (2004), 145
Song of Songs: The Watchmen Found Me (2016), 92
Sukkah (1995), 188
Synagogue Menorah Surmounted with Polish Eagle (2021), 241
Synagogue Tombstones (2021), 296

Temple in Jerusalem Bookplate (2021), 68
Temple in Ruins (1998), 101
That Old Song – Do You Still Know It? (2017), 292
The Altneuschul (2008), 169
The Ant (2020), 89
The Attic (2008), 233
The Burning Bush (1997), 117
The Enemy (2019), 249
The Four Holy Cities (2011), 100
The Golden Calf (2020), 65
The Jews Are All Gone, Never to Return (1980s), 269
The Master Race (2016), 228
The Scapegoat (2003), 137
The Seven Species of Israel (2014), 277
The Torah Is the Map of the World (1994), 216
This Is the Law of Moses (2008), 104
Titus Who Destroyed Herod's Temple (2004), 112
Torah Pointers and French Flag (2020), 217
Torah Shield Engraved with Chodorów Synagogue (2020), 289

Tower of Babel (1994), 52
Tower of David as a Spice Box
 (2021), 60
Tu B'Shevat (2003), 240
Twelve Tribes (2011), 76
Two Panels of a Triptych
 (2020), 161
Tyrants Sought to Destroy
 Us (1971), 125
Tyrants Sought to Destroy
 Us (2011), 221

Úštek School Book (2017), 173

Waiting for a Minyan (2020), 184
Western Portal (2020), 176
Western Wall (1978), 232
Where Time Stands Still (1997), 224
Why Did the Heavens Not
 Darken? (2013), 153
Wooden Synagogue of Zabludow
 (1999), 105

Yiddish Typewriter (2018), 32
Yom Kippur in the Altneuschul
 (2008), 180

Zbarazh (2021), 281
Zeus Defiling the Temple (1997),
 108

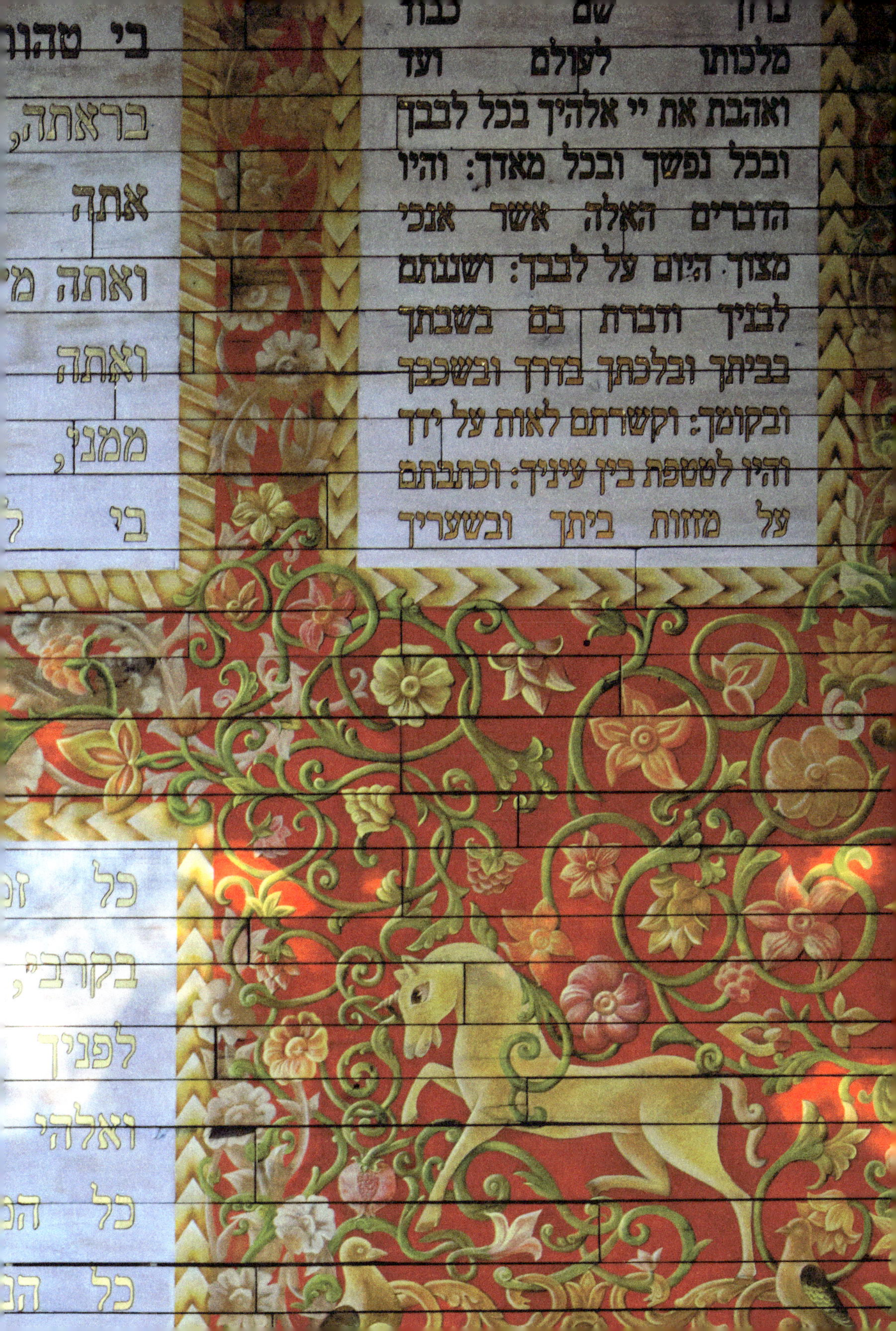

רוך שם כבוד
מלכותו לעולם ועד
ואהבת את יי אלהיך בכל לבבך
ובכל נפשך ובכל מאדך: והיו
הדברים האלה אשר אנכי
מצוך היום על לבבך: ושננתם
לבניך ודברת בם בשבתך
בביתך ובלכתך בדרך ובשכבך
ובקומך: וקשרתם לאות על ידך
והיו לטטפת בין עיניך: וכתבתם
על מזזות ביתך ובשעריך
בי טהור
בראתה,
אתה
ואתה מ
ואתה
ממני,
בי ל
כל ז
בקרבי,
לפניך
ואלהי
כל ה
כל ה

A Synagogue for Babyn Yar

Manuel Herz
Galina Andrusenko
Iwan Baan

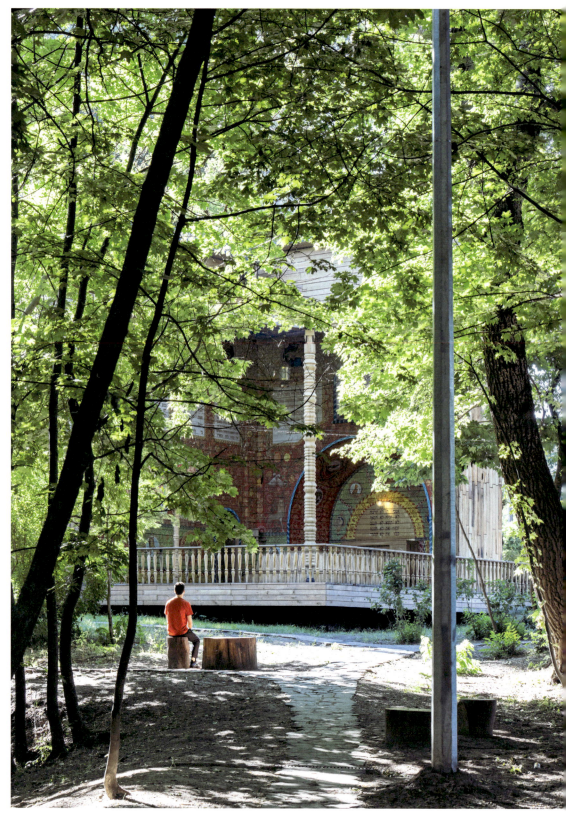

Holding Space

Marina Otero Verzier and Nick Axel

On May 14, 2021, the memorial Babyn Yar Synagogue was inaugurated with a performative event, a new collective ritual for the site in Kyiv that was witness to one of the most atrocious and unaccounted-for events of the Holocaust. Orchestrated by ten people moving to the sound of the shofar, the building's tall, confident, somber wooden walls were spread open like the covers of a book; its carved central column swung out; its vividly painted roof lifted up; and its bimah and women's balcony folded out.

The synagogue's literal opening preceded the eightieth anniversary of September 29–30, 1941—a two-day period when Nazi forces massacred approximately 33,771 Jews at the Babyn Yar ravine, on what was then the outskirts of the city. Over the following two years, nearly 70,000 more people were killed, making Babyn Yar one of the most historically significant sites of what Father Patrick Desbois, founder of Yahad-In Unum and head of the Academic Council of the Babyn Yar Holocaust Memorial Center, has called the "Holocaust by bullets." Today, that history, which is deeply entangled with that of the Soviet Union and what has followed since its dissolution, is still being written across eastern Europe. The synagogue is part of that process of memorialization.

Designed by Manuel Herz, the building is the first of a series of site-specific interventions commissioned by the Babyn Yar Holocaust Memorial Center to pay tribute to the site's history. Herz has distilled the idea of a synagogue down into its elemental, constituent parts and recomposed them into an intimately familiar yet wholly novel creation. Like any synagogue service, the structure itself needs the actions of ten bodies—the minyan—to be opened. Opening the structure, then, is like opening the Torah. Herz's architecture is itself an act of prayer, of worship. The building is the book. Persecuted since time immemorial, not allowed the conditions of permanence to inhabit or build architecture in any conventional sense, Jewish people have been historically called the People of the Book. Synagogues are, therefore, more ritual than architectural typology. And when considering them as a feature of our built environments today, we tend to think of synagogues as closed, unassuming buildings. The Babyn Yar Synagogue is modeled not just on the books of Judaism but also on another type of book that similarly holds wonderous worlds within its pages: a pop-up book. Set back slightly into the woods, its tall, dramatic wooden back faces the first Jewish memorial at Babyn Yar, a monumental bronze menorah erected in 1991. When the book of the synagogue is opened, a dynamic three-dimensional space looks out onto a preserved spur of the former ravine, welcoming the surroundings and making them an intrinsic part of the building. Herz's project resists traditional spatial dichotomies—inside-outside, interior-exterior, open-closed, temporary-permanent. Its boundaries undergo perpetual transformation through the integration of different perspectives, shifting climatic conditions, and processes of assembly and reassembly.

The unassuming wooden exterior unfolds to reveal a colorful world of beauty and wonder within. The interior walls are painted in the style of seventeenth- and eighteenth-century synagogues in western Ukraine, all of which were destroyed in the czarist pogroms and Nazi genocide. Decorating the surfaces of centuries-old oak, which was collected from all parts of Ukraine, are prayers and blessings of the Jewish liturgy, including one that speaks of the transformation of nightmares into good dreams. The ceiling, a surface typically adorned with icons from Judaic astrology, is painted as a specific map of the stars, depicting the night sky that was visible over Kyiv on the first night of the massacre. Beneath this midnight-blue skyscape ornamented with zodiac symbols, flowers, and geometric patterns, we are gently taken back to 1941 while breathing the air of Babyn Yar and listening to the movement of trees that continue to root into its ground.

Writings, drawings, and symbols inscribed on every surface of the interior reinforce the image of the building as a prayer book: a siddur or perhaps even the Talmud—the fluid and multidirectional text central to Judaism that is more a library than a book. Yet, perhaps what best describes Herz's synagogue is an annotated architecture: a palimpsest constructed from overlapping materials, knowledge, and histories made accessible once again. It is an architecture to be collectively opened and closed, experienced, modified, contemplated, and read. It memorializes not by allowing one to forget but by bringing the past back into the present, allowing it to live anew.

Heritage is not the conservation of objects or sites as if time does not pass through them. As scholar Laurajane Smith asserts in her book Uses of Heritage, heritage is a dynamic process and must be lived. It is an experience that involves acts and embodied practices of remembering. With such engagement, new collective memories can be created, shared, and passed to future generations. Heritage is, therefore, a performative act. The Babyn Yar Synagogue is conceived not as a monument but as a generative medium that engages with acts of remembering. Its value relies not only on the built object itself but also on the cultural and social bonds that it instigates. To give and transmit meaning across time and generations is to honor those whose lives were taken in its immediate surroundings.

Babyn Yar is the resting place of countless souls. Before the massacre of 1941, citizens of Kyiv would use the edge of the ravine to bury their dead. There were cemeteries for the city's Jewish, Eastern Orthodox, military, Mariavite, Muslim, Karaite, and Evangelical communities. Today, little remains visible of this history. A few burial markers from the Kyrylivska Orthodox cemetery still do populate the forest, but the Jewish cemetery was almost entirely erased. A handful of headstones, previously scattered across the site, were brought together in 2017 and arranged along the path that connects the former office of the Jewish cemetery with the memorial menorah and now the synagogue. But its historical grounds have largely been paved over and built upon. A TV station, a sports complex, a gas station, a bus depot, and a shooting range all currently stand upon the former resting places of Kyiv's Jewish community.

It is not just the cemetery that has been largely erased but also the landforms that articulated the site. Over the past eighty years, a series of large-scale terraforming operations conducted by both the Nazis and, later, the Soviet Union, largely erased its ancient topography. The approximately 150-hectare site is a heterogeneous territory today, with types of environments that range from relatively flat, clean, and ordered parklike spaces to the steep, wild remnants of the former ravine around which the city has grown. Babyn Yar is not only a site of memory but a public park used daily by the people of Kyiv.

Despite these transformations that have profoundly altered the conditions of Babyn Yar, the specific location of the 1941 shootings has been identified, in one of the most highly trafficked areas of the entire site, about a half kilometer away from the synagogue, not far from the Metro. However, the sites of the massacres that took place after those two first days, lasting until the Nazi occupying forces left Kyiv, have not been fully located. In Babyn Yar, it is not possible to say with certainty whether one is standing where someone died or where a body might rest. The entire site, in effect, is a burial place. Its ground demands reverence, a demand that any new architectural project on the site inevitably faces.

Buildings most often sustain violent relations with the ground they occupy and to which they are anchored. Inscribing architecture on a site generally involves soil excavation, removal, and displacement. As such, Halakhah, the collective body of Jewish religious laws, states that no new building, no new activity, should occur on the resting place of a Jewish person. Yet, as a religion, Judaism focuses on issues of behavior, not faith. The key question for Jews is not, as discussed earlier in this book, "What should I believe?" (the central issue in Christianity) but "What ought I do next?" Herz's synagogue responds to these questions, as well as to the troubled, uncertain condition of Babyn Yar's ground, with respect and honor. The synagogue does not have deep foundations. Instead, it sits on a concrete mass placed on top of the irregular topography. Its lightweight wooden platform is slightly elevated, rising over the ground, at once defining a place without fully enclosing it and turning the synagogue into a stage.

The synagogue's architecture, therefore, is enacted between inside and outside, between soil and sky, between present and past, between near and far. It is sacred and intimate, yet public and open. It is situated while conflating local realities and distant memories. It inspires emotion through its material, spatial, formal conditions. Yet, above all, it holds the space to generate new relations, new modes of negotiation within and beyond this contentious site—beyond its trauma. As worship sites become increasingly confined, surveilled, guarded, and inward-facing, the Babyn Yar Synagogue opens to the world in a vulnerable yet confident gesture.

Thoughts on the design process
Manuel Herz

To build on land that has seen more murder and devastation than most other places on this planet, places immense responsibility on the architect. How do we respect the dead? Can we develop a response that is appropriate to the gravity of the site's history? These questions were going through my head when I received the commission to design a synagogue on the grounds of Babyn Yar in October 2020. Of course, the echoes of Yevgeni Yevtushenko's majestic poem "There are no monuments over Babi Yar," written in 1961, accentuated my initial hesitation. Can, or should, we build here at all? Isn't the poem, and its extraordinary intonation by Shostakovich, the most profound commemoration we can imagine? While this is true to a certain extent, I also believe that architecture and the spatial disciplines can bring a quality of commemoration to Babyn Yar that is truly different from that wrought in such other artistic disciplines as literature and music.

One might think that the appropriate response to this unbelievably inhumane massacre should be an architecture that is somber, minimalist, and monumental. The architectural history of Holocaust memorials is full of such responses. But I wanted to approach the project in a very different way. I thought of a John Hejduk project that had made a strong impression on me when I was still an architecture student: "Victims," Hejduk's proposal for the site of the former Gestapo (Nazi secret police) headquarters in the center of Berlin. Instead of a single, monumental memorial, the proposal sketches out several small interventions, all of which have a performative and even playful character—interventions that are enacted, rather than just looked at. It was these qualities that I sought for the Babyn Yar Synagogue.

I wanted to create a project that has a transformative dimension and establishes a new ritual on the site. I strongly believe that a monumental, static approach—in view of the site, which is literally and metaphorically drenched with blood—would be wrong. We cannot respond to the massacre by designing a building that imposes itself onto the ground and onto the narrative of history. We will never match the monumental suffering of the massacre through a monumental architecture. The categorical and definitive message that a monumental and static building would suggest stands at odds with the tens of thousands of distinctive voices that perished in Babyn Yar. I was looking for a building that is multivalent, that does not demand a conclusive reading. Hence, the idea was born, to design an architecture that creates a new collective ritual, that has a performative and transformative quality, that is commemorative, just as it also creates a feeling of wonder and awe. And it would be a building that barely touches the ground.

Previously, in my Mainz synagogue, I had explored the intimate relationship between writing and the production of space in Jewish thought. With the Jewish people often referred to as the People of the Book, the idea of referencing a book in the design of the synagogue is perhaps not all that surprising. I was then thinking of pop-up books, which are so fascinating. From a flat, almost two-dimensional object, they unfold into three-dimensional volumes, revealing scenographies often architectural in character. Who can resist the temptation to open up these books and see how a new and surprising world unfolds? We can get lost in this new world, as in a cabinet of wonders. In a certain way, this is exactly what happens when we come together to pray in a synagogue: we open a book together (either the *siddur*, i.e., book of prayers; or the Bible). Reading this book in the collective of the congregation also opens a new world to us, a world of stories, of histories, of morals, of love, and of wisdom. The pop-up book, with its transformative quality, the collective ritual of opening and closing it, and the sense of wonder that emanates, seemed to provide the perfect starting point for designing the Babyn Yar Synagogue.

Early in the design process, I had suggested that the interiors of historic wooden synagogues from western Ukraine could be a source of inspiration for the interiors of the Babyn Yar Synagogue. Their use of ornament and writing on the walls was fascinating. One historic photograph, in particular, of the strikingly beautiful synagogue of Gwoździec, caught my interest. While studying it, I actually tried to identify the text that was visible in the photograph, expecting it to be one of the main prayers of the Jewish liturgy, such as the Kaddish, or the Shema Israel. A family member whom I asked for help came back to me a little bit later. Surprisingly, the Gwoździec text was a quite obscure blessing, dating back to the Talmudic period, concerning the interpretations of dreams. In fact, it was a blessing to transform nightmares into good dreams. When I heard this, I immediately thought that there could be no better leitmotif for the Babyn Yar Synagogue than this blessing for turning nightmares into good dreams. This blessing now occupies the main wall, written just above the *Aron ha'Kodesh*, where the Torah scrolls are kept.

I started working on the Babyn Yar Synagogue just two weeks after my wonderful wife, Xenia, gave birth to our son, Max. Hence, I was engaged in a topic of murder and unbearable suffering while at the same time marveling at this new, tender human life. When I looked into the beautiful face of our little son, I saw his curiosity and eagerness to know his new world, and his immense joy of experiencing life. My son taught me that the Babyn Yar Synagogue cannot be only about commemorating the past but must also be about opening up to a new future. It needs to be a project that turns a nightmare into a good dream. A project that is not entrenched in death and destruction but that celebrates the beauty of life.

Artist Statement
Galina Andrusenko

Modern examples of Jewish wooden synagogue painting do not exist, and most historical ones have been systematically destroyed by antisemitic movements over the recent centuries. But a handful of early black-and-white photographs exist, and there have been some historical reconstructions, including the painted ceilings of the Chodorow and Gwoździec synagogues in Poland. These reconstructions are a unique and living archive of this historical Jewish painting tradition.

    I started painting the Babyn Yar Synagogue by creating a quick compositional drawing, dividing the two main vertical surfaces into basic blocks in dialogue with the space's architectural features and blocks of text originally chosen and positioned by the architect. I then began roughly positioning the medallion-like elements that contain symbols from the Jewish zodiac—strongly prevalent in this decorative tradition—and sketching the ornamental infill. The symbolic animals and fantastic artifacts adorning the interior are intertwined with floral patterns and decorative squares. The interior is meant to feel like a portal into another world, where each element represents and glorifies the Almighty.

    The Chodorow synagogue provided compositional inspiration, which is colorful and polychromatic. Greens and blacks guide the lower and central band of the wall, while whites and blues create a transition upwards to the roof, which is distinct in its conception and was designed by the architect. Lions, bears, deer, elephants, squirrels, rabbits, lambs, leopards, eagles, camels, and more populate the walls and all speak to each other in their specific meaning and placement. The Bimah and the Women's Balcony are distinguished with the introduction of a bright red.

    As I was trained in monumental art, the painting was dictated by the texture of the old oak surface being painted on. I wanted to harmoniously place the image onto the wall. I am grateful to the work of the fifteen artists who painted this with me, including experts in mural painting, folk art, restoration, and students of the National Ukrainian Academy of Arts (АМУ).

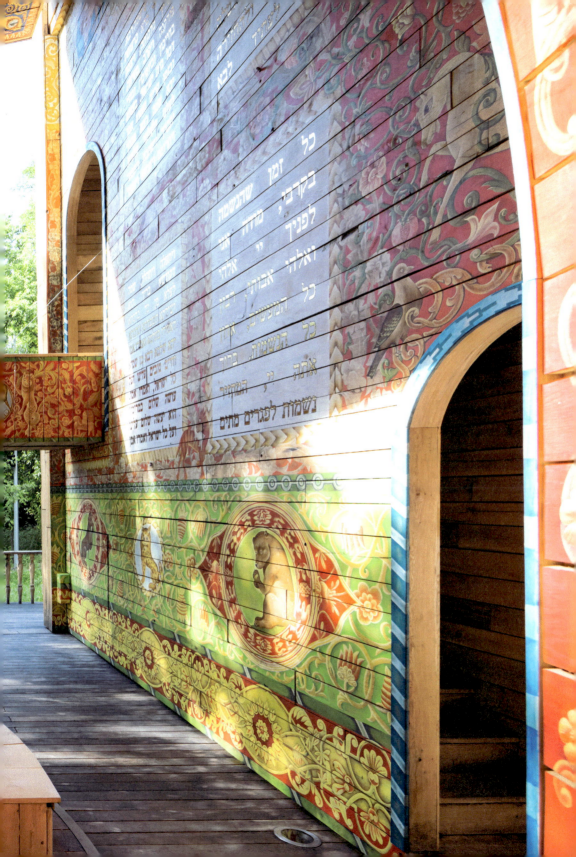

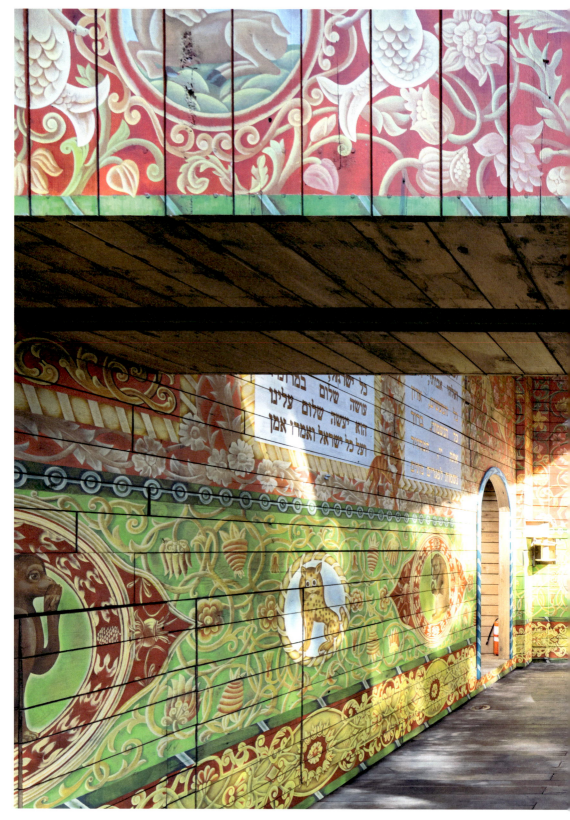

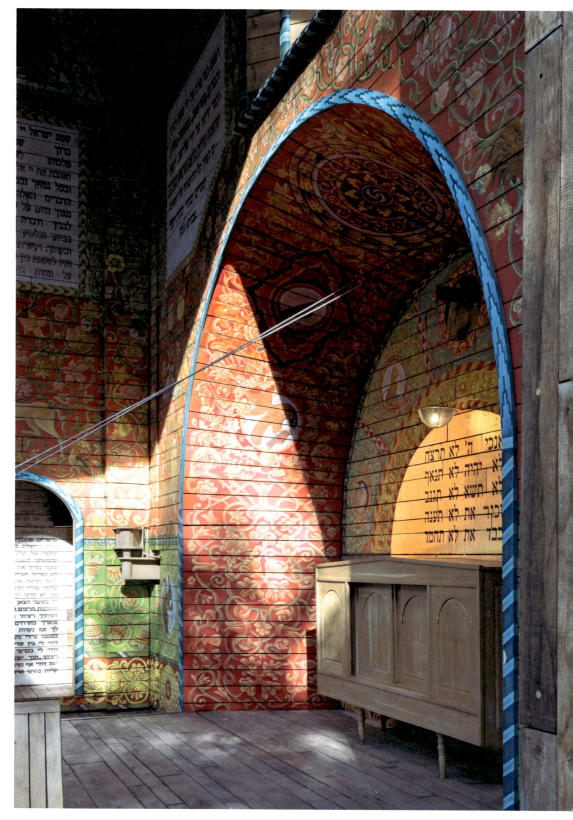

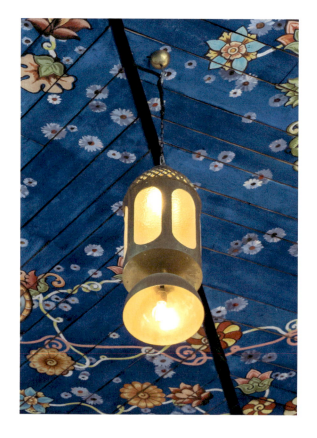

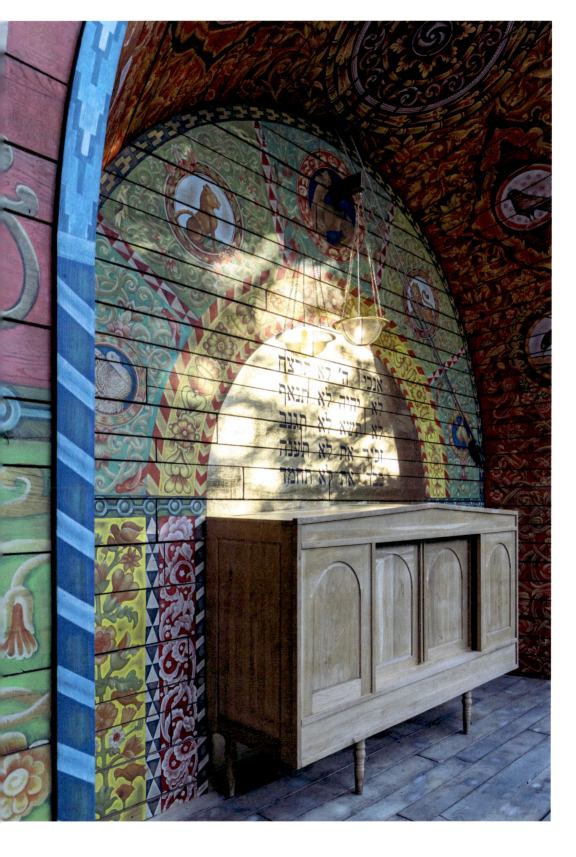

7

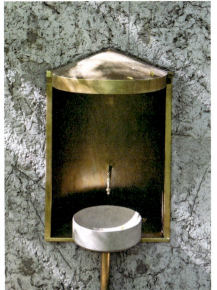

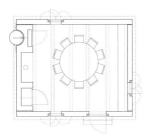

minar building, floor plan

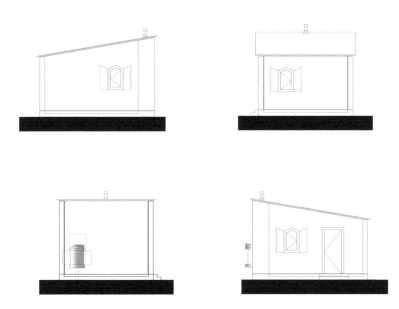

minar building, elevations

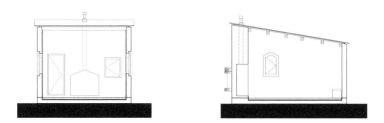

minar building, sections

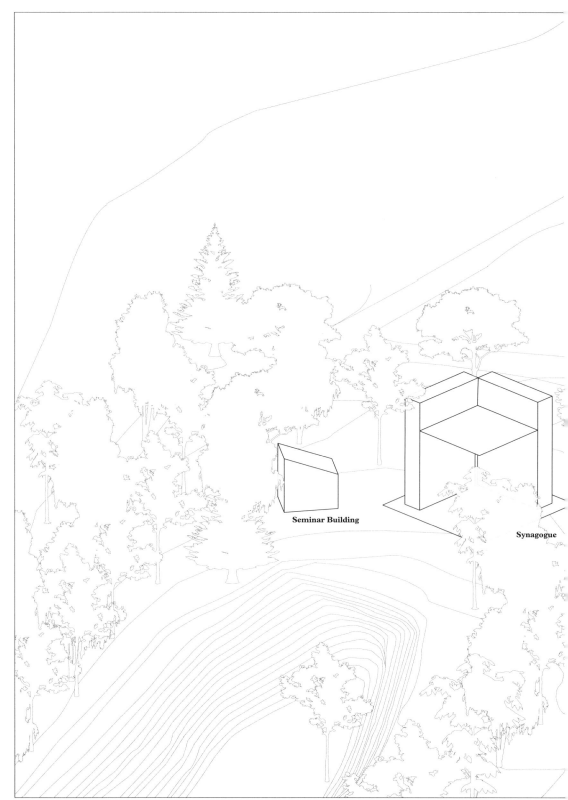

Site axonometric

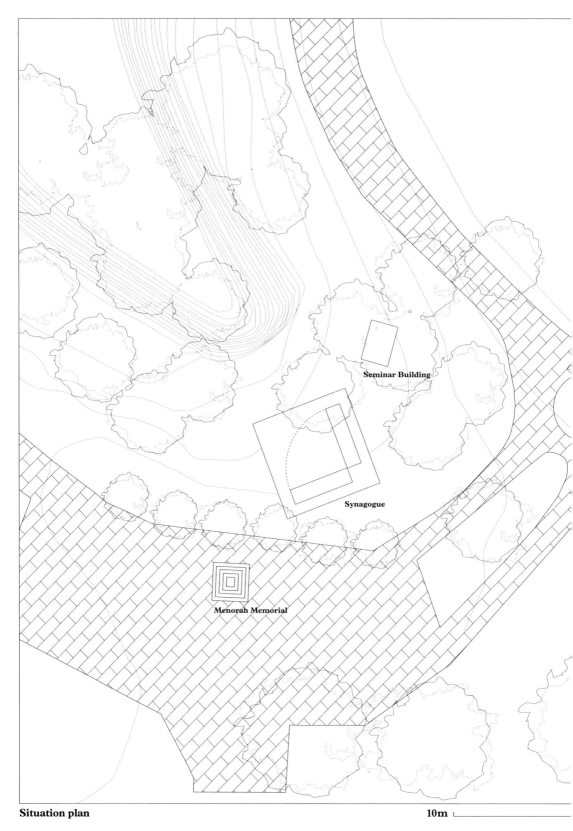

Situation plan   10m

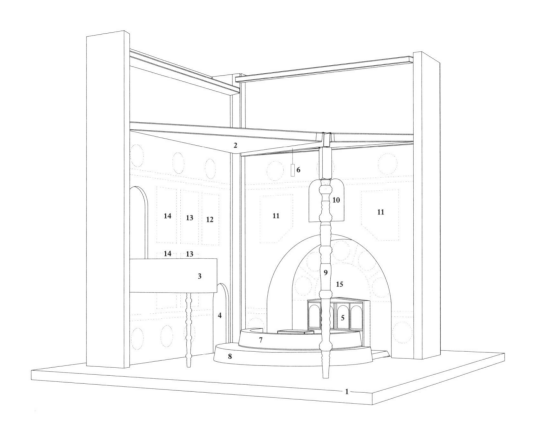

Platform
Ceiling with star constellation
Women's balcony
Stairs to women's balcony
Aron ha qodesh
Ner tamid (Eternal light)
Bima
Seats

9 **Zitzit (column)**
10 **Window**
11 **Dream blessing**
12 **Sh'ma yisrael**
13 **Morning blessing**
14 **Kaddish**
15 **Ten Commandments**

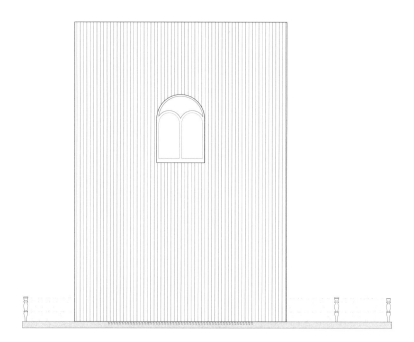

Elevation south (closed)

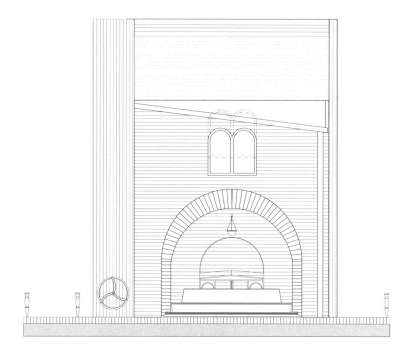

Elevation north (open)

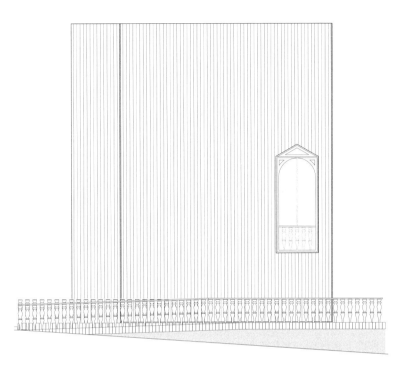

elevation east (open)

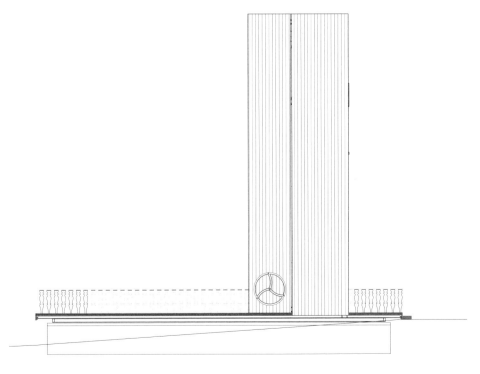

elevation west (closed)

0 1 2 3 4 5

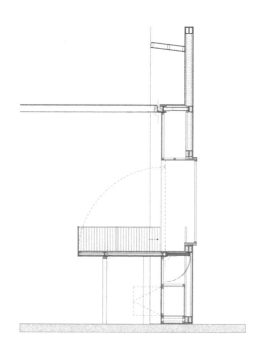

Section of moveable wall

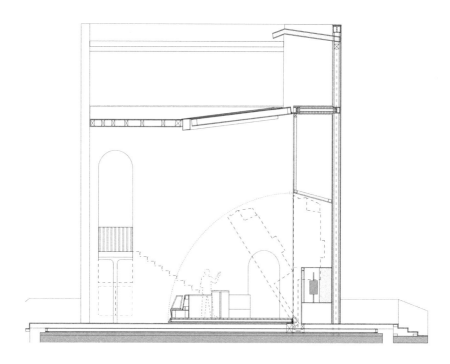

Section of fixed wall

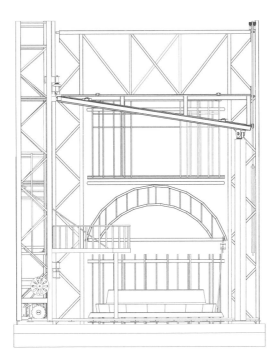

technical section of moveable wall

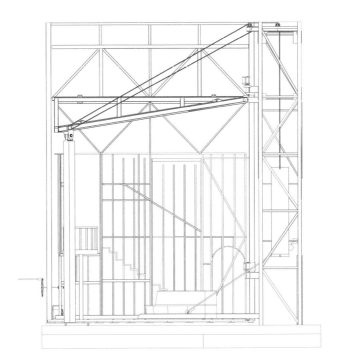

technical section of fixed wall

0 1 2 3 4 5

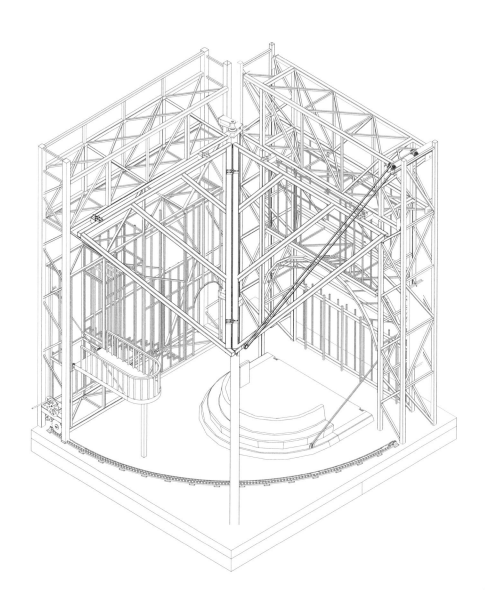

Technical axonometric

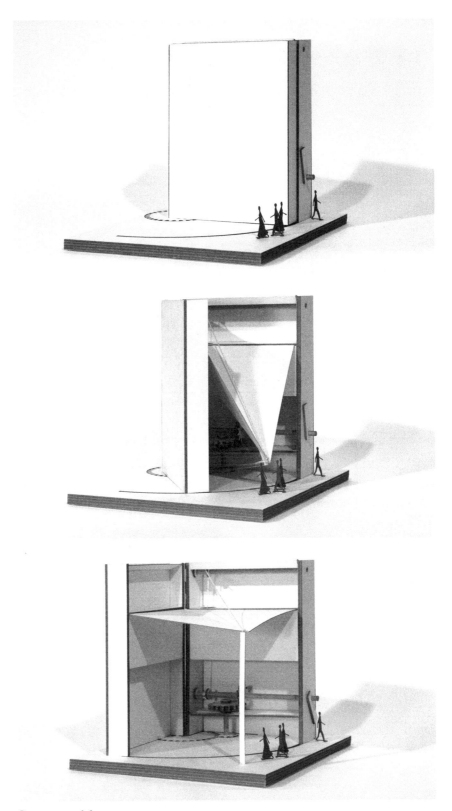

Concept model

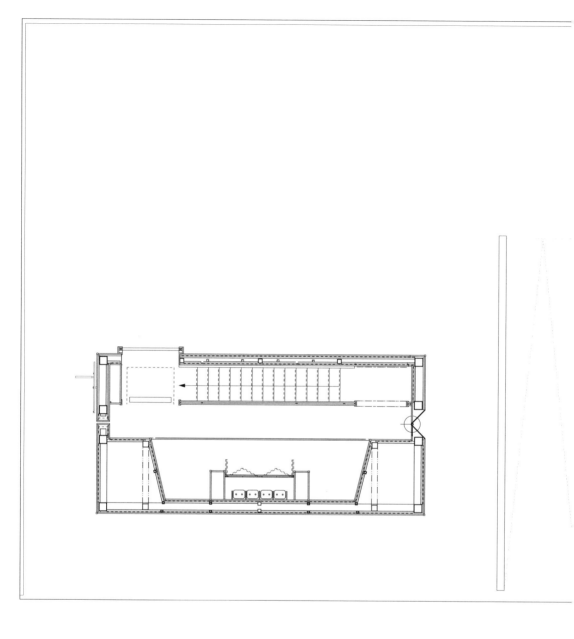

Floor plan (closed)

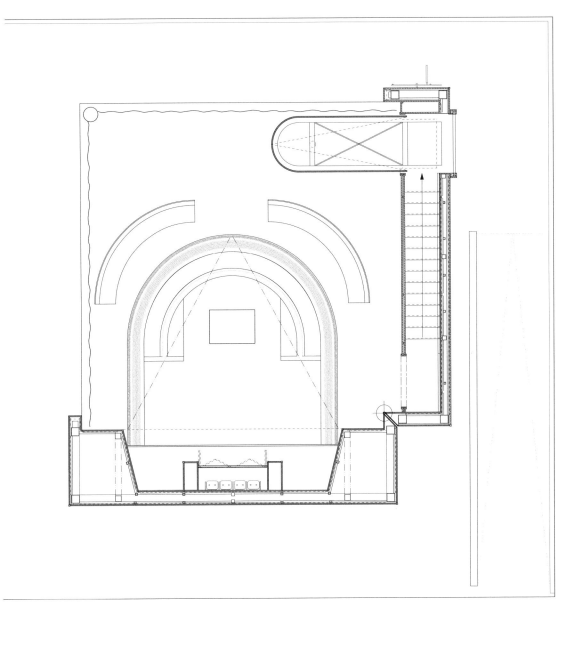

floor plan (open)

0 1 2 3 4 5

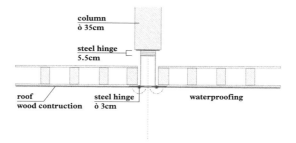

Hinge detail

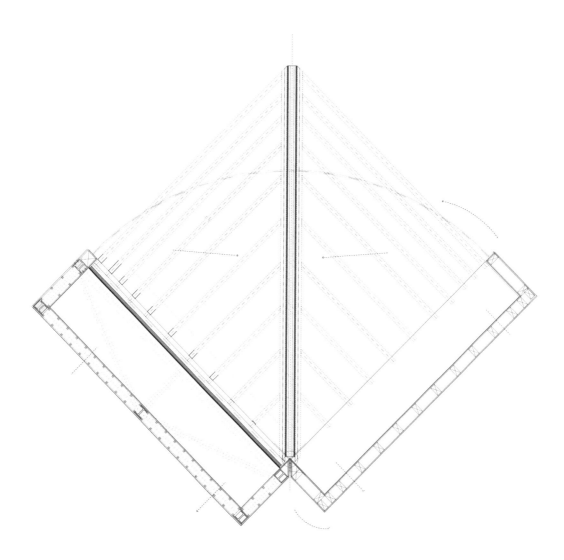

Roof plan

balcony window elevation

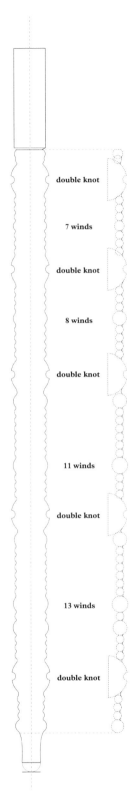

Zitzit column diagram

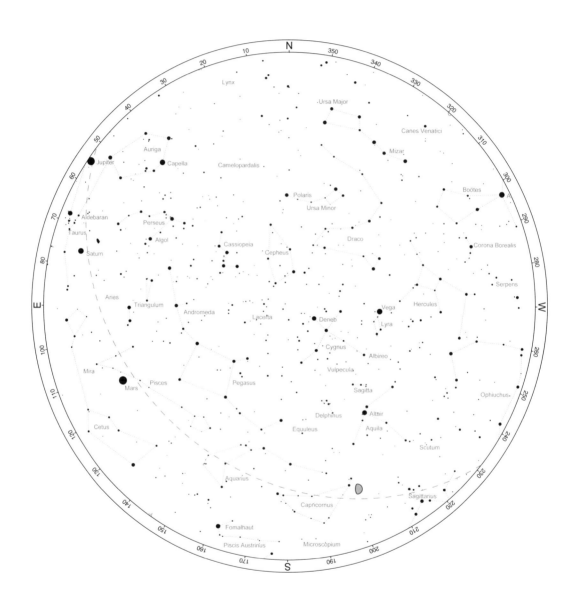

Skychart

**Kyiv, 50.4500°N, 30.5241°E
September 29, 1941, 21:00 (UTC +02:00)**

iling painting

Using the iconography of the Gwozdziec Synagogue, the ceiling of the Babyn Yar Synagogue recreates the precise star constellation that was visible in the night sky over Kyiv on September 29th, 1941.

The Park and the Box
Jean-Louis Cohen

As the Red Army was marching towards the West, the SS stationed in Auschwitz blew up the camp's crematories in late 1944 and early 1945 in a desperate attempt to destroy incriminating evidence of their mass murders committed during four long years. In Babyn Yar, crematories were constructed in 1943, shortly before the end of the Nazi occupation, as part of the process of erasure.

While the ruins of Birkenau and other parts of Auschwitz were left standing after the war, the ravine of Baby Yar was systematically filled with factory waste and water, a process which led to a new catastrophe just fifteen years after the war, the Kurenivka mudslide of 1961. It would take another fifteen years to see the erection of a first official monument on Babyn Yar. The monument, dedicated to the memory of "Soviet civilians and Red Army soldiers and officers—prisoners of war—who were shot at Babi Yar by the German occupiers" carefully avoided acknowledging, not to mention mourning the mass murder of Kyiv's Jewish population on September 29 and 30, 1941.

Symptomatically, the first tributes to Babyn Yar were not inscribed in the earth of Kyiv's suburb, but on paper. Texts were published by members of the city's Jewish community immediately following the liberation of Kyiv, within the context of Stalin's postwar antisemitic campaign. It took fifteen years for Yevgeny Yevtushenko's famous homonymous poem, with the provocative first line "There are no monuments over Babyn Yar," to be made public. This was followed by Anatoly Kuznetsov's Document in the Form of a Novel, which created a shock wave through the Soviet Union, despite its mutilation by the literary censors. More recently, Jonathan Littell's novel Les bienveillantes (The Kindly Ones) added a fictional layer to what Kuznetsov had defined as documentary literature. This layering of factual writings, poetic accounts, and official Soviet discourse excised the memory of Babyn Yar from Jews, turning it into a palimpsest.

A parallel can be drawn between this literary and political history with the sequence of transformations that has taken place on the site of Babyn Yar and its surroundings ever since the war. The nearly endless succession of landfills, exhumations, incinerations, dumping, terraforming, and overbuilding has left traces which can sometimes be seen today, but are in most cases difficult, if not impossible to detect. The transformations of the topography, the creation of infrastructure, and the development of a wide range of buildings have become one with the destruction of the various cemeteries present on the site since the eighteenth century.

The idea of restoring the site to its pre-war ecological, topographic, and geological condition would require a massive campaign of public works on a site that has already seen such incredible violence enacted on and to it. The recreation of the topographic conditions which were the stage for the brutal murders from 1941–1943 cannot be made on the ground. The suppression of the last layers of construction and the restitution of demolished buildings and graves would be a complex and costly task. The only imaginable strategy is the addition of a new layer on top of the existing palimpsest: a complex memorial park in which the former strategies of erasure themselves could be documented and made visible. This layer would be one of commemoration and recollection.

But what would it means to create this added level of use and perception? Viennese art historian Aloïs Riegl and his path-breaking essay on the Modern Cult of Monuments published by in the early years of the 20th century remains useful in this task of critical reflection and understanding.

Riegl examined the different characteristics of monuments either built or designated as such since Antiquity. In particular, he counterposed intentional monuments—ones deliberately loaded with a precise meaning—with unintentional ones—which have taken on value and meaning over time. If one applies this analytic framework to Babyn Yar, one can identify a lengthy phase, from 1941–1976, when the site was an unintentional, or even forbidden monument. Within that time as a series of memorials were designed for the site, but were never built.

It took more than three decades for this unintentional monument to assume both a historical and a commemorative value. This change of status over time is not exceptional, in particular for sites related to the two world wars. In the aftermath of the Great War, several of the main battlefields became unintentional monuments. One such case is the site of Verdun, in Northeastern France, where the bloodiest battle of the entire war had taken place. It almost immediately became a place of popular sightseeing and pilgrimage before the eventual erection of a massive, overwhelming ossuary inaugurated in 1932.

The case of Auschwitz is more complex and can more easily be compared to Babyn Yar. Not meant by the Nazis to become a place of visit, the former camp was opened to the public after a number of buildings had been demolished by the newly established Polish government, notably in Birkenau. A careful restoration program of the remaining ones, where permanent exhibits have been installed, complement the preserved section of the camps, and has led to the inclusion of Auschwitz I and II on UNESCO's world heritage list. However, Auschwitz III—or Monowitz—long remained an unintentional monument, housing one of Poland's largest chemical industry complex for decades, developed on the basis of the IG Farben plant.

In Auschwitz and in several former camp sites around Europe, commemorating the Holocaust with surviving buildings, infrastructure, and landscape features is made possible not only by the existence of compelling spatial evidence, but also by a significant quantity of visual testimonies, from objects and photographs to films. Nothing near this abundance of materials exists in the case of Babyn Yar, which remains largely undocumented in contrast to what is known about the situation of Kyiv at large during the war. Its traces are tenuous and for the most part written. Hence, new interventions on the area of the former ravine and its surroundings are needed.

Not all of Babyn Yar's historic features have been erased, yet they are scattered around the vastness of the area. Built objects coexist with wide zones in which abundant vegetation gives the illusion of a long-established natural landscape. After the ambitious plan for an over-scaled museum was abandoned in 2019, a step-by-step strategy has been developed by the Babyn Yar Holocaust Memorial Center and has already led to a handful of projects. The installation A Look Into the Past, a series of red granite stelae with monoculars, allows visitors to discover of the few original photographs of the site in 1941 and operates like peepholes responding to the scoping pulsion of the visitors. While the stones convey these rare images, the Menorah Monument Walk audio installation along the Road of Sorrow connects one of the site's main entrances on Oleny Telihy Street, next to the former office of the Jewish cemetery, to the giant bronze menorah which was installed in 1991, just one month after the independence of Ukraine. In 2016 the remaining gravestones from the former Jewish cemetery were collected and arranged along this path. The work, conceived by Maksym Demydenko, is the site's the first major work indexing the Jewish martyrs, broadcasting the 19,000 known names of victims of September 1941's executions.

In one of the glades parallel to the Road of Sorrow, Denis Shibanov's Mirror Field introduces key notions of Jewish culture through a set of stainless steel columns whose tops have been blown-up and pierced by bullet holes that radiate light at night. Their number, ten, and their arrangement on a steel disk alludes to the Kabbalistic sign of the Sefirot. Another expression of the Kabbala transpires from the ground, where Demydenko has installed an organ that plays the transposition of victims' names using the Gematria alphanumeric code, in which a numerical value is assigned to letters or words, and here, sound.

The Kurgan of Memory, the first museum structure built by the Babyn Yar Holocaust Memorial Center and designed by sub for the commemoration the massacre's 80th anniversary, is more modest and lighter than the massive facility originally envisioned in the 2019 competition. Modeled on the Neolithic burial mound typology typical to Ukraine, the kurgan, an artificial hill is lit at the base by long slits brings to mind Mario Fiorentino's collective grave at the Fosse Ardeatine in Rome. Within it sits a large-scale topographic model of the ravine inscribed into the ground, on top of which sit diorama-like forensic reconstructions of specific scenes that took place in 1941 and 1943. In order to respect the dead, the structure will float above ground, carried by a set of supports.

While the stelae trigger and focus imagination, and the museum reconstructs the topography of mass murder, the Crystal Wall of Crying, a long mineral structure designed by artist Marina Abramović, will at last create a place of mourning in a territory in which no space is left for labors of the soul. Singular objects such as these, spread out within the 130-hectare park, consider Babyn Yar in all its historical and human dimension. While each operate in their own realm, and speak to the faceted and deep meanings present in Babyn Yar, the Synagogue built by Manuel Herz stands out. Its vertical silhouette marks the end of the Road of Sorrow and echoes the menorah.

In contrast with art installations and with the museum that aspires to become part of the topography, this apparently frail parallelepiped speaks not of loss, or death, but of life, of joy, of wonder. Standing on a wooden platform, it seems to have landed from outer space—from the space of imagination—into a heavily loaded landscape. Only the window towards the access path, shaped like the Tables of the Law, gives incoming visitors a hint as to their destination.

The simplicity of this box, located at the intersection of commemoration and religion, is deceiving. At dusk, the apparently static and self-centered volume opens up to embrace the forest, becoming a place of worship on a side where no kaddish was recited when tens of thousands of Jews perished.

The collective process of reflection on the architecture of contemporary synagogues has been ongoing for decades. Before building his unique structure at Babyn Yar, Herz first contributed to this discourse in Mainz in 2011 with a synagogue whose acute geometry and contrast between the dark terracotta exterior and the generous daylight that bathes the interior is striking. Post-Cold War Germany has been fertile ground for this process, and other recent German buildings come to mind, such as the synagogue built in Dresden in 2001 by Rena Wandel-Hoefer and Wolfgang Lorch on the spot where Gottfried Semper's temple stood before its destruction during the Kristallnacht of 1938.

The history of modern and contemporary synagogues is a dense one, in which many significant architects have been engaged. Determined by binding rituals, synagogues were not one of the main laboratories of typological innovation over the course of the twentieth century, but a wave of new constructions did coincide with the emancipation of Jews throughout Europe and the emergence of new ideals in architecture. In the late nineteenth century the dominant language of European synagogues was eclectic Orientalism, which worked to differentiate them from the other religious buildings. Emmanuel Pontremoli's 1911 synagogue in Boulogne-sur-Seine, near Paris, for instance, used neo-Byzantine spatial and decorative patterns. Hector Guimard's synagogue on rue Pavée in Paris, built two years later, uses more dynamic shapes of Art Nouveau to frame a daylight-filled space inserted into a narrow Parisian lot.

Jews were well represented in the groups that shaped the Modern movement in European architecture, but very few synagogues of the time embodied its new design strategies. In 1917, however, Fritz Landauer, who worked in Munich from 1909 to 1934, built an impressive synagogue and community center in

Augsburg, in which Byzantine features were interpreted through the prism of Otto Wagner's designs. In 1930, Landauer built another, more radical synagogue in the Saxon city of Plauen: a sleek parallelepiped, the most explicit implementation of the language of the Neues Bauen (New Objectivity) to both the exterior and interior of a temple. Exiled in England, Landauer went on to build two more synagogues in the suburbs of London.

There are only a few instances where main figures in the modern architecture movement worked on synagogues. Peter Behrens' Neolog synagogue in Žilina, built from 1928–1931, is a solid concrete box crowned by a dome, and has become the defining monument of this Slovak city. Its generously daylit interior features bicolor horizontal bands, an elegant echo of the neo-Moorish patterns used in previous epochs. The Beth Sholom synagogue built in 1959 by Behrens' contemporary Frank Lloyd Wright in Elkins Park, a suburb of Philadelphia, instead gives primacy to natural light during the day, and to illumination at night. At dusk, the synagogue becomes a huge lantern, which Wright himself described as a "luminous Mount Sinai."

Perhaps more than in other sacral buildings, the synagogue is determined by the interaction of light and ornament. Modern architects of the following generation privileged the former, leaning towards abstraction and laconism in their designs. After emigrating to the United States from Berlin, Erich Mendelsohn built several religious and community centers before his death in 1953. The parabolic roof of Mendelsohn's B'nai Amoona synagogue in St. Louis, Missouri breaks with the recurrent centrality and the boxy character of Behrens' and Wright's designs. He also designed the Park Synagogue in Cleveland, Ohio, whose oversized copper-clad dome seems to be a caricature of conservative designs.

Other architects in the United States worked not so much at reinvention but at reforming current synagogue types. Philip Johnson's temple for the Congregation Kneses Tifereth Israel in Port Chester, New York—which has been seen as an attempt to redeem his prewar antisemitic leaning—belong to the boxy genre. Lit by narrow windows of colored glass, the interior supposedly alludes to the Flight from Egypt. In the same generation as Johnson, Louis I. Kahn designed several versions of a building meant to replace the Hurva synagogue, which had been blown up in 1948, after the 1967 war in Jerusalem. His unbuilt schemes envisioned a porous space created by high and solid stone-clad pillars that incorporate the remaining ruins of the destroyed temple and allow natural light to penetrate, creating an atmosphere hospitable to prayer.

Since the 1950s, scores of synagogues have been built in Israel, reflecting the main directions in the country's architecture, and a new wave of temples and community centers have built in Germany, both before and after reunification. Previous spatial types have been in most cases dropped in favor of experimental solutions in the response to the sites, to the creative handling of enclosure and light and to the challenge of conceiving contemporary geometric ornaments.

In contrast to these buildings, Manuel Herz's box-like design for the Babyn Yar Synagogue conveys a feeling of fragility. One of the preconditions of its construction was the avoidance of foundations, which would have desecrated the ground. The impossibility of building a permanent, solid structure in this context has led to what Robert Smithson called a "nonsite" work, but built on the site in reference to it.

Coexisting with the installations directly documenting the massacre, the small building manifests the reappearance of the Jews in Kyiv after slaughter, repression, and exile. The unfolding of the volume calls to mind the opening of a book's pages, combined with the deployment of an open room devoted to prayer. Once it has reached its maximal expansion, the building can be home to religious services, bringing to mind the projecting roof and altar of Le Corbusier's Notre Dame du Haut church in Ronchamp.

The cinematics of the building do not denote previous synagogue architecture. Rather, they recall some of the works of the Russian avant-garde, like Konstantin Melnikov's rotating devices for his 1924 entry to the Leningrad Pravda competition, his 1925 Pavilion at the Paris exposition—which was also a lightweight wooden structure—and Lyubov Popova's stage designs for Vsevolod Meyerhold's show The Magnificent Cuckhold, performed in 1922—a wooden mechanism with giant cogwheels. Seemingly set on its platform as if it were in transit from a previous location to another one, one could imagine a set of wheels being mounted on each side of Herz's building, transforming it into a moving object.

On the site, each time the mechanical devices are operated and the building's interior is fully deployed, a colorful world unfolds, conjuring up echoes of past synagogues as if components of past buildings have been transferred to Babyn Yar for this structure. As an intertextual architecture, a varied set of operations—explicit quotation, paraphrase, or condensation—are assembles these fragments of former synagogue into a new visual text, proposing a short anthology of the vanished world of Ukrainian and Polish decorated synagogues.

The Zodiac featured on the ceiling reproduces the configuration of the sky on the first night of the 1941 slaughter, with each sign projecting out from a background of flowers representing the stars. A joyful bestiary unfolds, with animals—real and mythical—reproduced from the walls of the main synagogue in Kyiv's Podil, and from the recreated roof and painted ceiling of the eighteenth century Gwoździec Synagogue, now in Warsaw's Museum of the History of Polish Jews. An expression of life radiates from the walls, stronger than the sorrow transpiring from the looming presence of ravine. The interplay of these images with the Hebrew texts featured on the walls also condenses the universe of Jewish tales, which a young El Lissitzky made a number of illustrated books about.

When considering the wooden volume and the wonders it contains, another connection with art cannot be dispelled. Despite its much larger size, the synagogue could be compared to Marcel Duchamp's Box in a suitcase, the miniature portable museum containing a collection of reproductions of his works, of which he conceived several iterations. One could elaborate on the meaning of the suitcase, thinking of those in which the victims of the 1941 massacre had packed their meager belongings before taking them on their long walk to the site of their death. In addition to the site-specific relevance of the original building in Kyiv, one could perhaps imagine other versions, identical or rethought in relationship with other historical contexts, which would convey the lively message of hope uttered in Babyn Yar: a synagogue in a suitcase.